Mastering Network Flow Traffic Analysis

I0049888

Implementing and analyzing flow data
across network topologies for threat detection

Gilberto Persico

bpb

www.bpbonline.com

First Edition 2025

Copyright © BPB Publications, India

ISBN: 978-93-65890-266

To View Complete
BPB Publications Catalogue
Scan the QR Code:

www.bpbonline.com

Dedicated to

*My partner **Tin**, my daughter **Flora**,
my father **Carlo** and my mother **Grazyna***

About the Author

Gilberto Persico is a Unix system, networking, and security engineer with over 30 years of experience in the IT world, working as a programmer, architect, security auditor, and systems and network engineer. He worked for IBM, Sun Microsystems, Oracle, and Huawei both as an employee and as a freelancer, designing, developing, and supporting production-ready enterprise-grade architectures for dozens of very important customers. He also conceived, designed, and developed Fl0wer, a new generation network flow analysis product, and deployed it in a big setup, successfully controlling two big data centers. He plays cello in his free time and raises a daughter when not hacking things in his lab. He also loves resurrecting old systems, retro-computing, and is currently works as a NOC team leader in Econocom.

About the Reviewer

Md Nahidul Kibria is currently staff engineer at HelloFresh. With over a decade of experience in software development and cloud infrastructure, he specializes in migrating legacy systems to cloud-native environments. He focuses on improving the synergy between DevOps and SecOps processes and enhancing infrastructure scalability, data streaming technologies, and security.

He has worked with companies of various sizes, designing and developing microservices-based platforms, implementing service mesh strategies, and leading cloud migration initiatives. His expertise includes cloud technologies such as AWS and Kubernetes, infrastructure as code, data streaming technologies, and application security.

He is also an active member of the global cybersecurity community, serving as a red team member and community lead, and has presented at prestigious conferences. He believes that learning is a lifelong journey and enjoys sharing his insights through writing and public speaking on topics such as data streaming, application scaling, and advanced threat hunting.

He holds a bachelor's degree in computer science and is passionate about building resilient, scalable, and secure systems. Outside work, he enjoys exploring emerging technologies and finding innovative ways to simplify and enhance complex operations.

Acknowledgement

I want to express my deepest gratitude to my family and friends for their unwavering support and encouragement throughout this book's writing, especially my partner Tin and my daughter Flora. I want to thank my father for teaching me the meaning of patience and determination, and my mother for helping me in my darkest moments. I love you all.

I am also grateful to BPB Publications for their guidance and expertise in bringing this book to fruition. It was a long journey of revising this book, with valuable participation and collaboration of reviewers, technical experts, and editors.

I would also like to acknowledge the valuable contributions of my colleagues and co-worker during many years working in the tech industry, who have taught me so much and provided valuable feedback on my work.

Finally, I would like to thank all the readers who have taken an interest in my book and for their support in making it a reality. Your encouragement has been invaluable.

Preface

Managing the enterprise network security is a complex task that requires a comprehensive understanding of the latest technologies. On one side, passive network traffic analysis still makes sense for several reasons, but what is going to provide a more scalable approach to network security is the analysis of network traffic flows.

The book aims to familiarize the readers with network traffic flows analysis technologies, giving a deep understanding on the difference between active and passive network traffic analysis, the advantages and disadvantages of each methodology, with a special focus about network flow traffic analysis, which due to its scalability, privacy, ease of implementation and effectiveness, is beginning to play a leader role in the field of network security. The book allows a reader to dive deep into tools and technologies that can be used and leveraged to effectively deploy a scalable and affordable network monitoring solution capable of giving a clear idea of all internal traffic flows and providing an effective, almost-real-time data breach detection mechanism.

Throughout the book, you will learn how common network infrastructures are built, how the flow protocols work, what kind of data is managed, and how you can effectively take advantage of it.

The book targets professionals with job roles such as incident responder, forensic investigator, SOC analyst, network administrator, or a student seeking to extend their knowledge on network flow analysis. The book assumes readers know network topologies, the OSI and TCP/IP models, and have a basic understanding of capturing network data. The book heavily relies on Linux knowledge.

The reader will learn to set up their infrastructure to obtain flow traffic data and make the most of this information. The reader will also learn to understand how to relate to normal and unknown traffic, how to set up tasks to automate network controls, and how to assess their network in a passive but proactive way. The reader will acquire the knowledge and skills that will allow them to be untied by limitations of traditional analysis tools and embrace a new and scalable way to improve security on high-speed networks.

I hope you will find this book informative and helpful.

Chapter 1: Foundation of Network Flow Analysis - This chapter lays the base for conducting network analysis using flow protocols, with a strong bias towards network security. The reader will learn about the essentials, important concepts of types of network analysis types, advantages, scalability, and sustainability of different types of analysis. Additionally, in this chapter, the reader will learn about the proper tools to get effective results in each of the different analysis types, focusing on the network flow analysis. The reader will familiarize himself with the differences between packet and flow analysis while learning the advantages and disadvantages of statistical flow analysis.

Chapter 2: Fixed and Dynamic Length Flow Protocols - This chapter will discuss both the fixed length flow protocols and the dynamic length flow protocols, their advantages, and drawbacks. The chapter describes NetFlow v1, NetFlow v5, NetFlow v9, sFlow v5, and IPFIX. By the end, the chapter will discuss case studies on the protocols' benefits or misuse and their identification.

Chapter 3: Network Topologies - This chapter primarily focuses on various network topologies found in companies and ways to implement proper flow analysis in different contexts, from classical flat infrastructure to frontend/backend/DMZ to Virtual Private Clouds and ways to discover blind points.

Chapter 4: Implementing Flow Export on Layer 2 Devices - This chapter will guide the reader to implement flow data export on the most widespread Layer 2 devices (switches and access points) from most vendors on the market, and will also describe a solution to get NetFlow/IPFIX data from a switch using port mirroring.

Chapter 5: Implementing Flow Export on Layer 3 Devices - This chapter will guide the reader to implement flow data export on the most widespread Layer 3 devices like firewalls, routers, load balancers, and wireless gateways from most vendors on the market.

Chapter 6: Implementing Flow Export on Servers - This chapter focuses on solutions for implementing flow export on servers, which may be required in contexts where you want to see the flow traffic but cannot manage network infrastructure, like cloud environments or hosting services.

Chapter 7: Implementing Flow Export on Virtualization Platforms - This chapter focuses on solutions for implementing flow export on virtualization systems like VMware and Proxmox, which can give you network visibility in traffic not crossing the network infrastructure (imagine traffic between different virtual machines on the same hypervisor).

Chapter 8: Ingesting Data into Clickhouse and Elasticsearch - This chapter shows the user how to ingest raw flow data into more usable and structured analysis platforms like Elasticsearch and Clickhouse (open-source high-performance OLAP).

Chapter 9: Flow Data Analysis: Exploring Data for Fun and Profit - This chapter will discuss how we can do interesting analysis of the flow data we are getting from the network, and will teach the reader to understand better what is happening inside their network infrastructure, by showing a lot of examples. It will also give the reader further in-depth knowledge about identifying patterns and anomalies, and how to detect security threats.

Chapter 10: Understanding the Flow Matrix - This chapter introduces an often too underestimated concept, the matrix of flows happening inside the company network. A deep dive into the concept will allow the reader to take advantage of it to improve the security posture of the whole network.

Chapter 11: Firewall Rules Optimization Use Case - This chapter describes a real use case of NetFlow data to approach a quite complex problem of firewall optimization rules in a complex (but now becoming quite common) environment.

Chapter 12: Simple Network Anomaly Detection System Based on Flow Data Analysis - This chapter focuses on how to identify network anomalies and data breaches by using the flow matrix and some Python scripting using Pandas. It will show the reader how to automate continuous checking, trying to address the problem of the slowness in identifying a breach.

Code Bundle and Coloured Images

Please follow the link to download the
Code Bundle and the *Coloured Images* of the book:

https://rebrand.ly/46sqwki

The code bundle for the book is also hosted on GitHub at
https://github.com/bpbpublications/Mastering-Network-Flow-Traffic-Analysis.
In case there's an update to the code, it will be updated on the existing GitHub repository.

We have code bundles from our rich catalogue of books and videos available at
https://github.com/bpbpublications. Check them out!

Errata

We take immense pride in our work at BPB Publications and follow best practices to ensure the accuracy of our content to provide with an indulging reading experience to our subscribers. Our readers are our mirrors, and we use their inputs to reflect and improve upon human errors, if any, that may have occurred during the publishing processes involved. To let us maintain the quality and help us reach out to any readers who might be having difficulties due to any unforeseen errors, please write to us at :

errata@bpbonline.com

Your support, suggestions and feedbacks are highly appreciated by the BPB Publications' Family.

Did you know that BPB offers eBook versions of every book published, with PDF and ePub files available? You can upgrade to the eBook version at www.bpbonline. com and as a print book customer, you are entitled to a discount on the eBook copy. Get in touch with us at :

business@bpbonline.com for more details.

At **www.bpbonline.com**, you can also read a collection of free technical articles, sign up for a range of free newsletters, and receive exclusive discounts and offers on BPB books and eBooks.

Piracy

If you come across any illegal copies of our works in any form on the Internet, we would be grateful if you would provide us with the location address or website name. Please contact us at **business@bpbonline.com** with a link to the material.

If you are interested in becoming an author

If there is a topic that you have expertise in, and you are interested in either writing or contributing to a book, please visit **www.bpbonline.com**. We have worked with thousands of developers and tech professionals, just like you, to help them share their insights with the global tech community. You can make a general application, apply for a specific hot topic that we are recruiting an author for, or submit your own idea.

Reviews

Please leave a review. Once you have read and used this book, why not leave a review on the site that you purchased it from? Potential readers can then see and use your unbiased opinion to make purchase decisions. We at BPB can understand what you think about our products, and our authors can see your feedback on their book. Thank you!

For more information about BPB, please visit **www.bpbonline.com**.

Join our book's Discord space

Join the book's Discord Workspace for Latest updates, Offers, Tech happenings around the world, New Release and Sessions with the Authors:

https://discord.bpbonline.com

Table of Contents

CHAPTER 1

Foundation of Network Flow Analysis

Introduction

This chapter introduces you to network flow analysis, ways of performing it, techniques and technologies involved in network security, and their advantages. Nowadays, technology is playing a pivotal role in the success of most companies. Moreover, computer-based technology relies on a strong foundation: computer networks. A famous computer slogan used by *Sun Microsystems*[1] once said *The network is the computer*. When you browse the Internet, your computer uses the company's network to connect to various websites. Maybe you can reach only some websites, in which case it means that some sort of network control is already in place, or maybe you can go anywhere (which does not suggest that controls are not in place). In any case, if you are in your office, you are connected to the company's internal network unless you are doing smart work. A network is simply made by computers with network interfaces, cables, and networking devices (like hubs, switches, routers, firewalls, etc.), each performing exactly the task they were developed for.

But what is network security? Simple, with the advent of computer networks first and the Internet later, protecting internal data and users from theft and fraud has become increasingly complicated than before. And in current times, if you read about network security news, there is always a company that has been hacked or was the victim of malware or data theft.

_____
1. https://spectrum.ieee.org/does-repurposing-of-sun-microsystems-slogan-honor-history

The interesting fact is that normally, everyone assumes that the internal network of the company is a safe place without risks or menaces. It is no surprise that searching zero trust online yields numerous articles; we will get back to it in the following chapters, but let us just assume that to keep a network perimeter safe, you must work on it in some way!

Structure

In this chapter we will discuss the following topics:

- Computer network
- Computer network analysis
- Common network security threats to company networks
- Network security traffic analysis
- Techniques for performing network security traffic analysis
- Packet-inspection network traffic analysis
- Network flow-based traffic analysis
- Basics of network protection
- Firewalls and packet filters
- Network proxies
- Intrusion detection systems
- Intrusion prevention systems
- Pros and cons of packet-inspection network traffic analysis
- Open-source and commercial solutions
- Pros and cons of network flow-based traffic analysis
- Open-source and commercial solutions
- Challenge of analyzing 800Gbps networks

Objectives

This chapter will introduce the user to the world of corporate network security, corporate networking, and the different types of network traffic analysis, as well as introduce the network flow traffic analysis.

Computer network

A computer network is a collection of interconnected computers and devices that can communicate with each other, share resources, and exchange data. These networks can be as small as a few devices at home or office or as large as the global Internet, connecting billions of devices worldwide. Computer networks enable the sharing of information, resources, and services, facilitating communication and collaboration between users and systems.

Usually, depending on the size of the company, inside networks are split and deployed in different ways, both on the physical and logical levels. Normally there are distinct designs for logical and physical, because modern network devices allow this split distinction. This has several benefits from the perspective of security and availability of the network service.

An example of a simple logical split can be in terms of frontend, backend, and employee networks. These networks can be split into Layer 2 (switches or VLANs) and interconnected by routers or firewalls in Layer 3.

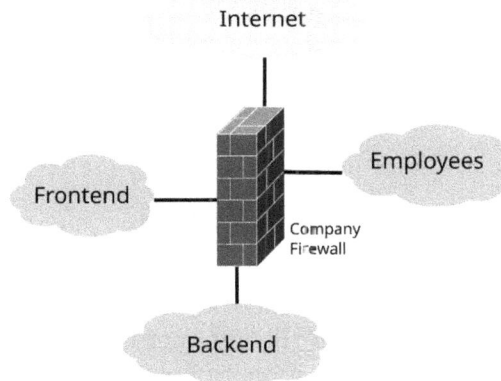

Figure 1.1: *Logical network view*

The same network infrastructure, considered on the physical design, can have different ways to be deployed. In our example, implementing full redundancy (using proper protocols and configurations) can be as presented in *Figure 1.2*:

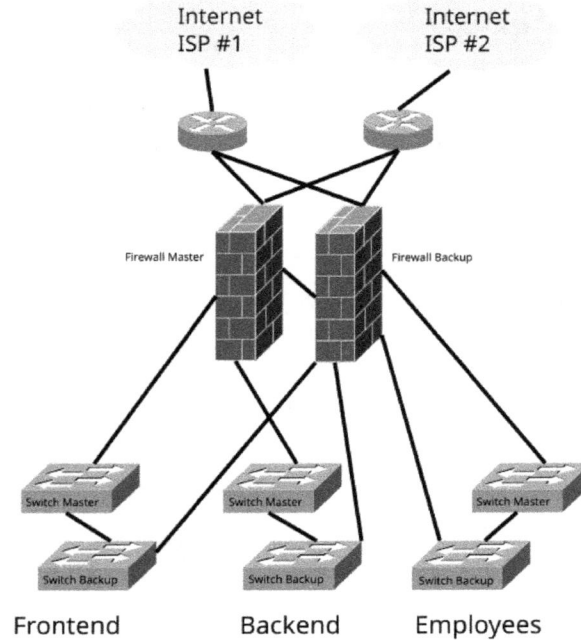

Figure 1.2: Physical network view

Computer network analysis

Computer network analysis refers to examining and evaluating computer networks to understand their performance, security, efficiency, and overall functionality. It involves various techniques and tools to gain insights into network behavior and make informed decisions about network design, optimization, troubleshooting, and security.

Here are some key aspects of computer network analysis:

- **Performance monitoring**: Network administrators and analysts use various monitoring tools to track the performance of a network. This includes measuring bandwidth utilization, latency, packet loss, and network throughput. Performance analysis helps in identifying bottlenecks and optimizing network resources.

- **Security analysis**: Network analysis is crucial for identifying and mitigating security threats. It involves monitoring network traffic for suspicious activities, such as intrusion attempts, malware infections, and unauthorized access. Security analysts use **intrusion detection systems** (**IDS**), firewalls, and other security tools to analyze network traffic patterns and detect anomalies.

- **Troubleshooting**: When network issues occur, network analysis is used to diagnose and resolve problems. By examining network traffic, logs, and configuration settings, administrators can pinpoint the root causes of network outages, connectivity problems, or performance issues. This process is essential for maintaining network reliability.

- **Optimization**: Network analysis helps in optimizing network resources and configurations. By studying traffic patterns and usage data, administrators can make informed decisions about network design, capacity planning, and load balancing. This ensures that the network operates efficiently and cost-effectively.

- **Capacity planning**: Analyzing network usage trends over time helps forecast future capacity requirements. This is important for ensuring that the network can handle increased traffic and new applications without degradation in performance.

- **Protocol analysis**: Network analysts often use packet sniffers and protocol analyzers to capture and analyze network traffic at a granular level. This is useful for diagnosing protocol-related issues and ensuring that network protocols are functioning as expected.

- **QoS analysis**: **Quality of service (QoS)** analysis involves assessing the network's ability to deliver different types of traffic with varying levels of priority. This is crucial for ensuring that real-time applications like voice and video conferencing receive the bandwidth and low latency to perform well.

- **Traffic engineering**: Network analysis is used to optimize traffic routing and distribution within a network. This is particularly important in large-scale networks to balance traffic loads and minimize congestion.

- **Network visualization**: Visualization tools and techniques are often used to represent network data graphically. This helps network administrators and analysts better understand network topologies, traffic flows, and dependencies.

- **Compliance and auditing**: Network analysis is also important for ensuring that a network complies with regulatory requirements and internal policies. It helps in auditing network activity and maintaining compliance records.

In summary, computer network analysis is a multidisciplinary field that involves the use of various tools and methodologies to gain insights into the performance, security, and efficiency of computer networks. It plays a crucial role in maintaining the reliability and integrity of modern networks in an ever-evolving technological landscape. In this book, we are focusing on the network security topics.

Common network security threats to company networks

Common network security threats, often referred to as cybersecurity threats or menaces, pose significant risks to computer networks and the data they contain. These threats can lead to data breaches, financial losses, and reputational damage for organizations. Here are some of the most common network security threats:

- **Malware**: Malware, short for malicious software, includes viruses, worms, Trojans, ransomware, spyware, and adware. Malware infects systems and devices, often intending to steal data, damage systems, or engage in other malicious activities.

- **Phishing**: Phishing attacks involve sending deceptive emails or messages that appear from legitimate sources but are designed to trick recipients into revealing sensitive information, such as login credentials or financial details.

- **Social engineering**: Social engineering tactics manipulate individuals into divulging confidential information or performing actions compromising security. This can include techniques like pretexting, baiting, and tailgating.

- **DoS and DDoS attacks**: **Denial-of-service** (**DoS**) attacks flood a network or system with traffic to overwhelm and disrupt services. **Distributed denial-of-service** (**DDoS**) attacks involve multiple devices coordinating an attack, making it even more challenging to mitigate.

- **Insider threats**: Insider threats can come from employees, contractors, or other individuals with authorized access to a network. These individuals may intentionally or unintentionally compromise network security, steal data, or engage in malicious activities.

- **Data breaches**: Data breaches occur when unauthorized parties gain access to sensitive or confidential data. Breaches can result from various attacks, including hacking, malware infections, and insider threats.

- **SQL injection**: SQL injection attacks target web applications by manipulating input fields to execute malicious SQL queries against a database. This can lead to unauthorized access to or modification of data.

- **MITM attacks**: In **man-in-the-middle** (**MITM**) attacks, an attacker intercepts and potentially alters communications between two parties without their knowledge. This can be used to steal data or gain unauthorized access.

- **Zero-day exploits**: Zero-day vulnerabilities are software vulnerabilities that are not yet known to the software vendor or the public. Attackers can exploit these vulnerabilities before patches or fixes are available.

- **Brute force attacks**: Brute force attacks involve attempting to guess passwords or encryption keys by systematically trying all possible combinations. These attacks can be time-consuming but may eventually succeed if weak passwords are used.

- **Credential theft**: Attackers may steal user credentials through various means, such as keyloggers, credential harvesting, or password reuse attacks. Once obtained, these credentials can be used for unauthorized access.

- **IoT vulnerabilities**: **Internet of Things** (**IoT**) devices, often lacking robust security measures, can be vulnerable to attacks. Compromised IoT devices can be used as entry points into a network.

- **Eavesdropping and sniffing**: Attackers may intercept and monitor network traffic to capture sensitive information, such as login credentials or data transmitted in plaintext.

- **XSS**: **Cross-site scripting** (**XSS**) attacks exploit vulnerabilities in web applications to inject malicious scripts into web pages viewed by other users. These scripts can steal information or perform actions on behalf of the victim.

- **Misconfigured security settings**: Incorrectly configured security settings on network devices, servers, or applications can create vulnerabilities that attackers can exploit.

To defend against these network security threats, organizations implement a combination of security measures, including firewalls, **intrusion detection and prevention systems** (**IDPS**), antivirus software, encryption, access controls, regular software patching, and security awareness training for employees. Regular monitoring and incident response planning are also essential to detect and respond to threats promptly.

Network security traffic analysis

Network security traffic analysis is the process of monitoring and inspecting network traffic to identify and assess potential security threats, anomalies, and suspicious activities. It involves the examination of data packets, network flows, and communication patterns to gain insights into the security posture of a network. The primary goal of network security traffic analysis is to detect and respond to security incidents in real-time or post-incident analysis.

Here are key aspects of network security traffic analysis:

- **Traffic monitoring**: Network security analysts use specialized tools to capture and monitor network traffic across various network segments, such as **local area networks** (**LANs**) and **wide area networks** (**WANs**). These tools collect data packets as they traverse the network.

- **Packet-level analysis**: At the most granular level, network security analysts can examine individual data packets to inspect their content, source, and destination addresses, port numbers, and protocols. This level of analysis allows for detailed inspection of network communication.

- **Flow-level analysis**: Network flows represent conversations or interactions between devices or systems. Flow analysis involves tracking these interactions, identifying the participants, and analyzing the volume and duration of data exchanged. Flow analysis can help detect patterns indicative of security threats.

- **Protocol analysis**: Analysts scrutinize network protocols to identify deviations from expected behavior. This includes examining the behavior of protocols like HTTP, FTP, SMTP, and DNS to detect suspicious or malicious activity.

- **Anomaly detection**: Network security traffic analysis includes using anomaly detection techniques to identify unusual or unexpected network behavior. Deviations from established baselines or statistical norms may indicate security threats or network issues.

- **Signature-based detection**: Like IDS, network traffic analysis tools often use signature-based detection to match observed traffic patterns against known attack signatures. When a match is found, alerts are generated.

- **Behavioral analysis**: Behavioral analysis focuses on the behavior of network entities, such as devices, users, and applications. It seeks to identify unusual or malicious behavior based on historical data and behavior profiles.

- **Threat intelligence integration**: Threat intelligence feeds and databases are integrated into traffic analysis tools to provide up-to-date information about known threats, malware, and **indicators of compromise (IoCs)**.

- **Alerting and reporting**: When suspicious or malicious activity is detected, the network security analysis tools generate alerts or notifications. These alerts are sent to security personnel for investigation and response. Detailed reports may also be generated for post-incident analysis and compliance purposes.

- **Incident response**: Network security traffic analysis is a critical component of incident response. When a security incident is confirmed, analysts use the insights gained from traffic analysis to understand the scope and impact of the incident and to develop mitigation strategies.

- **Continuous monitoring**: Effective network security traffic analysis involves continuous, real-time monitoring to detect threats as they happen. Continuous monitoring allows for swift response and containment of security incidents.

Network security traffic analysis is vital for identifying and mitigating various security threats, including malware infections, intrusion attempts, data exfiltration, and other malicious activities. It plays a crucial role in enhancing an organization's overall cybersecurity posture by providing visibility into network traffic and helping security teams proactively defend against cyber threats.

Techniques for performing network security traffic analysis

Network security traffic analysis is a critical aspect of maintaining the security of computer networks. It involves monitoring and examining network traffic to identify and mitigate potential threats, anomalies, and vulnerabilities. Here are some techniques for performing network security traffic analysis:

- **Packet inspection**: It normally works by analyzing all traffic contents, inspecting every single traffic packet, at different levels depending on packet type.

  o **DPI**: Analyzing the content of individual network packets to detect suspicious or malicious activity. **Deep packet inspection (DPI)** can identify specific protocols, applications, and even malware signatures.

- **Flow analysis**:

  o **NetFlow analysis**: Examining **network flow (NetFlow)** records to understand traffic patterns, detect anomalies, and identify potential security incidents.

  o **sFlow/J-Flow/IPFIX**: Similar to NetFlow, the protocols **Sampled Flow (sFlow), Juniper Flow (J-Flow), Internet Protocol Flow Information Export (IPFIX)** provide flow data for analysis.

- **Signature-based detection**:

  o **IDS**: Utilizing predefined signatures or patterns to identify known attacks and threats. Examples include Snort and Suricata.

- **Behavioral analysis**:

  o **Anomaly detection**: Establishing a baseline of normal network behavior and then flagging any deviations from that baseline as potential threats. Tools like anomaly-based IDS or **security information and event management (SIEM)** systems are used.

- **Heuristic analysis**:

  o **Heuristic IDS/IPS**: Employing rule-based systems that look for patterns or behaviors indicative of attacks. These are more flexible than signature-based methods but can generate false positives.

- **Machine learning and AI**:

  o **Machine learning models**: Training models to recognize unusual network behavior by analyzing historical data and identifying deviations from established norms.

- **AI-powered threat detection**: Using artificial intelligence to identify complex and evolving threats that may not have known signatures.

- **Protocol and port analysis**:

  o Monitoring network protocols and port usage to detect unusual or unauthorized network traffic.

- **Payload inspection**:

  o Examining the payload of network packets or packets themselves for malicious content or IoCs.

- **DNS analysis**:
  - o Investigating **Domain Name System** (**DNS**) traffic for signs of malicious domains, DNS tunneling, or data exfiltration.

- **SSL/TLS decryption**:
  - o Decrypting and inspecting encrypted traffic ensures that malicious activities are not hiding within encrypted connections.

- **NetFlow and packet capture**:
  - o Collecting and storing network traffic data for analysis and forensic purposes. Tools like Wireshark are commonly used for packet capture.

- **Log analysis**:
  - o Reviewing logs generated by network devices, servers, and applications for indications of security incidents.

- **SIEM integration**:
  - o Integrating network security traffic analysis with SIEM systems to correlate network events with other security data sources.

- **Threat intelligence feeds**:
  - o Subscribing to threat intelligence feeds to stay updated on known threats and IoCs and then using this data for analysis.

- **User and entity behavior analytics (UEBA)**:
  - o Focusing on analyzing user and entity behavior to detect insider threats and unusual user activities.

- **Packet filtering and firewall rules**:
  - o Implementing **access control lists** (**ACLs**) and firewall rules to restrict or allow traffic based on predefined criteria.

- **Honeypots and honeytokens**:
  - o Deploying honeypots or honeytokens within the network to attract and identify malicious activity and potential attackers.

- **Vulnerability scanning**:
  - o Scanning the network for known vulnerabilities and assessing their potential impact on security.

- **Continuous monitoring**:
  - o Maintaining ongoing, real-time monitoring of network traffic to quickly respond to emerging threats.

- **Incident response**:

    o   Developing incident response plans and procedures to effectively respond to and mitigate security incidents identified through traffic analysis.

These techniques can be used individually or in combination to create a comprehensive network security traffic analysis strategy tailored to the specific needs and risks of an organization. Regularly updating and adapting these techniques is essential to keep pace with evolving cyber threats.

Packet inspection network traffic analysis

Packet inspection, also known as **packet-level network traffic analysis** or **passive network analysis**, is a method of analyzing individual network packets to gain insights into network activities, identify potential security threats, and troubleshoot network issues. This technique involves capturing and inspecting the content of packets as they traverse a network. Here is a more detailed description of packet inspection in network traffic analysis:

- **Packet capture**: Packet inspection begins with the collection of network packets. This can be done using tools such as packet capture software (for example, Wireshark) or network monitoring devices (for example, network taps or packet brokers).

- **DPI**: DPI is the process of analyzing the actual content of each packet, including its headers and payload. This in-depth examination allows for the identification of specific protocols, applications, and potentially malicious content within the packets.

- **Protocol identification**: DPI can determine the protocols being used within the network traffic, including HTTP, SMTP, FTP, DNS, and more. This information is crucial for understanding the nature of the traffic and identifying any anomalies.

- **Application recognition**: DPI can also identify specific applications and services based on the traffic patterns and signatures within the packets. For example, it can distinguish between web browsing, email traffic, and file transfers.

- **Signature-based threat detection**: Signature-based detection involves comparing the content of packets against known patterns or signatures of known threats, such as malware or intrusion attempts. If a match is found, it can trigger an alert.

- **Content inspection**: DPI allows for the inspection of packet payloads, which can reveal potentially malicious content, such as malware downloads, command and control communications, or sensitive data being transmitted.

- **Traffic analysis**: By examining packet headers, DPI can provide insights into the source and destination IP addresses, ports, and traffic patterns. This information can help detect suspicious or unauthorized network activities.

- **Real-time monitoring**: Packet inspection is often performed in real-time, enabling network administrators and security analysts to respond quickly to emerging threats or issues.

- **Log generation and reporting**: Logs and reports are typically generated as a result of packet inspection. These logs can be used for compliance, forensics, and incident response purposes.

- **Performance considerations**: Packet inspection can be resource-intensive, especially in high-traffic networks. It may impact network performance, so careful planning and optimization are necessary.

- **Encrypted traffic decryption**: In cases where traffic is encrypted (for example, HTTPS), decryption may be necessary to perform effective packet inspection. SSL/TLS decryption tools are used for this purpose.

Packet inspection is a powerful technique for understanding network behavior, identifying security incidents, and ensuring network performance. However, it is important to use it responsibly and in compliance with privacy and legal considerations, especially when dealing with the content of network communications. Additionally, combining packet inspection with other network security measures, such as IDS and **intrusion prevention systems (IPS)**, can provide a more comprehensive defense against threats.

Network flow-based traffic analysis

Network flow-based traffic analysis is a technique used to monitor and analyze network traffic by examining data flows or connections between devices or systems on a network. Instead of inspecting individual packets, this approach focuses on aggregating and analyzing information about these flows. Here is a more detailed description of network flow-based traffic analysis:

- **Flow definition**: A network flow typically represents a unidirectional sequence of packets between a source and a destination over time. A flow is identified by several attributes, including source and destination IP addresses, source and destination ports, protocol (for example, TCP or UDP), and the ingress and egress interfaces.

- **Flow data collection**: Flow-based analysis relies on collecting flow data from network devices, such as routers, switches, and specialized flow collectors. Common flow data formats include NetFlow (used by *Cisco* devices), sFlow, J-Flow, and IPFIX.

- **Flow record generation**: Network devices (but not only) generate flow records, which contain information about each observed flow. These records typically include details like timestamps, packet and byte counts, TCP flags, and various metadata.

- **Aggregation and summarization**: Flow records are aggregated and summarized to provide a high-level view of network traffic. This can include statistics on top talkers, top applications, and traffic volume between specific endpoints.

- **Traffic profiling**: By analyzing flow data, network administrators can profile network traffic patterns. This helps in understanding typical usage, peak usage times, and identifying deviations or anomalies.

- **Anomaly detection**: Network flow-based analysis can be used to detect anomalies in network traffic, such as unusually large amounts of traffic, unexpected communication patterns, or changes in protocol usage. These anomalies may indicate security incidents or network issues.

- **Bandwidth monitoring**: Flow analysis can provide insights into bandwidth utilization. By examining flow records, administrators can identify bandwidth hogs or network congestion issues.

- **Application identification**: Flow data can be used to identify the applications and services running on the network. This is done by mapping flow characteristics to known application behaviors and signatures.

- **Threat detection**: Flow-based analysis can help detect certain network threats, including DDoS attacks, port scans, and suspicious communication patterns that may indicate malware infections.

- **Flow correlation**: Correlating flow data with other security information, such as intrusion detection alerts or log data, can provide a more comprehensive view of network security incidents.

- **Capacity planning**: Understanding network flow patterns and trends can aid in capacity planning, helping organizations scale their network infrastructure to meet future demands.

- **Compliance and reporting**: Flow data can generate reports for compliance purposes, such as demonstrating adherence to security policies or data retention requirements.

Network flow-based traffic analysis (for example, Source IP: 192.168.1.1, Source Port: 53215, Dest IP: 10.0.0.1, Protocol: TCP, Dest. Port: 80, Bytes: 500 and so on) offers a more scalable and less resource-intensive approach compared to DPI. It is particularly valuable for gaining insights into overall network behavior and identifying trends and potential issues. However, it may not provide the same level of detail as DPI when inspecting the content of individual packets, making it more suitable for certain types of analysis, such as traffic profiling and trend analysis.

Basics of network protection

As of today, it is almost certain that every company deployed some type of network protection to try to mitigate some of the more common threats we described before. The first form of protection is a good network design, both on the physical and both on the logical point of view. Once this design is implemented, it is quite common for companies to deploy one or more of the following solutions to protect their inside networks.

Firewalls and packet filters

A firewall is a network security device or software application designed to monitor and control incoming and outgoing network traffic based on an organization's predefined security rules or policies. The primary purpose of a firewall is to act as a barrier between a trusted internal network (such as a corporate network) and untrusted external networks (such as the Internet), allowing authorized traffic to pass while blocking or inspecting potentially harmful or unauthorized traffic.

Firewalls can be implemented in various forms, including hardware appliances, software applications, and virtual appliances. They operate at different layers of the network stack, including:

- **Packet filtering firewall**: These firewalls examine individual packets of data as they travel through the network and make filtering decisions based on criteria such as source and destination IP addresses, port numbers, and protocol types. Packet filtering firewalls are typically the simplest and fastest type of firewall but provide limited security because they don't inspect the content of packets.

- **Stateful inspection firewall**: Also known as dynamic packet filtering firewalls, these devices keep track of the state of active connections and make filtering decisions based on the state of the connection. They are more advanced than packet-filtering firewalls and provide improved security because they understand the context of network traffic.

- **Proxy firewall**: Proxy firewalls act as intermediaries between internal and external networks. They receive and forward network requests on behalf of clients, making it more challenging for attackers to directly access internal resources. Proxy firewalls can also inspect and filter application-layer traffic, providing better security for specific applications.

- **NGFW**: **Next-generation firewall** (**NGFWs**) combines traditional firewall features with advanced security capabilities such as intrusion detection and prevention, deep packet inspection, and application-layer filtering. They can identify and control specific applications and perform more granular security checks.

Firewalls use a set of rules or policies to determine which traffic should be allowed, denied, or inspected. These rules are typically based on factors like source and destination

IP addresses, port numbers, protocol types, and application-layer information. Firewalls can be configured to allow or block traffic based on a default-deny or default-allow policy, depending on the organization's security requirements.

Key functions and benefits of firewalls include:

- **Access control**: Firewalls control access to a network, allowing administrators to define which systems and services are accessible from the outside world.

- **Traffic inspection**: They inspect network traffic for suspicious patterns or known threats and can block or alert about malicious activity.

- **Protection from unauthorized access**: Firewalls protect against unauthorized access and help prevent data breaches and cyberattacks.

- **Network segmentation**: They can segment networks into different security zones, isolating sensitive systems from less secure areas.

- **Logging and reporting**: Firewalls often provide logging and reporting capabilities, allowing administrators to monitor network activity and analyze security events.

In summary, firewalls are a fundamental component of network security, serving as a crucial defense mechanism to protect networks and the data they contain from unauthorized access and cyber threats. They are a key element of any organization's cybersecurity strategy.

Network proxies

Another key security tool is the network proxy, acting as an intermediary between users and the Internet. A network proxy, often simply referred to as a proxy, is an intermediary server or software application that acts as a gateway between a user's device (such as a computer or smartphone) and the Internet. When a user makes a request to access a website or a service on the Internet, the request is first sent to the proxy server, which then forwards the request to the target server or resource on behalf of the user. Here are some key functions and purposes of network proxies:

- **Anonymity**: Proxies can hide a user's real IP address and location from the websites or services they access. This is often used for privacy and security reasons.

- **Content filtering**: Proxies can be configured to filter and block access to specific websites or content categories. This is commonly used in organizations to enforce Internet usage policies.

- **Load balancing**: In a network with multiple servers providing the same service (for example, web servers), a proxy can distribute incoming requests among these servers to balance the load, improve performance, and ensure high availability.

- **Caching**: Proxies can store copies of frequently accessed web pages and resources locally. When a user requests a cached resource, the proxy can serve it directly, reducing the load on the target server and speeding up access to content.

- **Security**: Proxies can act as a security layer by inspecting incoming and outgoing traffic for malicious content, such as malware or phishing attempts. They can block or filter out threats before they reach the user.

- **Access control**: Proxies can enforce access controls and authentication, allowing or denying access to specific users or groups based on predefined policies.

- **Bypassing geographical restrictions**: Users can use proxies to access content or services that may be restricted or geo-blocked in their region. By connecting to a proxy server in a different location, they can appear to be browsing from that location.

- **Monitoring and logging**: Proxies can record and log network traffic, providing administrators with visibility into user activities and potential security incidents.

- **Network optimization**: Proxies can compress and optimize data traffic, reducing bandwidth consumption and improving the performance of slow or congested network connections.

- **Protocol conversion**: Some proxies can translate between network protocols, allowing incompatible devices or applications to communicate effectively. As example, this could allow older systems to use certain modern applications.

There are various types of proxies, including HTTP proxies, SOCKS proxies, transparent proxies, and reverse proxies, each with specific use cases and functionalities. The choice of proxy type depends on the intended purpose, such as web browsing, anonymous browsing, or network security. Proxies are commonly used in both corporate environments and personal settings to achieve different networking and security goals.

Intrusion detection systems

An IDS is a security technology used to monitor and analyze network traffic or system activity for signs of unauthorized access, misuse, or malicious activities. The primary purpose of an IDS is to detect security incidents and potential security threats within a network or on a host system. It is a crucial component of an organization's overall cybersecurity strategy.

Here is how an IDS works:

- **Data collection**: The IDS collects data from various sources within a network or on a host system. These sources can include network traffic, system logs, and event data generated by applications, devices, and other network components.

- **Traffic analysis**: In the case of a **network-based IDS** (**NIDS**), the system continuously analyzes network traffic passing through it. It examines packets of data to identify suspicious patterns, such as known attack signatures, anomalies, or deviations from normal network behavior In the case of a **host-based IDS** (**HIDS**), the system monitors activities on a specific host or server. It reviews system logs, file system changes, registry modifications, and other host-related events.

- **Signature-based detection**: One common method used by IDS is signature-based detection. This approach involves comparing observed data patterns to a database of known attack signatures. If a match is found, the IDS generates an alert. Signature-based detection is effective against known threats but may not detect new or previously unseen attacks.

- **Anomaly-based detection**: Anomaly-based detection involves establishing a baseline of normal network or system behavior and then flagging deviations from this baseline as potential threats. Anomalies can indicate novel or previously unknown attacks, making this approach valuable for detecting zero-day vulnerabilities. However, it can also produce false positives if the baseline is not well-defined.

- **Heuristic and behavioral analysis**: Some IDS use heuristic analysis to identify patterns of behavior indicative of attacks. This approach looks for patterns that may not match known signatures but still exhibit suspicious or malicious characteristics.

- **Alert generation**: When the IDS detects suspicious activity or a potential intrusion, it generates alerts. These alerts may include information about the nature of the activity, the source and destination addresses, and the severity of the threat. Alerts are typically sent to a **security operations center** (**SOC**) or a designated security team for further investigation.

- **Response and mitigation**: After receiving an alert, security analysts investigate the incident to determine its severity and impact. Depending on the organization's policies and the nature of the threat, various actions may be taken, such as isolating affected systems, blocking malicious IP addresses, or implementing security patches.

- **Logging and reporting**: IDS systems maintain logs of detected events and incidents. These logs are crucial for post-incident analysis, compliance reporting, and continuous improvement of security policies.

There are two main types of IDS:

- **NIDS**: NIDS monitors network traffic at key points on the network, such as at the perimeter or within critical network segments. It is well-suited for detecting threats that traverse the network, such as network attacks and malicious traffic.

- **HIDS**: HIDS is installed on individual host systems, such as servers or endpoints. It focuses on monitoring activities specific to the host it protects, making it effective at detecting host-level threats, such as unauthorized access or malware infections.

In summary, an IDS is a critical cybersecurity tool that helps organizations identify and respond to security threats by monitoring and analyzing network traffic or host activity. It plays a vital role in maintaining network and system security and is often used with other security measures like firewalls and IPS.

Intrusion prevention systems

Building on IDS concepts, IPS take the proactive approach instead of a monitoring only one. An IPS is a network security technology and device or software application that goes beyond the capabilities of an IDS by actively preventing and blocking potential security threats and attacks in real time. While an IDS focuses on detecting and alerting suspicious or malicious network activity, an IPS takes a proactive approach by automatically taking action to stop or mitigate identified threats.

Here is how IPS works:

- **Traffic inspection**: The IPS continuously inspects network traffic, examining packets, sessions, and application-layer data to identify patterns or behaviors that may indicate an attack or security breach.

- **Signature-based detection**: Similar to an IDS, an IPS uses signature-based detection to compare observed traffic patterns with a database of known attack signatures. If it identifies a match, it generates an alert and takes predefined actions to block or mitigate the threat.

- **Anomaly-based detection**: An IPS can also employ anomaly-based detection by establishing a baseline of normal network behavior. Deviations from this baseline are flagged as potential threats. Anomaly-based detection is useful for identifying unknown or zero-day attacks but may produce false positives.

- **Behavioral analysis**: Some IPS systems use behavioral analysis to identify suspicious behavior that may not match known signatures but still indicates malicious intent. This approach looks for patterns that deviate from expected behavior.

- **Automatic blocking**: The key differentiator of an IPS is its ability to automatically block or mitigate threats in real-time. When the IPS detects a potential attack, it can take various actions, including:

- **Dropping or blocking malicious packets**: The IPS can prevent malicious packets from reaching their intended destination, effectively stopping the attack at the network level.

- **Alerting**: The IPS can generate alerts to notify security teams of detected threats and actions taken.

- **Connection reset**: In the case of an established connection determined to be malicious, the IPS can send a reset signal to terminate the connection.

- **Rate limiting**: The IPS can limit the rate of certain types of traffic to prevent flooding attacks, such as DDoS attacks.

- **Logging and reporting**: Like an IDS, an IPS maintains logs of detected events and actions taken. These logs are essential for incident analysis, compliance reporting, and auditing.

- **Integration**: IPS solutions can often integrate with other security technologies, such as firewalls and SIEM systems, to provide a more comprehensive security posture.

IPS are deployed at various points within a network, including at the network perimeter, within network segments, and on individual endpoints. They are an important component of a multi-layered security strategy and work alongside firewalls, antivirus software, and other security measures to protect against a wide range of cyber threats.

By actively blocking malicious traffic and attacks in real-time, IPS systems help organizations enhance their network security and reduce the risk of security breaches and data loss.

Pros and cons of packet inspection network traffic analysis

Packet inspection network traffic analysis, often referred to as packet-level analysis or packet inspection, involves examining the individual packets of data that flow through a network to gain insights into network activity. This approach has its own set of pros and cons.

The pros are as follows:

- **Granular visibility**: Packet inspection provides the most detailed level of visibility into network traffic. It allows you to see the actual data packets, including their contents, headers, and source/destination information. This granularity is crucial for troubleshooting and security analysis.

- **Accurate threat detection**: Packet inspection is highly effective for detecting network threats and anomalies. It can identify malware, intrusion attempts, and suspicious traffic patterns that may be missed by other, less granular monitoring techniques.

- **Forensic analysis**: When a security incident occurs, packet-level analysis is invaluable for forensic investigation. It provides a detailed record of network activity, which can be crucial for understanding the scope and impact of a security breach.

- **Protocol analysis**: Packet inspection allows for in-depth analysis of network protocols, helping to identify protocol-specific issues, misconfigurations, or performance bottlenecks.

- **Customization**: Analysts can customize packet inspection tools and filters to focus on specific aspects of network traffic, which is particularly useful for meeting the unique needs of an organization or network.

The cons are as follows:

- **Resource intensive**: Packet inspection can be very resource intensive. It requires specialized hardware and software tools to capture, store, and analyze large volumes of network packets. This can lead to high infrastructure costs.

- **Privacy concerns**: Examining the contents of network packets can raise privacy concerns. It may involve inspecting sensitive data, such as user communications or application payloads, which can lead to legal and ethical issues if not handled carefully.

- **Complexity**: Analyzing network packets is complex and requires expertise. Network administrators and security analysts need a deep understanding of networking protocols and packet-level details, which can be a barrier to entry for some organizations.

- **Performance impact**: In high-traffic networks, capturing and inspecting every packet can introduce latency and affect network performance. It is important to strike a balance between visibility and performance.

- **Limited scalability**: Packet inspection is challenging to scale for large networks with high volumes of traffic. It may not be feasible to inspect every packet in such environments, which can limit its effectiveness.

- **Encrypted traffic**: With the increasing use of encryption (for example, TLS/SSL), packet inspection becomes less effective at inspecting the contents of encrypted packets. This can make it challenging to detect threats hiding within encrypted traffic.

In summary, packet inspection network traffic analysis provides unparalleled visibility and accuracy for network monitoring and security but comes with significant resource and complexity challenges. Organizations should consider their specific needs and limitations before implementing packet-level analysis as part of their network monitoring and security strategy.

Open-source and commercial solutions

Packet-level network analysis is crucial for understanding network traffic and diagnosing issues. Several open-source tools are available for performing packet-level network analysis. Here are some popular ones:

- **Wireshark**: Wireshark is one of the most widely used and powerful open-source packet analyzers available. It allows you to capture, dissect, and analyze network packets in real-time. Wireshark is available for various platforms and supports a wide range of protocols.

- **tcpdump**: tcpdump is a command line packet analyzer available for Unix-based systems. It can capture packets and display them in a human-readable format. tcpdump is often used in combination with other tools for more in-depth analysis.

- **Tshark**: Tshark is the command line version of Wireshark and comes bundled with Wireshark. It provides similar packet analysis capabilities but is intended for use in scripts and automated tasks.

- **Arkime**[2]: Arkime is an open-source full packet capture and indexing system that can also be used for flow-based network traffic analysis. It provides capabilities for storing and querying flow data.

- **Suricata**: Suricata is an open-source IDS and IPS that can capture and analyze network packets. It is primarily focused on detecting network threats and malicious activity.

- **Snort**: Snort is another open-source IDS that can be used for packet analysis. It is highly configurable and can be used to monitor network traffic for suspicious patterns and signatures.

- **ChopShop**[3]: ChopShop is an extensible packet analysis framework that allows you to create and share packet analysis modules. It is designed for security researchers and analysts.

- **NetworkMiner**: NetworkMiner is a network forensic analysis tool that can parse captured network traffic and extract useful information like hostnames, usernames, and file artifacts.

- **Xplico**[4]: Xplico is an open-source network forensic analysis tool that can extract data from captured network traffic and provide insights into various protocols, such as HTTP, SIP, and IMAP.

- **Darkstat**: Darkstat is a network traffic analyzer that collects network statistics and presents them in a web-based interface. It is useful for monitoring and visualizing network traffic trends.

---

2. https://arkime.com/
3. https://www.mitre.org/our-impact/intellectual-property/chopshop
4. https://www.xplico.org

These open-source tools vary in features, complexity, and use cases, so you should choose the one that best suits your specific requirements for packet-level network analysis.

There are also several commercial products available that can perform packet-level network analysis. Here are some popular options:

- **SolarWinds network performance monitor**: SolarWinds offers various network monitoring and analysis tools, including **network performance monitor (NPM)**. NPM can provide packet-level analysis capabilities to help diagnose and troubleshoot network issues.

- **Riverbed SteelCentral Packet Analyzer**: This commercial product by Riverbed offers packet-level analysis for network troubleshooting and performance monitoring. It provides insights into network traffic and helps identify problems affecting network performance.

- **NETSCOUT nGeniusONE**: NETSCOUT'S nGeniusONE platform offers packet-level analysis and real-time monitoring of network traffic. It is designed to help organizations optimize network performance and troubleshoot issues.

- **Colasoft Capsa**: Capsa is a network analyzer by Colasoft that provides packet-level analysis and network monitoring. It is available in various editions, including a free version with limited features.

- **WildPackets (Savvius) Omnipeek**: Omnipeek is a packet-level network analyzer that offers comprehensive network troubleshooting and analysis capabilities. It can capture and dissect packets in real time.

- **NETSCOUT InfiniStreamNG**: This product by NETSCOUT is designed for high-speed packet capture and analysis. It is suitable for organizations with large and complex networks.

- **Cisco Stealthwatch**: Cisco's Stealthwatch is a network traffic analysis solution that offers both flow-based and packet-level analysis for security monitoring and threat detection.

- **ExtraHop Reveal(x)**: ExtraHop's Reveal(x) provides real-time network traffic analysis, including packet-level insights. It focuses on security and threat detection within the network.

- **Plixer Scrutinizer**: Plixer offers Scrutinizer, a network traffic analysis and flow monitoring solution that provides packet-level analysis for in-depth troubleshooting.

Remember that the choice of a packet-level network analysis tool should be based on your specific needs, budget, and the scale of your network. Additionally, some tools may offer additional features beyond packet-level analysis, such as security monitoring, application performance management, and historical data retention, so consider those factors when making your decision.

Pros and cons of network flow-based traffic analysis

Network flow-based traffic analysis is a method used to monitor and analyze network traffic by examining the flow of data packets within a network. It involves collecting information about the source, destination, volume, and timing of data flows. While it has several advantages, it also has its limitations. Here are the pros and cons of network flow-based traffic analysis.

The pros are as follows:

- **Efficient data reduction**: Network flow analysis reduces the vast amount of raw network traffic data into manageable and meaningful flow records. This helps in efficient storage and processing of network traffic information.

- **Scalability**: Flow-based analysis can scale effectively to large and complex networks, making it suitable for enterprise-level and data center environments.

- **Anomaly detection**: It is effective for identifying anomalies in network traffic patterns. Sudden spikes in data volume or unusual communication patterns can be detected, which may indicate security threats or network issues.

- **Resource efficiency**: Flow-based analysis consumes fewer network resources compared to full packet capture and inspection, making it less intrusive and more suitable for high-speed networks.

- **Real-time monitoring**: It provides real-time visibility into network traffic, allowing network administrators to promptly respond to issues and security threats.

- **Compliance and reporting**: Flow data can be useful for compliance requirements and generating network performance reports.

The cons are as follows:

- **Limited payload data**: Network flow analysis typically does not capture the content of packets, including the payload. This means that it cannot detect threats or anomalies that are hidden within encrypted traffic or require packet-level inspection.

- **Lack of granularity**: Flow-based analysis may not provide detailed information about specific packet-level events, making it less suitable for in-depth packet-level troubleshooting or forensic analysis.

- **False positives**: Depending on the flow aggregation and sampling rate, network flow analysis can produce false positives or miss subtle network anomalies.

- **Resource intensive**: While less resource-intensive than full packet capture, flow-based analysis still requires dedicated hardware and storage for processing and storing flow records, especially in high-traffic environments.

- **Limited protocol support**: Flow-based analysis may not capture information about all protocols, particularly if the network uses non-standard or proprietary protocols.

- **Intrusive sampling**: To manage resource consumption, flow-based analysis often relies on sampling, which means not all traffic is analyzed. This could lead to some traffic being missed.

In summary, network flow-based traffic analysis offers a balance between efficiency and visibility in monitoring network traffic. It is valuable for detecting certain network issues and anomalies but may not be suitable for all use cases, especially those requiring deep packet inspection or analysis of encrypted traffic. Organizations should consider their specific needs and constraints when choosing a network traffic analysis approach.

Open-source and commercial solutions

There are several open-source network flow-based analysis tools available that allow organizations to monitor and analyze network traffic using flow data. These tools offer various features for gaining insights into network behavior, identifying anomalies, and enhancing security. Here are some of the main open-source network flow-based analysis tools:

- **nfdump**: nfdump is a popular open-source tool that collects and processes flow data, such as NetFlow and IPFIX. It provides options for visualization, reporting, and querying flow records.

- **Yet Another Flowmeter (YAF)**: YAF is an open-source flow-based network traffic analysis tool that can process and analyze various flow formats. It offers features for network monitoring, security analysis, and reporting.

- **System for Internet-Level Knowledge (SiLK)**: SiLK is an open-source suite of flow analysis tools developed by the *CERT Division of the Software Engineering Institute*. It supports flow collection, storage, and analysis for security and network monitoring purposes.

- **Softflowd**: Softflowd is an open-source flow exporter that captures flow data and exports it in NetFlow format. It is designed to be lightweight and efficient for resource-constrained environments.

- **Argus**: Argus is an open-source network audit tool that collects and processes flow data, providing insights into network communication, behavior, and performance.

Keep in mind that open-source tools might require more hands-on setup and customization compared to commercial solutions, but they offer flexibility and cost savings for organizations willing to invest time in deployment and maintenance.

Several commercial network flow-based analysis tools are also available to help organizations monitor and analyze network traffic using flow data. These tools offer various features for understanding network behavior, identifying anomalies, and enhancing security. Here are some of the main commercial network flow-based analysis tools:

- **SolarWinds NetFlow traffic analyzer**: SolarWinds offers a NetFlow traffic analyzer that provides real-time monitoring and analysis of network traffic using flow data. It offers insights into network bandwidth usage, application traffic, and communication patterns.

- **Plixer Scrutinizer**: Plixer's Scrutinizer is a flow analysis and network monitoring tool that supports various flow formats, including NetFlow and IPFIX. It offers real-time visualization, reporting, and security insights.

- **Kentik network observability cloud**: Kentik's platform offers flow-based network observability, helping organizations monitor and analyze network performance, detect anomalies, and optimize network resources.

- **ManageEngine NetFlow analyzer**: NetFlow analyzer by *ManageEngine* provides comprehensive flow-based analysis for network traffic monitoring, application identification, capacity planning, and security threat detection.

- **Flowmon solution**: Flowmon offers network performance and security monitoring solutions that leverage flow data to provide insights into network behavior, application usage, and potential security incidents.

- **Riverbed SteelCentral NetProfiler**: Riverbed's NetProfiler is a flow analysis solution that offers visibility into network performance, application behavior, and communication patterns for troubleshooting and optimization.

- **InfoVista Ipanema SD-WAN**: InfoVista's Ipanema SD-WAN platform uses flow data to monitor application performance, analyze network traffic, and prioritize critical applications over the network.

- **Cisco Stealthwatch**: Cisco's Stealthwatch is a network security solution that leverages flow data for threat detection, anomaly detection, and incident response. It focuses on identifying malicious activities and potential security breaches.

- **NETSCOUT nGeniusONE**: NETSCOUT'S nGeniusONE platform combines flow-based analysis with packet-level visibility to provide insights into network performance, security, and application behavior.

- **ExtraHop Reveal(x)**: ExtraHop offers a network detection and response platform that uses flow data along with real-time packet analysis to provide security insights, threat detection, and investigation capabilities.

- **Flower**[5] : It is a hybrid commercial/open-source solution that has several

---
5. https://fl0wer.me

innovations not yet seen in big players, very innovative and focusing on network security. Simple and easy flow-matrix creation, **Network Probabilistic Application Recognition (NPAR)** and traffic classification rules (beside tons of other features) are very effective in network understanding and monitoring.

When evaluating commercial network flow-based analysis tools, consider factors such as the supported flow formats, scalability, real-time analysis capabilities, reporting features, integration options, and pricing. It is also important to assess whether the tool aligns with your organization's specific network environment, security requirements, and performance monitoring needs.

As you have probably seen, there are several tools, techniques and ways to improve network security. Tools nowadays are not strictly so vertical on one technology and often incorporate different ones. As an example, let us consider Darktrace, it works basically using packet-level network analysis but makes use of machine learning to improve its detection mechanism. What should be clear is that there is not a single good for everything tool or technique that suits all needs, but you need to understand very well what you are planning to control, its bandwidth, your budget and concrete facts.

Traffic encryption

Over time, a significant portion of Internet traffic has shifted to using encryption, primarily through protocols like HTTPS (TLS/SSL) for web traffic, which prevents the content of the communication from being easily readable by network sniffers. This encryption is intended to enhance security and privacy by ensuring that sensitive data is transmitted securely.

Consider the following reasons:

- **Rapid growth**: The adoption of encrypted protocols, such as HTTPS, has been steadily increasing over the years. Major initiatives like *Let's Encrypt* have contributed to this growth by making it easier for website owners to obtain and implement SSL/TLS certificates for their domains.

- **Browser push**: Major web browsers, including *Google Chrome, Mozilla Firefox*, and others, have been actively pushing for secure connections. They often mark non-encrypted websites with warnings and prioritize encrypted sites in search rankings.

- **HTTPS usage**: By 2020, a significant portion of web traffic already used HTTPS. According to the Mozilla Observatory's statistics, over 90% of page loads in the United States were encrypted using HTTPS.

- **Popular websites**: Many popular websites and online services have transitioned to HTTPS, including social media platforms, e-commerce websites, and online banking services.

- **Encrypted applications**: Beyond web traffic, many applications and services, including messaging apps and VPNs, use encryption to secure data in transit.

- **Regulatory compliance**: Various regulations and privacy laws, such as the **General Data Protection Regulation** (**GDPR**) in Europe, encourage encryption to protect user data.

The widespread adoption of encryption does indeed pose a challenge for passive network traffic analysis, as traditional packet sniffing tools are unable to decipher the encrypted content directly. While encryption makes it more difficult to analyze the actual payload of the traffic, there are still aspects of network traffic that can be analyzed, even when encrypted:

- **Metadata analysis**: Even when the content of the communication is encrypted, metadata such as source and destination IP addresses, port numbers, packet sizes, and communication patterns can still be captured and analyzed. This information can provide insights into the nature of communication, the parties involved, and the volume of traffic, revealing recurring patterns like **command and control** (**C&C**), **The Onion Router** (**TOR**) connections and/or DDoS traffic by simply investigating spikes in small patterns

- **TLS inspection**: Some security solutions, like IDPS and NGFW, are equipped with TLS inspection capabilities. In certain conditions, they can decrypt and analyze encrypted traffic to detect malicious payloads or activities. However, this process requires careful implementation and can raise privacy and compliance concerns.

- **Certificate analysis**: Analyzing the certificates used in encryption can provide information about the websites being accessed, the entities providing the certificates, and the encryption protocols being used.

- **Flow analysis**: Flow-based analysis, which focuses on tracking the connections and behaviors between endpoints, can provide insights into communication patterns and anomalies, even when the actual payload is encrypted.

- **Threat intelligence and behavior analysis**: Some security solutions leverage threat intelligence and behavioral analysis to identify potential threats based on patterns of communication, known malicious domains, or other indicators.

- **Anomaly detection**: By establishing baselines of normal network behavior, anomalies in encrypted traffic can still be detected, such as unusual patterns of traffic volume or communication.

- **Endpoints and host analysis**: Endpoint-based security solutions can analyze encrypted traffic once it reaches the endpoint, allowing for more comprehensive inspection and analysis.

While encryption does pose challenges to traditional passive network traffic analysis, the security community continues to develop methods and techniques to adapt to this evolving landscape. Organizations looking to perform network analysis in encrypted environments often turn to a combination of traffic analysis techniques, behavioral analysis, and endpoint security solutions to gain meaningful insights despite the encryption barriers.

Network bandwidth increase

The average backbone speeds within networks can vary significantly based on factors such as geographic location, network infrastructure, technology advancements, and the type of network (for example, enterprise, data center, ISP backbone). However, we can provide you with a general overview of the trends and speeds that were commonly seen in network backbones up to that point:

- **Enterprise networks**: In enterprise environments, backbone speeds typically ranged from 1 **Gbps** (**Gigabit per second**) to 10 Gbps. Many organizations were transitioning to 10 Gbps backbones to accommodate increasing data traffic and the demand for higher bandwidth due to the proliferation of devices and applications.

- **Data centers**: Data center networks commonly employed backbone speeds of 10 Gbps, 40 Gbps, and 100 Gbps. The adoption of 100 Gbps was increasing, driven by the need to support high-density virtualization, cloud services, and the rapid movement of data within data center environments.

- **ISP backbones**: **Internet Service Provider** (**ISP**) backbone speeds have evolved over time to meet the growing demand for high-speed Internet access. Backbones were commonly operating at 100 Gbps, and some larger ISPs were already exploring 400 Gbps and even 1 **Terabit per second** (**Tbps**) speeds to handle the massive data traffic across their networks.

- **Research and education networks**: Research and education networks often had higher backbone speeds due to their focus on advanced data-intensive applications. Speeds of 100 Gbps and beyond were not uncommon in these environments.

Note: These speeds are not stagnant and continue to evolve as technology advances. The deployment of faster networking technologies, such as 400 Gbps and 800 Gbps, is actual, and even higher speeds may have become more prevalent since then.

Challenge of analyzing 800 Gbps networks

To consider, performing network traffic analysis on 800 Gbps networks presents unique challenges due to the sheer volume of data involved. This technology is already available nowadays, just look for it with an Internet search engine.

Even using the fastest hardware and CPUs available nowadays, they would be spending all their time dealing with the huge quantity of interrupts just for handling packets if the **Network Interface Cards** (**NICs**) would not provide offloading of a lot of TCP/IP functions on them.

So, to efficiently perform traffic analysis using DPI, you would need:

- **High-speed capture hardware**: To handle the high data rates, you need specialized network capture hardware capable of capturing and processing data at 800 Gbps. This hardware should have multiple high-speed network interfaces and ample storage capacity to accommodate the captured data.

- **Traffic filtering**: Given the volume of data, it is important to filter the captured traffic to focus on specific areas of interest. Use filters to capture only the relevant traffic, such as traffic to and from critical servers, communication between specific IP ranges, or traffic using specific protocols.

- **Sampling**: Due to the high speed, you might consider using sampling techniques to capture a subset of the traffic for analysis. Sampling involves capturing a fraction of the total traffic, which can help manage the volume of data while still providing insights into network behavior.

- **Advanced analysis tools**: Deploy advanced network analysis tools that can handle high-speed data rates and provide in-depth insights. These tools should offer features like behavioral analysis, anomaly detection, and the ability to generate meaningful reports.

- **Parallel processing**: Use multi-threading and parallel processing techniques to distribute the analysis workload across multiple CPU cores or machines. This can help improve analysis speed and efficiency.

- **Hybrid approach**: Consider a hybrid approach that combines real-time analysis with storage for historical analysis. Store captured data for later analysis when specific incidents or anomalies need further investigation.

- **Bandwidth throttling**: If capturing the entire network is not feasible, consider using network devices to throttle or shape traffic to a manageable level for analysis purposes.

Performing network traffic analysis on 800 Gbps networks requires a combination of specialized hardware, high-performance analysis tools, and careful planning to ensure that the analysis process is effective and efficient. It is important to stay updated with advancements in network analysis technology to address the challenges posed by high-speed networks.

But if we adopt a different approach like network flow analysis, things are quite different. We do not need any more to analyze every single packet in the thousands or million flows crossing the high-speed connection, but we have a single flow to consider. It is true that we do not have the details of the packet's payload, but there is an 80% possibility it would have been encrypted, so it would not have been very useful to deal with anyway. And instead of worrying about dealing with about a billion packets per second, we can think about understanding if that single flow (in the middle of so many flows) is meaningful for our business just by looking at the tuple of {IP Source, IP Destination, IP Protocol, Source Port and Destination Port}.

The downside of network flow analysis is that the flow is emitted by the crossing device when the communication is completed, so it is almost near real-time. But in the end, it is not very different from an IPS that could block a connection (even valid) only when it matches some well-known pattern. Putting it simply, network flow analysis can scale much more than passive DPI analysis. It can also build the foundation and rules for a better network policy, being proactive, while DPI struggles with high-speed connection links and is quite useless against encrypted traffic.

Conclusion

We introduced some of the already-known concepts, depending on your skill, but it is better to have a good understanding of how things work in combination with the kind of problems we both must solve and the ones we will have to face. Network flow analysis is not yet well-known and documented like DPI. It was not much used until recently, but we hope that in this book, you will learn enough to take advantage of it.

In the next chapter, we are going to delve into flow protocol descriptions to have a solid foundation and understanding of what we can do and what we cannot with the provided information.

Join our book's Discord space

Join the book's Discord Workspace for Latest updates, Offers, Tech happenings around the world, New Release and Sessions with the Authors:

https://discord.bpbonline.com

## CHAPTER 2

Fixed and Dynamic Length Flow Protocols

Introduction

Let us start diving into the core of network flow analysis. In *Chapter 1, Foundation of Network Flow Analysis,* you have learned that packet-inspection traffic analysis is like listening to a phone call, while network flow traffic analysis is like checking the phone bill (you do not know the content of the phone call, but you know both the parties, that is, the source and destination IP address, involved in conversation, how long it lasted (timestamp of begin and end of conversation), in which language they talked about, that is, the IP protocol; the topics, mainly the destination ports, and how meaningful the conversation was (bytes and packets). So, flow data is the single entry in the phone bill.

The first thing we need to understand is how flow data is transmitted over the network in a way that can be efficiently used for both general and security purposes. We need to identify who are the actors in communication and their scope. There are flow exporters, which are commonly operating on network devices (but not only), and consumers of this kind of information, which are widely called flow collectors. Normally, you configure the flow exporters to send flow data to flow collectors and choose (if possible) the network protocol to use.

A network protocol is a set of rules, conventions, and procedures that govern how data is formatted, transmitted, received, and acknowledged within a network. It defines the standards and guidelines for communication between devices, ensuring that they can understand and exchange information with each other efficiently and accurately. In the case of flow protocols, they can be thought of as a sort of data streaming of information from the flow exporter to the collector; it is a sort of unidirectional conversation, usually happening over UDP protocol, although in rare cases, **Stream Control Transmission Protocol (SCTP)** could be used.

Structure

In this chapter, we will discuss the following topics:

- Different kinds of network flow exporters
- Network flow collectors
- NetFlow version 1
- NetFlow version 5
- NetFlow version 9
- IPFIX
- sFlow v5
- Differences between fixed and dynamic flow protocols

Objectives

The chapter will discuss both the fixed length flow protocols, both dynamic length flow protocols, their advantages and drawbacks. The chapter describes in depth NetFlow v1, NetFlow v5, NetFlow v9, sFlow v5 and IPFIX. By the end of this chapter, the user will have a good understanding of the different protocols and protocols misuse.

Different kinds of network flow exporters

A network flow exporter is a device or software component that collects, aggregates, and exports network flow data to a designated collector or analyzer. Network flow data consists of summarized information about communication patterns and traffic within a network, and it is crucial for network monitoring, analysis, and security.

Here are the key aspects and functions of a network flow exporter:

- **Data collection**: Gathers flow data by examining packets passing through a network interface or interfaces. Flow data is typically collected based on defined criteria, such as source and destination IP addresses, ports, protocols, and timestamps.

- **Flow aggregation**: Aggregates individual packets or observed flows based on specific attributes (for example, IP addresses, ports) to create summarized flow records. Aggregation helps reduce the volume of data to be processed and transmitted.

- **Flow record generation**: Generates flow records containing information about each aggregated flow, such as source and destination addresses, ports, byte and packet counts, and timestamps. These records provide a concise representation of network activity.

- **Exporting flow records**: Transmits the flow records to a designated flow collector for further analysis. The export process may use protocols such as NetFlow, IPFIX, sFlow, or others to transfer the flow data from the exporter to the collector.

- **Protocol support**: Supports specific flow export protocols, such as NetFlow (v5, v9), IPFIX, sFlow, J-Flow (a variation of NetFlow v9, specific to Juniper devices), and others, depending on the capabilities and configuration of the exporter.

- **Configurable parameters**: Allows configuration of parameters like sampling rate (for sampled flow data), record format, export interval, and destination collector(s) to suit the network monitoring requirements.

- **Timestamping**: Assigns accurate timestamps to each flow record to provide insights into when the communication occurred, aiding in time-sensitive analysis.

- **Flow sampling (optional)**: Optionally employs flow sampling techniques to select a subset of flows for monitoring. Sampling helps reduce resource overhead while providing a representative view of network traffic.

- **Efficient resource utilization**: Ensures efficient usage of system resources (CPU, memory, network bandwidth) to handle the collection, aggregation, and export of flow data without impacting the overall network performance.

Network flow exporters play a critical role in network monitoring and analysis by providing valuable insights into traffic patterns, helping detect anomalies, assessing network performance, and facilitating informed decision-making regarding network management and security. Flow collectors analyse the exported flow data to derive meaningful insights and actionable intelligence for optimizing network operations.

Normally, Layer 2 devices like switches or virtual switches make use of sFlow v5 protocol, while Layer 3 devices (like routers, firewalls, servers, load balancers or virtualization platforms) make use of some NetFlow variant or IPFIX protocol, depending on the system.

Although there are many variants and evolutions of the NetFlow protocols, in this book we will focus on the v1, v5, v9, IPFIX and sFlow protocols.

Network flow collectors

Network flow collectors are specialized devices or software applications responsible for gathering, storing, and analyzing network flow data generated by flow exporters. They play a vital role in network monitoring and management, providing valuable insights into network traffic, usage patterns, and security events. Here are the key aspects and functions of network flow collectors:

- **Data reception**: Receive and accumulate network flow data transmitted by flow exporters across the network. Flow data is sent using specific flow export protocols such as NetFlow, IPFIX, sFlow, J-Flow, etc.

- **Flow data storage**: Store the received flow data in a structured and organized manner, often using databases or specialized storage systems optimized for efficient data storage and retrieval.

- **Data aggregation and correlation**: Aggregate and correlate flow data to create summaries or reports that provide an overview of network traffic patterns, usage trends, and behaviour. Aggregated data aids in identifying anomalies and detecting potential security threats.

- **Data analysis and visualization**: Can analyze the flow data to derive meaningful insights, generate reports, and visualize network traffic trends. Data can be presented in various graphical formats, dashboards, or tables for easy interpretation.

- **Anomaly detection and alerting**: Can utilize algorithms and heuristics to detect anomalies or unusual patterns in network traffic that may indicate potential security incidents or abnormal behaviour. Alerts and notifications are often generated for further investigation.

- **Historical data retention**: Retain historical flow data for a specified duration to support trend analysis, historical comparisons, and forensic investigations into past network activities.

- **Integration with other systems**: Integrate with other network management and security systems to enhance overall network visibility and provide a comprehensive view of the network environment.

- **Security analysis**: Assist in security analysis by identifying suspicious network behavior, potential DDoS attacks, malware infections, and other security-related events based on flow data patterns.

- **Capacity planning**: Can aid in network capacity planning by analyzing trends and traffic patterns to forecast future network requirements and optimize network resources.

- **Compliance and reporting**: Can generate compliance reports based on regulatory requirements or organizational policies. Provide audit trails and evidence of network activity for compliance purposes.

- **Customization and configuration**: Allow customization of reports, dashboards, and analysis parameters to suit specific organizational requirements and preferences.

Network flow collectors are a critical component of network monitoring and analysis infrastructure. They help organizations maintain optimal network performance, improve security posture, and make informed decisions to ensure efficient network operations.

NetFlow version 1

NetFlow version 1 (NetFlow v1) was the initial implementation of the protocol, and it laid the foundation for subsequent versions with more features and improvements. NetFlow v1 is the first iteration of the NetFlow protocol, focusing on exporting basic flow information for network analysis. While it laid the groundwork for subsequent versions, it has limitations in terms of features and scalability. Organizations looking for more advanced capabilities typically use newer versions of the protocol. Here is a detailed description of the NetFlow v1 protocol:

- **NetFlow v1 protocol overview**: NetFlow v1 is a lightweight protocol designed to export network traffic information from network devices, such as routers and switches, to a collector for analysis. It focuses on sending information about individual packets or flows as they traverse the device.

- **Key concepts**:

  - **Flow**: A flow represents a unidirectional sequence of packets between a specific source IP address and a specific destination IP address. Flows are defined by their network-layer attributes and can include fields such as source IP, destination IP, source port, destination port, protocol, and so on.

  - **NetFlow exporter**: This network device (for example, router or switch) generates and sends NetFlow records to a collector. The exporter identifies and aggregates flow data to be exported.

  - **NetFlow collector**: This is the server that receives NetFlow records from one or more exporters. It stores and analyzes the data to provide insights into network traffic patterns.

  - **NetFlow record**: A NetFlow record is a data structure that contains information about a flow. It includes fields such as source IP, destination IP, source port, destination port, protocol, bytes sent, packets sent, and so on.

- **NetFlow v1 packet structure**: A NetFlow v1 packet consists of a header followed by a sequence of flow records.

  - **Header**:

    - **Version number**: 1 (indicating NetFlow v1).

    - **Count**: Number of flow records in the packet.

  - **Flow record format**: Each flow record contains the following fields:

    - **Source IP address**: The source IP address of the flow.

    - **Destination IP address**: The destination IP address of the flow.

    - **IP protocol**: The IP protocol number (for example, TCP = 6, UDP = 17).

- **Source port**: The source port of the flow (0 if not applicable).

- **Destination port**: The destination port of the flow (0 if not applicable).

- **Packet count**: Number of packets in the flow.

- **Byte count**: Total number of bytes in the flow.

- **First switched**: Timestamp when the first packet of the flow was observed.

- **Last switched**: Timestamp when the last packet of the flow was observed.

- **NetFlow v1 protocol operation**:

  o **Flow identification**: The NetFlow exporter monitors incoming packets and identifies unique flows based on their attributes.

  o **Flow aggregation**: The exporter aggregates data for each identified flow, maintaining counters for packets and bytes sent.

  o **Flow timeout**: When a flow is no longer active (no packets seen for that flow within the scheduled timeout, which usually is around 30/60 seconds), it is considered inactive. The exporter maintains a timeout mechanism to clear inactive flows from its cache.

  o **Record generation**: Once a flow becomes inactive or when a NetFlow export timer expires, the exporter generates NetFlow records for the flow.

  o **Record export**: The exporter encapsulates NetFlow records into NetFlow v1 packets and sends them to the collector using UDP.

  o **Collection and analysis**: The collector receives the NetFlow packets, extracts the records, and processes the data for analysis, reporting, and monitoring purposes.

Limitations of NetFlow v1

NetFlow v1 lacks some of the advanced features found in later versions, such as flow sampling, support for IPv6, and additional flow attributes. It also has limitations in terms of scalability and extensibility compared to later NetFlow versions like NetFlow v5, v9, and **Internet Protocol Flow Information Export** (**IPFIX**).

Here we can see a Wireshark dissected NetFlow V1 protocol packet. In this example, a Mikrotik RB2011 (Firmware 7.11.2) with IP address 10.1.30.101 was configured to send packets to collector on 10.1.30.210 on port 2056 (which Wireshark labels as service omnisky). It is a 394 bytes UDP packet containing 7 **Protocol Data Units** (**PDUS**, in our case, flows). Refer to the following:

```
No.       VLAN Time             Source                Destination
Protocol DST Port Length Info
     1        0.000000         10.1.30.101            10.1.30.210
CFLOW     omnisky  394     total: 7 (v1) flows
```

Frame 1: 394 bytes on wire (3152 bits), 394 bytes captured (3152 bits)

Ethernet II, Src: Routerbo_d8:3f:d7 (d4:ca:6d:d8:3f:d7), Dst:
HewlettP_15:9c:45 (2c:27:d7:15:9c:45)

Internet Protocol Version 4, Src: 10.1.30.101, Dst: 10.1.30.210

User Datagram Protocol, Src Port: omnisky (2056), Dst Port: omnisky (2056)

Cisco NetFlow/IPFIX

    Version: 1

    Count: 7

    SysUptime: 59155.920000000 seconds

    Timestamp: Oct 15, 2023 15:22:19.861512015 CEST

    pdu 1/7

        SrcAddr: 10.1.30.101

        DstAddr: 10.1.30.210

        NextHop: 0.0.0.0

        InputInt: 11

        OutputInt: 11

        Packets: 3

        Octets: 564

        [Duration: 13.520000000 seconds]

        SrcPort: 2056

        DstPort: 2056

        Padding: 0000

        Protocol: UDP (17)

        IP ToS: 0x00

        TCP Flags: 0x00

        Padding: 00001e

        Reserved: 00000000

    pdu 2/7

        SrcAddr: 10.1.30.210

        DstAddr: 10.1.30.101

        NextHop: 0.0.0.0

        InputInt: 11

        OutputInt: 0

        Packets: 3

        Octets: 648

        [Duration: 13.520000000 seconds]

```
            SrcPort: 0
            DstPort: 0
            Padding: 0000
            Protocol: ICMP (1)
            IP ToS: 0xc0
            TCP Flags: 0x00
            Padding: 000021
            Reserved: 00000000
pdu 3/7
            SrcAddr: 10.1.50.100
            DstAddr: 10.1.30.101
            NextHop: 0.0.0.0
            InputInt: 11
            OutputInt: 0
            Packets: 3
            Octets: 648
            [Duration: 13.520000000 seconds]
            SrcPort: 0
            DstPort: 0
            Padding: 0000
            Protocol: ICMP (1)
            IP ToS: 0xc0
            TCP Flags: 0x00
            Padding: 000000
            Reserved: 00000000
pdu 4/7
            SrcAddr: 10.1.20.201
            DstAddr: 10.1.30.101
            NextHop: 0.0.0.0
            InputInt: 11
            OutputInt: 0
            Packets: 3
            Octets: 648
            [Duration: 13.520000000 seconds]
            SrcPort: 0
            DstPort: 0
            Padding: 0000
            Protocol: ICMP (1)
            IP ToS: 0xc0
            TCP Flags: 0x00
```

```
    Padding: 006dd8
    Reserved: 00000000
pdu 5/7
    SrcAddr: 10.1.20.200
    DstAddr: 10.1.30.101
    NextHop: 0.0.0.0
    InputInt: 11
    OutputInt: 0
    Packets: 3
    Octets: 648
    [Duration: 13.520000000 seconds]
    SrcPort: 0
    DstPort: 0
    Padding: 0000
    Protocol: ICMP (1)
    IP ToS: 0xc0
    TCP Flags: 0x00
    Padding: 000000
    Reserved: 00000000
pdu 6/7
    SrcAddr: 10.1.20.202
    DstAddr: 10.1.30.101
    NextHop: 0.0.0.0
    InputInt: 11
    OutputInt: 0
    Packets: 3
    Octets: 648
    [Duration: 13.520000000 seconds]
    SrcPort: 0
    DstPort: 0
    Padding: 0000
    Protocol: ICMP (1)
    IP ToS: 0xc0
    TCP Flags: 0x00
    Padding: 000000
    Reserved: 00000000
pdu 7/7
    SrcAddr: 10.1.20.203
    DstAddr: 10.1.30.101
    NextHop: 0.0.0.0
```

```
InputInt: 11
OutputInt: 0
Packets: 3
Octets: 648
[Duration: 13.520000000 seconds]
SrcPort: 0
DstPort: 0
Padding: 0000
Protocol: ICMP (1)
IP ToS: 0xc0
TCP Flags: 0x00
Padding: 000000
Reserved: 00000000
```

NetFlow version 5

NetFlow version 5 (**NetFlow v5**) is an enhanced version of the NetFlow v1 protocol, developed by *Cisco*, that provides more detailed information about network flows compared to the original NetFlow v1. Building on v1's simplicity, v5 introduced support for Border Gateway Protocol information and flow sequence numbers. It is widely used for network monitoring, security analysis, and traffic analysis. Here is a comprehensive description of the NetFlow v5 protocol:

- **NetFlow v5 protocol overview**: NetFlow v5 builds upon the foundation of NetFlow v1 by introducing additional attributes and features to provide a richer view of network traffic flows. It captures and exports data on individual flows traversing network devices for analysis by network administrators and security professionals.

- **Key concepts**:

  o **Flow**: Similar to NetFlow v1, a flow in NetFlow v5 represents a unidirectional sequence of packets between a specific source IP address and a specific destination IP address. Flows are characterized by their network-layer attributes, including source and destination IP, source and destination port, and protocol.

  o **NetFlow exporter**: The network device (router, switch, and so on) generating and transmitting NetFlow records to a collector. The exporter identifies, aggregates, and exports flow data.

  o **NetFlow collector**: The server that receives NetFlow records from one or more exporters. It stores, processes, and analyzes the data to offer insights into network traffic behavior.

- o **NetFlow record**: A data structure representing a flow. It contains attributes such as source IP, destination IP, source port, destination port, protocol, packet and byte counts, and additional information.

- **NetFlow v5 packet structure**: A NetFlow v5 packet comprises a header followed by a sequence of flow records.

  - o **Header**:

    - **Version Number**: 5 (indicating NetFlow v5).

    - **Count**: Number of flow records in the packet.

    - **System uptime**: Time in milliseconds since the device was booted.

    - **UNIX timestamp**: Seconds since the UNIX epoch (usually January 1, 1970) when the packet was sent.

    - **Sequence number**: A monotonically increasing value used for packet ordering.

    - **Source ID**: A field used to differentiate between multiple exporters when packets are sent to a single collector.

  - o **Flow record format**: Each flow record contains attributes similar to NetFlow v1 and introduces a few new attributes:

    - Source IP address

    - Destination IP address

    - Source port

    - Destination port

    - IP protocol

    - **Type of Service** (**ToS**)

    - IP Next Hop (the IP address of the next hop router in the path)

    - Source **Autonomous System** (**AS**) number

    - Destination AS number

    - Input interface (incoming interface on the exporting device)

    - Output interface (outgoing interface on the exporting device)

    - Packet count

    - Byte count

    - First switched

    - Last switched

    - TCP flags

    - Router and source mask

- **NetFlow V5 operation**:

  o **Flow identification**: Similar to NetFlow v1, the NetFlow exporter monitors incoming packets to identify distinct flows based on their attributes.

  o **Flow aggregation**: Flow data is aggregated, and counters for packets and bytes are updated for each flow.

  o **Flow timeout**: When a flow becomes inactive (no packets seen), it is marked as inactive and eventually removed from the exporter's cache.

  o **Record generation**: Inactive flows or when the export timer triggers, NetFlow records are generated for each flow.

  o **Record export**: NetFlow records are encapsulated into NetFlow v5 packets and transmitted to the collector using UDP.

  o **Collection and analysis**: The collector receives NetFlow packets, extracts records, processes the data, and generates reports for network analysis, monitoring, and security purposes.

Advantages of NetFlow v5

NetFlow v5 offers more attributes and information compared to v1, allowing for a deeper understanding of network traffic patterns, application usage, and potential security threats. It strikes a balance between feature richness and simplicity, making it a popular choice for network administrators. It is still very widely used, performs very well but it lacks support for extended attributes and IPv6 protocol.

Here we can see a Wireshark dissected NetFlow V5 protocol packet. In this example, a Mikrotik RB2011 (Firmware 7.11.2) with IP address 10.1.30.101 was configured to send packets to collector on 10.1.30.210 on port 2056 (which Wireshark labels as service omnisky). It is a 114 bytes UDP packet containing 1 PDU (flows). Refer to the following:

```
No.      VLAN Time            Source              Destination
Protocol DST Port Length Info
      1      0.000000       10.1.30.101          10.1.30.210
CFLOW    omnisky  114     total: 1 (v5) flow

Frame 1: 114 bytes on wire (912 bits), 114 bytes captured (912 bits)
    Encapsulation type: Ethernet (1)
    Arrival Time: Oct 15, 2023 21:26:33.385431000 CEST
    [Time shift for this packet: 0.000000000 seconds]
    Epoch Time: 1697397993.385431000 seconds
    [Time delta from previous captured frame: 0.000000000 seconds]
    [Time delta from previous displayed frame: 0.000000000 seconds]
    [Time since reference or first frame: 0.000000000 seconds]
```

```
    Frame Number: 1
    Frame Length: 114 bytes (912 bits)
    Capture Length: 114 bytes (912 bits)
    [Frame is marked: False]
    [Frame is ignored: False]
    [Protocols in frame: eth:ethertype:ip:udp:cflow]
    [Coloring Rule Name: UDP]
    [Coloring Rule String: udp]
Ethernet II, Src: Routerbo_d8:3f:d7 (d4:ca:6d:d8:3f:d7), Dst:
HewlettP_15:9c:45 (2c:27:d7:15:9c:45)
    Destination: HewlettP_15:9c:45 (2c:27:d7:15:9c:45)
        [Destination (resolved): HewlettP_15:9c:45]
        [Destination OUI: 2c:27:d7 (Hewlett Packard)]
        [Destination OUI (resolved): Hewlett Packard]
        Address: HewlettP_15:9c:45 (2c:27:d7:15:9c:45)
        [Address (resolved): HewlettP_15:9c:45]
        [Address OUI: 2c:27:d7 (Hewlett Packard)]
        [Address OUI (resolved): Hewlett Packard]
        .... ..0. .... .... .... .... = LG bit: Globally unique address
(factory default)
        .... ..0. .... .... .... .... = LG bit: Globally unique address
(factory default)
        .... ...0 .... .... .... .... = IG bit: Individual address
(unicast)
        .... ...0 .... .... .... .... = IG bit: Individual address
(unicast)
    Source: Routerbo_d8:3f:d7 (d4:ca:6d:d8:3f:d7)
        [Source (resolved): Routerbo_d8:3f:d7]
        [Source OUI: d4:ca:6d (Routerboard.com)]
        [Source OUI (resolved): Routerboard.com]
        Address: Routerbo_d8:3f:d7 (d4:ca:6d:d8:3f:d7)
        [Address (resolved): Routerbo_d8:3f:d7]
        [Address OUI: d4:ca:6d (Routerboard.com)]
        [Address OUI (resolved): Routerboard.com]
        .... ..0. .... .... .... .... = LG bit: Globally unique address
(factory default)
        .... ..0. .... .... .... .... = LG bit: Globally unique address
(factory default)
        .... ...0 .... .... .... .... = IG bit: Individual address
(unicast)
        .... ...0 .... .... .... .... = IG bit: Individual address
(unicast)
```

```
    Type: IPv4 (0x0800)
Internet Protocol Version 4, Src: 10.1.30.101, Dst: 10.1.30.210
    0100 .... = Version: 4
    .... 0101 = Header Length: 20 bytes (5)
    Differentiated Services Field: 0x00 (DSCP: CS0, ECN: Not-ECT)
        0000 00.. = Differentiated Services Codepoint: Default (0)
        .... ..00 = Explicit Congestion Notification: Not ECN-Capable
Transport (0)
    Total Length: 100
    Identification: 0xbf76 (49014)
    Flags: 0x0000
        0... .... .... .... = Reserved bit: Not set
        .0.. .... .... .... = Don't fragment: Not set
        ..0. .... .... .... = More fragments: Not set
    Fragment offset: 0
    Time to live: 255
    Protocol: UDP (17)
    Header checksum: 0xaad9 [validation disabled]
    [Header checksum status: Unverified]
    Source: 10.1.30.101
    Source or Destination Address: 10.1.30.101
    [Source Host: 10.1.30.101]
    [Source or Destination Host: 10.1.30.101]
    Destination: 10.1.30.210
    Source or Destination Address: 10.1.30.210
    [Destination Host: 10.1.30.210]
    [Source or Destination Host: 10.1.30.210]
User Datagram Protocol, Src Port: omnisky (2056), Dst Port: omnisky (2056)
    Source Port: omnisky (2056)
    Destination Port: omnisky (2056)
    Source or Destination Port: omnisky (2056)
    Source or Destination Port: omnisky (2056)
    Length: 80
    [Checksum: [missing]]
    [Checksum Status: Not present]
    [Stream index: 0]
    [Timestamps]
        [Time since first frame: 0.000000000 seconds]
        [Time since previous frame: 0.000000000 seconds]
Cisco NetFlow/IPFIX
```

```
Version: 5
Count: 1
SysUptime: 81009.440000000 seconds
Timestamp: Oct 15, 2023 21:26:33.381530544 CEST
    CurrentSecs: 1697397993
    CurrentNSecs: 381530544
FlowSequence: 13
EngineType: RP (0)
EngineId: 0
00.. .... .... .... = SamplingMode: No sampling mode configured (0)
..00 0000 0000 0000 = SampleRate: 0
pdu 1/1
    SrcAddr: 10.1.61.2
    DstAddr: 255.255.255.255
    NextHop: 0.0.0.0
    InputInt: 218
    OutputInt: 0
    Packets: 1
    Octets: 190
    [Duration: 0.000000000 seconds]
        StartTime: 80993.160000000 seconds
        EndTime: 80993.160000000 seconds
    SrcPort: 5678
    DstPort: 5678
    Padding: 00
    TCP Flags: 0x00
    Protocol: UDP (17)
    IP ToS: 0x00
    SrcAS: 0
    DstAS: 0
    SrcMask: 0 (prefix: 0.0.0.0/32)
    DstMask: 0 (prefix: 0.0.0.0/32)
    Padding: 0000
```

NetFlow version 9

NetFlow version 9 (NetFlow v9) is an advanced version of the NetFlow protocol developed by *Cisco*. It significantly enhances the flexibility, extensibility, and capabilities of flow data export compared to earlier versions. NetFlow v9 allows for the export of customizable flow templates, enabling the collection of various types of flow data. Instead of using a fixed format with fixed fields, NetFlow v9 describes the information that will be exchanged in the so called template packets. The template packet contains a list of information fields that will be sent to the collector, that needs it for proper decoding of the flow traffic. Templates are dynamic and can change during the export process of information. NetFlow v9 represents a significant evolution over its predecessors, NetFlow v1 and v5. It introduces a template-based mechanism that offers greater flexibility in exporting flow data attributes, allowing for the capture of diverse information about network traffic flows. NetFlow v9 is often used in more complex network environments where the need for customizable flow data is high. Here is a comprehensive description of the NetFlow v9 protocol:

- **Key concepts**:
  - **Flow**: Similar to earlier NetFlow versions, a flow in NetFlow v9 represents a unidirectional sequence of packets between a specific source and destination. Flows are defined by their attributes, including source and destination IP, ports, protocol, and additional details.
  - **NetFlow exporter**: The network device generating and exporting NetFlow v9 records to a collector. The exporter defines and exports flow templates to convey the structure of the data.
  - **NetFlow collector**: The server that receives NetFlow v9 records from exporters. It processes the data according to the templates and provides insights into network behavior.
  - **NetFlow record**: The data structure representing a flow, similar to previous versions, with the added flexibility of customizable attributes.
  - **Flow template**: A key feature of NetFlow v9, flow templates define the structure of exported data. They specify which attributes are included in the flow records.
- **NetFlow v9 packet structure**: NetFlow v9 packets consist of a header, flow templates, and flow data records.
  - **Header**:
    - **Version number**: 9 (indicating NetFlow v9).
    - **Count**: Number of flow data records and template records in the packet.
    - **System uptime**: Time in milliseconds since the device was booted.
    - **UNIX timestamp**: Seconds since the UNIX epoch when the packet was sent.
    - **Sequence number**: An increasing value used for packet sequencing.
    - **Source ID**: A field to differentiate exporters in cases of multiple exporters sending data to a single collector.

- o **Flow template format**: Flow templates are used to describe the attributes included in flow data records. They include:

    - **Template ID**: An identifier for the template.

    - **Field count**: The number of fields included in the template.

    - **Scope count**: The number of fields that are part of the template's scope.

    - **Field type and length**: For each field, the type of attribute and its length.

- **Flow data record format**: Flow data records follow the structure defined by the templates and include attributes specified in the templates. These attributes include source IP, destination IP, ports, protocol, packet and byte counts, and more.

- **NetFlow operation**:

    - o **Flow template definition**: The exporter defines and sends flow templates to the collector. These templates specify the attributes to be included in flow data records.

    - o **Flow identification and aggregation**: Similar to earlier versions, the exporter monitors incoming packets, aggregates flow data, and updates counters.

    - o **Flow timeout and record generation**: Inactive flows or when the export timer triggers, the exporter generates flow data records using the templates.

    - o **Record export**: Flow data records are encapsulated into NetFlow v9 packets and transmitted to the collector via UDP.

    - o **Template management**: The collector maintains a template cache and uses received templates to parse and interpret flow data records.

    - o **Collection and analysis**: The collector extracts and processes flow data records based on templates, enabling in-depth network analysis, monitoring, and security.

Advantages of NetFlow v9

NetFlow v9 offers unparalleled flexibility through template-based export. This enables the collection of customized flow data attributes, making it suitable for complex network environments, cloud environments, and applications requiring specific flow attributes. It is a still very widely used protocol and it finally provides support for IPv6 and extended attributes. Although being a proprietary protocol, it became an industry standard like its fixed version NetFlow V5 and Cisco wrote several **Request for Comments (RFC)** related to NetFlow Version 9 (NetFlow v9) protocol, literally building the foundation for the IETF standard IPFIX (which is also ironically called NetFlow v10). Here are some key RFCs related to NetFlow v9:

- **RFC 3954:**
  - o **Title:** Cisco Systems NetFlow Services Export Version 9
  - o **URL:** RFC 3954 (**https://datatracker.ietf.org/doc/html/rfc3954**)
  - o **Note:** This RFC specifies the NetFlow v9 protocol and defines the structure of NetFlow v9 records.

- **RFC 3955:**
  - o **Title:** Evaluation of Candidate Protocols for IPFIX
  - o **URL:** RFC 3955 (**https://datatracker.ietf.org/doc/html/rfc3955**)
  - o **Note:** This RFC compares and evaluates flow export protocols, including NetFlow v9.

- **RFC 5470:**
  - o **Title:** Architecture for IP Flow Information Export
  - o **URL:** RFC 5470 (**https://datatracker.ietf.org/doc/html/rfc5470**)
  - o **Note:** This RFC provides an architecture for IPFIX, which is related to NetFlow v9.

- **RFC 5471:**
  - o **Title:** Guidelines for IPFIX Testing
  - o **URL:** RFC 5471 (**https://datatracker.ietf.org/doc/html/rfc5471**)
  - o **Note:** This RFC provides guidelines for testing IPFIX implementations, which includes NetFlow v9.

- **RFC 6313:**
  - o **Title:** Export of Structured Data in IPFIX
  - o **URL:** RFC 6313 (**https://datatracker.ietf.org/doc/html/rfc6313**)
  - o **Note:** This RFC covers exporting structured data within IPFIX, a framework related to NetFlow v9.

These RFCs define the standards, architecture, evaluation, and export mechanisms related to NetFlow v9. They are important references for understanding the protocol and implementing NetFlow v9 in network monitoring and analysis systems.

Here we can see a couple of Wireshark dissected NetFlow V9 protocol packet. In this example, a Mikrotik RB2011 (Firmware 7.11.2) with IP Address 10.1.30.101 was configured to send packets to the collector on 10.1.30.210 on port 2056 (which Wireshark labels as service omnisky). The first packet contains real data and the second packet contains the templates to decode data. Normally, the network flow exporter sends first the templates and then the data. Templates are normally exported periodically and could have their dedicated packets or can be mixed with data packets; normally, it is up to the vendor implementation. Refer to the following:

```
No.     VLAN Time              Source               Destination
Protocol DST Port Length Info
     1       0.000000          10.1.30.101          10.1.30.210
CFLOW    omnisky 842     total: 9 (v9) records Obs-Domain-ID=    0
[Data:256]

Frame 1: 842 bytes on wire (6736 bits), 842 bytes captured (6736 bits)
    Encapsulation type: Ethernet (1)
    Arrival Time: Oct 18, 2023 22:45:22.582126000 CEST
    [Time shift for this packet: 0.000000000 seconds]
    Epoch Time: 1697661922.582126000 seconds
    [Time delta from previous captured frame: 0.000000000 seconds]
    [Time delta from previous displayed frame: 0.000000000 seconds]
    [Time since reference or first frame: 0.000000000 seconds]
    Frame Number: 1
    Frame Length: 842 bytes (6736 bits)
    Capture Length: 842 bytes (6736 bits)
    [Frame is marked: False]
    [Frame is ignored: False]
    [Protocols in frame: eth:ethertype:ip:udp:cflow]
    [Coloring Rule Name: UDP]
    [Coloring Rule String: udp]
Ethernet II, Src: Routerbo_d8:3f:d7 (d4:ca:6d:d8:3f:d7), Dst:
HewlettP_15:9c:45 (2c:27:d7:15:9c:45)
    Destination: HewlettP_15:9c:45 (2c:27:d7:15:9c:45)
        [Destination (resolved): HewlettP_15:9c:45]
        [Destination OUI: 2c:27:d7 (Hewlett Packard)]
        [Destination OUI (resolved): Hewlett Packard]
        Address: HewlettP_15:9c:45 (2c:27:d7:15:9c:45)
        [Address (resolved): HewlettP_15:9c:45]
        [Address OUI: 2c:27:d7 (Hewlett Packard)]
        [Address OUI (resolved): Hewlett Packard]
        .... ..0. .... .... .... .... = LG bit: Globally unique address
(factory default)
        .... ..0. .... .... .... .... = LG bit: Globally unique address
(factory default)
        .... ...0 .... .... .... .... = IG bit: Individual address
(unicast)
        .... ...0 .... .... .... .... = IG bit: Individual address
```

```
(unicast)
    Source: Routerbo_d8:3f:d7 (d4:ca:6d:d8:3f:d7)
        [Source (resolved): Routerbo_d8:3f:d7]
        [Source OUI: d4:ca:6d (Routerboard.com)]
        [Source OUI (resolved): Routerboard.com]
        Address: Routerbo_d8:3f:d7 (d4:ca:6d:d8:3f:d7)
        [Address (resolved): Routerbo_d8:3f:d7]
        [Address OUI: d4:ca:6d (Routerboard.com)]
        [Address OUI (resolved): Routerboard.com]
        .... ..0. .... .... .... .... = LG bit: Globally unique address
(factory default)
        .... ..0. .... .... .... .... = LG bit: Globally unique address
(factory default)
        .... ...0 .... .... .... .... = IG bit: Individual address
(unicast)
        .... ...0 .... .... .... .... = IG bit: Individual address
(unicast)
    Type: IPv4 (0x0800)
Internet Protocol Version 4, Src: 10.1.30.101, Dst: 10.1.30.210
    0100 .... = Version: 4
    .... 0101 = Header Length: 20 bytes (5)
    Differentiated Services Field: 0x00 (DSCP: CS0, ECN: Not-ECT)
        0000 00.. = Differentiated Services Codepoint: Default (0)
        .... ..00 = Explicit Congestion Notification: Not ECN-Capable
Transport (0)
    Total Length: 828
    Identification: 0xce43 (52803)
    Flags: 0x0000
        0... .... .... .... = Reserved bit: Not set
        .0.. .... .... .... = Don't fragment: Not set
        ..0. .... .... .... = More fragments: Not set
    Fragment offset: 0
    Time to live: 255
    Protocol: UDP (17)
    Header checksum: 0x9934 [validation disabled]
    [Header checksum status: Unverified]
    Source: 10.1.30.101
    Source or Destination Address: 10.1.30.101
    [Source Host: 10.1.30.101]
    [Source or Destination Host: 10.1.30.101]
    Destination: 10.1.30.210
```

```
    Source or Destination Address: 10.1.30.210
    [Destination Host: 10.1.30.210]
    [Source or Destination Host: 10.1.30.210]
```

Here begins the NetFlow v9 data describing the different flows. Notice that in order to decode a NetFlow v9 data packet, you first need to receive the NetFlow v9 Template describing how to interpret the data in the packet. As you can see, the data packet contains the FlowSet ID 256, which is the number of the template ID, and the packet will be decoded according to its contents. The so-called template packets can arrive in any order, sometimes they are even embedded in different FlowSets inside the same packet, sometimes before the data, or sometimes after, depending on when the NetFlow data collection started on the device.

```
User Datagram Protocol, Src Port: omnisky (2056), Dst Port: omnisky (2056)
    Source Port: omnisky (2056)
    Destination Port: omnisky (2056)
    Source or Destination Port: omnisky (2056)
    Source or Destination Port: omnisky (2056)
    Length: 808
    [Checksum: [missing]]
    [Checksum Status: Not present]
    [Stream index: 0]
    [Timestamps]
        [Time since first frame: 0.000000000 seconds]
        [Time since previous frame: 0.000000000 seconds]
Cisco NetFlow/IPFIX
    Version: 9
    Count: 9
    SysUptime: 344938.640000000 seconds
    Timestamp: Oct 18, 2023 22:45:22.000000000 CEST
        CurrentSecs: 1697661922
    FlowSequence: 17
    SourceId: 0
    FlowSet 1 [id=256] (9 flows)
        FlowSet Id: (Data) (256)
        FlowSet Length: 780
        [Template Frame: 125 (received after this frame)]
        Flow 1
            [Duration: 71.760000000 seconds (switched)]
                StartTime: 344850.240000000 seconds
                EndTime: 344922.000000000 seconds
            Packets: 20
```

```
        Octets: 7596
        InputInt: 11
        OutputInt: 11
        SrcAddr: 10.1.30.101
        DstAddr: 10.1.30.210
        Protocol: UDP (17)
        IP ToS: 0x00
        SrcPort: 2056 (omnisky)
        DstPort: 2056 (omnisky)
        NextHop: 0.0.0.0
        DstMask: 0
        SrcMask: 0
        TCP Flags: 0x00
            00.. .... = Reserved: 0x0
            ..0. .... = URG: Not used
            ...0 .... = ACK: Not used
            .... 0... = PSH: Not used
            .... .0.. = RST: Not used
            .... ..0. = SYN: Not used
            .... ...0 = FIN: Not used
        Sampling interval: 0
        Sampling algorithm: Deterministic sampling (1)
        Destination Mac Address: 00:00:00_00:00:00 (00:00:00:00:00:00)
        Source Mac Address: Routerbo_d8:3f:d7 (d4:ca:6d:d8:3f:d7)
        Post Destination Mac Address: 00:00:00_00:00:00
(00:00:00:00:00:00)
        Post Source Mac Address: Routerbo_d8:3f:d7 (d4:ca:6d:d8:3f:d7)
```

As you can see in the following FlowSet, it describes a flow that is subject to a **Network Address Translation** (**NAT**), thus making use of the advanced flexibility of the NetFlow v9 protocol.

```
        Post NAT Source IPv4 Address: 10.1.30.101
        Post NAT Destination IPv4 Address: 10.1.30.210
        Post NAPT Source Transport Port: 2056
        Post NAPT Destination Transport Port: 2056
    Flow 2
        [Duration: 17.680000000 seconds (switched)]
            StartTime: 344904.320000000 seconds
            EndTime: 344922.000000000 seconds
        Packets: 6
        Octets: 2060
```

```
            InputInt: 11
            OutputInt: 0
            SrcAddr: 10.1.30.210
            DstAddr: 10.1.30.101
            Protocol: ICMP (1)
            IP ToS: 0xc0
            SrcPort: 0
            DstPort: 0
            NextHop: 0.0.0.0
            DstMask: 0
            SrcMask: 0
            TCP Flags: 0x00
                00.. .... = Reserved: 0x0
                ..0. .... = URG: Not used
                ...0 .... = ACK: Not used
                .... 0... = PSH: Not used
                .... .0.. = RST: Not used
                .... ..0. = SYN: Not used
                .... ...0 = FIN: Not used
```

As you can see, the NetFlow v9 also supports sampling, and it can even provide the way the sampling was applied.

```
            Sampling interval: 0
            Sampling algorithm: Deterministic sampling (1)
            Destination Mac Address: Routerbo_d8:3f:d7 (d4:ca:6d:d8:3f:d7)
            Source Mac Address: Routerbo_d8:3f:d7 (d4:ca:6d:d8:3f:d7)
            Post Destination Mac Address: HewlettP_15:9c:45
(2c:27:d7:15:9c:45)
            Post Source Mac Address: 00:00:00_00:00:00 (00:00:00:00:00:00)
            Post NAT Source IPv4 Address: 10.1.30.210
            Post NAT Destination IPv4 Address: 10.1.30.101
            Post NAPT Source Transport Port: 0
            Post NAPT Destination Transport Port: 0
        Flow 3
            [Duration: 71.760000000 seconds (switched)]
                StartTime: 344850.240000000 seconds
                EndTime: 344922.000000000 seconds
            Packets: 20
            Octets: 6260
            InputInt: 11
```

```
OutputInt: 0
SrcAddr: 10.1.50.100
DstAddr: 10.1.30.101
Protocol: ICMP (1)
IP ToS: 0xc0
SrcPort: 0
DstPort: 0
NextHop: 0.0.0.0
DstMask: 0
SrcMask: 0
TCP Flags: 0x00
    00.. .... = Reserved: 0x0
    ..0. .... = URG: Not used
    ...0 .... = ACK: Not used
    .... 0... = PSH: Not used
    .... .0.. = RST: Not used
    .... ..0. = SYN: Not used
    .... ...0 = FIN: Not used
Sampling interval: 0
Sampling algorithm: Deterministic sampling (1)
Destination Mac Address: Routerbo_d8:3f:d7 (d4:ca:6d:d8:3f:d7)
Source Mac Address: Routerbo_d8:3f:d7 (d4:ca:6d:d8:3f:d7)
Post Destination Mac Address: a2:55:f5:b3:27:ba
```
(a2:55:f5:b3:27:ba)
```
Post Source Mac Address: 00:00:00_00:00:00 (00:00:00:00:00:00)
Post NAT Source IPv4 Address: 10.1.50.100
Post NAT Destination IPv4 Address: 10.1.30.101
Post NAPT Source Transport Port: 0
Post NAPT Destination Transport Port: 0
```
```
Flow 4
    [Duration: 71.760000000 seconds (switched)]
        StartTime: 344850.240000000 seconds
        EndTime: 344922.000000000 seconds
    Packets: 20
    Octets: 6260
```

In previous versions of NetFlow, the input interface and output interface are provided. Their numbering is normally related to the SNMP view of the device, so **InputInt** 11 does not mean like the example, GigabitEthernet 0/11 but it is the interface number 11 reported by the SNMP agent of the system.

```
        InputInt: 11
        OutputInt: 0
        SrcAddr: 10.1.20.201
        DstAddr: 10.1.30.101
        Protocol: ICMP (1)
        IP ToS: 0xc0
        SrcPort: 0
        DstPort: 0
        NextHop: 0.0.0.0
        DstMask: 0
        SrcMask: 0
        TCP Flags: 0x00
            00.. .... = Reserved: 0x0
            ..0. .... = URG: Not used
            ...0 .... = ACK: Not used
            .... 0... = PSH: Not used
            .... .0.. = RST: Not used
            .... ..0. = SYN: Not used
            .... ...0 = FIN: Not used
        Sampling interval: 0
        Sampling algorithm: Deterministic sampling (1)
        Destination Mac Address: Routerbo_d8:3f:d7 (d4:ca:6d:d8:3f:d7)
        Source Mac Address: Routerbo_d8:3f:d7 (d4:ca:6d:d8:3f:d7)
        Post Destination Mac Address: a2:55:f5:b3:27:ba
(a2:55:f5:b3:27:ba)
        Post Source Mac Address: 00:00:00_00:00:00 (00:00:00:00:00:00)
        Post NAT Source IPv4 Address: 10.1.20.201
        Post NAT Destination IPv4 Address: 10.1.30.101
        Post NAPT Source Transport Port: 0
        Post NAPT Destination Transport Port: 0
    Flow 5
        [Duration: 71.760000000 seconds (switched)]
```

As strange as it can seem, the reported start time and stop time of the flow are not reported as absolute times but in terms of clock ticks of the router beginning from the standard Unix epoch (1/1/1970), and the calculation needed to understand it changes between the different versions of NetFlow and IPFIX.

```
        StartTime: 344850.240000000 seconds
        EndTime: 344922.000000000 seconds        Packets: 20
    Octets: 6260
    InputInt: 11
```

```
                    OutputInt: 0
                    SrcAddr: 10.1.20.200
                    DstAddr: 10.1.30.101
                    Protocol: ICMP (1)
                    IP ToS: 0xc0
                    SrcPort: 0
                    DstPort: 0
                    NextHop: 0.0.0.0
                    DstMask: 0
                    SrcMask: 0
                    TCP Flags: 0x00
                        00.. .... = Reserved: 0x0
                        ..0. .... = URG: Not used
                        ...0 .... = ACK: Not used
                        .... 0... = PSH: Not used
                        .... .0.. = RST: Not used
                        .... ..0. = SYN: Not used
                        .... ...0 = FIN: Not used
                    Sampling interval: 0
                    Sampling algorithm: Deterministic sampling (1)
                    Destination Mac Address: Routerbo_d8:3f:d7 (d4:ca:6d:d8:3f:d7)
                    Source Mac Address: Routerbo_d8:3f:d7 (d4:ca:6d:d8:3f:d7)
                    Post Destination Mac Address: a2:55:f5:b3:27:ba
(a2:55:f5:b3:27:ba)
                    Post Source Mac Address: 00:00:00_00:00:00 (00:00:00:00:00:00)
                    Post NAT Source IPv4 Address: 10.1.20.200
                    Post NAT Destination IPv4 Address: 10.1.30.101
                    Post NAPT Source Transport Port: 0
                    Post NAPT Destination Transport Port: 0
                Flow 6
                    [Duration: 71.760000000 seconds (switched)]
                        StartTime: 344850.240000000 seconds
                        EndTime: 344922.000000000 seconds
                    Packets: 20
                    Octets: 6260
                    InputInt: 11
                    OutputInt: 0
                    SrcAddr: 10.1.20.202
                    DstAddr: 10.1.30.101
                    Protocol: ICMP (1)
```

```
IP ToS: 0xc0
SrcPort: 0
DstPort: 0
NextHop: 0.0.0.0
DstMask: 0
SrcMask: 0
```

In our example, most flows are ICMP ones, so the following field is not used, but in the case of a TCP protocol flow, this reports the fields seen during the flow.

```
TCP Flags: 0x00
    00.. .... = Reserved: 0x0
    ..0. .... = URG: Not used
    ...0 .... = ACK: Not used
    .... 0... = PSH: Not used
    .... .0.. = RST: Not used
    .... ..0. = SYN: Not used
    .... ...0 = FIN: Not used
Sampling interval: 0
Sampling algorithm: Deterministic sampling (1)
Destination Mac Address: Routerbo_d8:3f:d7 (d4:ca:6d:d8:3f:d7)
Source Mac Address: Routerbo_d8:3f:d7 (d4:ca:6d:d8:3f:d7)
Post Destination Mac Address: a2:55:f5:b3:27:ba
(a2:55:f5:b3:27:ba)
Post Source Mac Address: 00:00:00_00:00:00 (00:00:00:00:00:00)
Post NAT Source IPv4 Address: 10.1.20.202
Post NAT Destination IPv4 Address: 10.1.30.101
Post NAPT Source Transport Port: 0
Post NAPT Destination Transport Port: 0
Flow 7
[Duration: 71.760000000 seconds (switched)]
    StartTime: 344850.240000000 seconds
    EndTime: 344922.000000000 seconds
Packets: 20
Octets: 6260
InputInt: 11
OutputInt: 0
SrcAddr: 10.1.20.203
DstAddr: 10.1.30.101
Protocol: ICMP (1)
IP ToS: 0xc0
SrcPort: 0
```

```
DstPort: 0
NextHop: 0.0.0.0
DstMask: 0
SrcMask: 0
TCP Flags: 0x00
    00.. .... = Reserved: 0x0
    ..0. .... = URG: Not used
    ...0 .... = ACK: Not used
    .... 0... = PSH: Not used
    .... .0.. = RST: Not used
    .... ..0. = SYN: Not used
    .... ...0 = FIN: Not used
Sampling interval: 0
Sampling algorithm: Deterministic sampling (1)
Destination Mac Address: Routerbo_d8:3f:d7 (d4:ca:6d:d8:3f:d7)
Source Mac Address: Routerbo_d8:3f:d7 (d4:ca:6d:d8:3f:d7)
Post Destination Mac Address: a2:55:f5:b3:27:ba
```
(a2:55:f5:b3:27:ba)
```
Post Source Mac Address: 00:00:00_00:00:00 (00:00:00:00:00:00)
Post NAT Source IPv4 Address: 10.1.20.203
Post NAT Destination IPv4 Address: 10.1.30.101
```

The NetFlow v9 also allows reporting the **Source Transport Port** and **Destination Transport Port** in case of Port Address Translation, which can be implemented in some network scenarios.

```
Post NAPT Source Transport Port: 0
Post NAPT Destination Transport Port: 0
Flow 8
    [Duration: 70.010000000 seconds (switched)]
        StartTime: 344852.270000000 seconds
        EndTime: 344922.280000000 seconds
    Packets: 40
    Octets: 10916
    InputInt: 11
    OutputInt: 0
    SrcAddr: 10.1.30.220
    DstAddr: 10.1.30.101
    Protocol: ICMP (1)
    IP ToS: 0xc0
    SrcPort: 0
    DstPort: 0
    NextHop: 0.0.0.0
```

```
        DstMask: 0
        SrcMask: 0
        TCP Flags: 0x00
            00.. .... = Reserved: 0x0
            ..0. .... = URG: Not used
            ...0 .... = ACK: Not used
            .... 0... = PSH: Not used
            .... .0.. = RST: Not used
            .... ..0. = SYN: Not used
            .... ...0 = FIN: Not used
        Sampling interval: 0
        Sampling algorithm: Deterministic sampling (1)
        Destination Mac Address: Routerbo_d8:3f:d7 (d4:ca:6d:d8:3f:d7)
        Source Mac Address: Routerbo_d8:3f:d7 (d4:ca:6d:d8:3f:d7)
        Post Destination Mac Address: HewlettP_15:9c:45
(2c:27:d7:15:9c:45)
        Post Source Mac Address: 00:00:00_00:00:00 (00:00:00:00:00:00)
        Post NAT Source IPv4 Address: 10.1.30.220
        Post NAT Destination IPv4 Address: 10.1.30.101
        Post NAPT Source Transport Port: 0
        Post NAPT Destination Transport Port: 0
    Flow 9
        [Duration: 72.060000000 seconds (switched)]
            StartTime: 344851.370000000 seconds
            EndTime: 344923.430000000 seconds
        Packets: 18
        Octets: 5108
        InputInt: 11
        OutputInt: 0
        SrcAddr: 192.168.254.1
        DstAddr: 10.1.30.101
        Protocol: ICMP (1)
        IP ToS: 0xc0
        SrcPort: 0
        DstPort: 0
        NextHop: 0.0.0.0
        DstMask: 0
        SrcMask: 0
        TCP Flags: 0x00
            00.. .... = Reserved: 0x0
```

```
           ..0. .... = URG: Not used
           ...0 .... = ACK: Not used
           .... 0... = PSH: Not used
           .... .0.. = RST: Not used
           .... ..0. = SYN: Not used
           .... ...0 = FIN: Not used
     Sampling interval: 0
     Sampling algorithm: Deterministic sampling (1)
     Destination Mac Address: Routerbo_d8:3f:d7 (d4:ca:6d:d8:3f:d7)
     Source Mac Address: Routerbo_d8:3f:d7 (d4:ca:6d:d8:3f:d7)
     Post Destination Mac Address: a2:55:f5:b3:27:ba
(a2:55:f5:b3:27:ba)
     Post Source Mac Address: 00:00:00_00:00:00 (00:00:00:00:00:00)
     Post NAT Source IPv4 Address: 192.168.254.1
     Post NAT Destination IPv4 Address: 10.1.30.101
     Post NAPT Source Transport Port: 0
     Post NAPT Destination Transport Port: 0
  Padding: 0000
```

The following frame describes a template packet for NetFlow v9, containing all the information used to decode the frames matching the template ID used in subsequent packets.

```
No.     VLAN Time            Source             Destination
Protocol DST Port Length Info
   125      14.560320        10.1.30.101        10.1.30.210
CFLOW    omnisky 278    total: 2 (v9) records Obs-Domain-ID=    0 [Data-
Template:256,257]

Frame 125: 278 bytes on wire (2224 bits), 278 bytes captured (2224 bits)
    Encapsulation type: Ethernet (1)
    Arrival Time: Oct 18, 2023 22:45:37.142446000 CEST
    [Time shift for this packet: 0.000000000 seconds]
    Epoch Time: 1697661937.142446000 seconds
    [Time delta from previous captured frame: 1.039961000 seconds]
    [Time delta from previous displayed frame: 1.039961000 seconds]
    [Time since reference or first frame: 14.560320000 seconds]
    Frame Number: 125
    Frame Length: 278 bytes (2224 bits)
    Capture Length: 278 bytes (2224 bits)
    [Frame is marked: False]
    [Frame is ignored: False]
    [Protocols in frame: eth:ethertype:ip:udp:cflow]
```

```
    [Coloring Rule Name: UDP]
    [Coloring Rule String: udp]
Ethernet II, Src: Routerbo_d8:3f:d7 (d4:ca:6d:d8:3f:d7), Dst:
HewlettP_15:9c:45 (2c:27:d7:15:9c:45)
    Destination: HewlettP_15:9c:45 (2c:27:d7:15:9c:45)
        [Destination (resolved): HewlettP_15:9c:45]
        [Destination OUI: 2c:27:d7 (Hewlett Packard)]
        [Destination OUI (resolved): Hewlett Packard]
        Address: HewlettP_15:9c:45 (2c:27:d7:15:9c:45)
        [Address (resolved): HewlettP_15:9c:45]
        [Address OUI: 2c:27:d7 (Hewlett Packard)]
        [Address OUI (resolved): Hewlett Packard]
        .... ..0. .... .... .... .... = LG bit: Globally unique address
(factory default)
        .... ..0. .... .... .... .... = LG bit: Globally unique address
(factory default)
        .... ...0 .... .... .... .... = IG bit: Individual address
(unicast)
        .... ...0 .... .... .... .... = IG bit: Individual address
(unicast)
    Source: Routerbo_d8:3f:d7 (d4:ca:6d:d8:3f:d7)
        [Source (resolved): Routerbo_d8:3f:d7]
        [Source OUI: d4:ca:6d (Routerboard.com)]
        [Source OUI (resolved): Routerboard.com]
        Address: Routerbo_d8:3f:d7 (d4:ca:6d:d8:3f:d7)
        [Address (resolved): Routerbo_d8:3f:d7]
        [Address OUI: d4:ca:6d (Routerboard.com)]
        [Address OUI (resolved): Routerboard.com]
        .... ..0. .... .... .... .... = LG bit: Globally unique address
(factory default)
        .... ..0. .... .... .... .... = LG bit: Globally unique address
(factory default)
        .... ...0 .... .... .... .... = IG bit: Individual address
(unicast)
        .... ...0 .... .... .... .... = IG bit: Individual address
(unicast)
    Type: IPv4 (0x0800)
Internet Protocol Version 4, Src: 10.1.30.101, Dst: 10.1.30.210
    0100 .... = Version: 4
    .... 0101 = Header Length: 20 bytes (5)
    Differentiated Services Field: 0x00 (DSCP: CS0, ECN: Not-ECT)
        0000 00.. = Differentiated Services Codepoint: Default (0)
```

```
        .... ..00 = Explicit Congestion Notification: Not ECN-Capable
Transport (0)
    Total Length: 264
    Identification: 0xd29e (53918)
    Flags: 0x0000
        0... .... .... .... = Reserved bit: Not set
        .0.. .... .... .... = Don't fragment: Not set
        ..0. .... .... .... = More fragments: Not set
    Fragment offset: 0
    Time to live: 255
    Protocol: UDP (17)
    Header checksum: 0x970d [validation disabled]
    [Header checksum status: Unverified]
    Source: 10.1.30.101
    Source or Destination Address: 10.1.30.101
    [Source Host: 10.1.30.101]
    [Source or Destination Host: 10.1.30.101]
    Destination: 10.1.30.210
    Source or Destination Address: 10.1.30.210
    [Destination Host: 10.1.30.210]
    [Source or Destination Host: 10.1.30.210]
User Datagram Protocol, Src Port: omnisky (2056), Dst Port: omnisky (2056)
    Source Port: omnisky (2056)
    Destination Port: omnisky (2056)
    Source or Destination Port: omnisky (2056)
    Source or Destination Port: omnisky (2056)
    Length: 244
    [Checksum: [missing]]
    [Checksum Status: Not present]
    [Stream index: 0]
    [Timestamps]
        [Time since first frame: 14.560320000 seconds]
        [Time since previous frame: 1.040291000 seconds]
Cisco NetFlow/IPFIX
    Version: 9
    Count: 2
    SysUptime: 344953.200000000 seconds
    Timestamp: Oct 18, 2023 22:45:37.000000000 CEST
        CurrentSecs: 1697661937
    FlowSequence: 21
    SourceId: 0
```

Here begins the template definition, template IDs are 256 and 257. The field meanings are described in a table published in the already mentioned RFCs, and the data size is reported.

```
FlowSet 1 [id=0] (Data Template): 256,257
    FlowSet Id: Data Template (V9) (0)
    FlowSet Length: 216
    Template (Id = 256, Count = 26)
        Template Id: 256
        Field Count: 26
        Field (1/26): LAST_SWITCHED
            Type: LAST_SWITCHED (21)
            Length: 4
        Field (2/26): FIRST_SWITCHED
            Type: FIRST_SWITCHED (22)
            Length: 4
        Field (3/26): PKTS
            Type: PKTS (2)
            Length: 4
        Field (4/26): BYTES
            Type: BYTES (1)
            Length: 4
        Field (5/26): INPUT_SNMP
            Type: INPUT_SNMP (10)
            Length: 4
        Field (6/26): OUTPUT_SNMP
            Type: OUTPUT_SNMP (14)
            Length: 4
```

These are of course (given the data size) related to IPv4 addresses; other field codes with proper size are used in case of IPv6 addresses.

```
        Field (7/26): IP_SRC_ADDR
            Type: IP_SRC_ADDR (8)
            Length: 4
        Field (8/26): IP_DST_ADDR
            Type: IP_DST_ADDR (12)
            Length: 4
        Field (9/26): PROTOCOL
            Type: PROTOCOL (4)
            Length: 1
        Field (10/26): IP_TOS
```

```
        Type: IP_TOS (5)
        Length: 1
Field (11/26): L4_SRC_PORT
        Type: L4_SRC_PORT (7)
        Length: 2
Field (12/26): L4_DST_PORT
        Type: L4_DST_PORT (11)
        Length: 2
Field (13/26): IP_NEXT_HOP
        Type: IP_NEXT_HOP (15)
        Length: 4
Field (14/26): DST_MASK
        Type: DST_MASK (13)
        Length: 1
Field (15/26): SRC_MASK
        Type: SRC_MASK (9)
        Length: 1
Field (16/26): TCP_FLAGS
        Type: TCP_FLAGS (6)
        Length: 1
Field (17/26): SAMPLING_INTERVAL
        Type: SAMPLING_INTERVAL (34)
        Length: 4
Field (18/26): SAMPLING_ALGORITHM
        Type: SAMPLING_ALGORITHM (35)
        Length: 1
Field (19/26): DESTINATION_MAC
        Type: DESTINATION_MAC (80)
        Length: 6
Field (20/26): SRC_MAC
        Type: SRC_MAC (56)
        Length: 6
```

Although not strictly related to Layer 3 from the ISO/OSI network stack, the source and destination MAC Addresses of the flow can also be reported. Keep in mind that if devices are not directly connected, the source or the destination MAC address could be one of the routing devices connected to the flow exporter.

```
Field (21/26): DST_MAC
        Type: DST_MAC (57)
        Length: 6
Field (22/26): SOURCE_MAC
```

```
            Type: SOURCE_MAC (81)
            Length: 6
        Field (23/26): postNATSourceIPv4Address
            Type: postNATSourceIPv4Address (225)
            Length: 4
        Field (24/26): postNATDestinationIPv4Address
            Type: postNATDestinationIPv4Address (226)
            Length: 4
        Field (25/26): postNAPTSourceTransportPort
            Type: postNAPTSourceTransportPort (227)
            Length: 2
        Field (26/26): postNAPTDestinationTransportPort
            Type: postNAPTDestinationTransportPort (228)
            Length: 2
    Template (Id = 257, Count = 25)
        Template Id: 257
        Field Count: 25
        Field (1/25): IP_PROTOCOL_VERSION
            Type: IP_PROTOCOL_VERSION (60)
            Length: 1
        Field (2/25): IPV6_SRC_ADDR
            Type: IPV6_SRC_ADDR (27)
            Length: 16
        Field (3/25): IPV6_SRC_MASK
            Type: IPV6_SRC_MASK (29)
            Length: 1
        Field (4/25): INPUT_SNMP
            Type: INPUT_SNMP (10)
            Length: 4
```

As you can see, in this example, template ID 256 is used for IPv4 flows, while template ID 257 is used for IPv6 flows.

```
        Field (5/25): IPV6_DST_ADDR
            Type: IPV6_DST_ADDR (28)
            Length: 16
        Field (6/25): IPV6_DST_MASK
            Type: IPV6_DST_MASK (30)
            Length: 1
        Field (7/25): OUTPUT_SNMP
            Type: OUTPUT_SNMP (14)
            Length: 4
```

```
Field (8/25): IPV6_NEXT_HOP
    Type: IPV6_NEXT_HOP (62)
    Length: 16
Field (9/25): PROTOCOL
    Type: PROTOCOL (4)
    Length: 1
Field (10/25): TCP_FLAGS
    Type: TCP_FLAGS (6)
    Length: 1
Field (11/25): SAMPLING_INTERVAL
    Type: SAMPLING_INTERVAL (34)
    Length: 4
Field (12/25): SAMPLING_ALGORITHM
    Type: SAMPLING_ALGORITHM (35)
    Length: 1
Field (13/25): IP_TOS
    Type: IP_TOS (5)
    Length: 1
Field (14/25): L4_SRC_PORT
    Type: L4_SRC_PORT (7)
    Length: 2
Field (15/25): L4_DST_PORT
    Type: L4_DST_PORT (11)
    Length: 2
Field (16/25): FLOW_LABEL
    Type: FLOW_LABEL (31)
    Length: 4
Field (17/25): IPV6_OPTION_HEADERS
    Type: IPV6_OPTION_HEADERS (64)
    Length: 4
Field (18/25): LAST_SWITCHED
    Type: LAST_SWITCHED (21)
    Length: 4
Field (19/25): FIRST_SWITCHED
    Type: FIRST_SWITCHED (22)
    Length: 4
Field (20/25): BYTES
    Type: BYTES (1)
    Length: 4
Field (21/25): PKTS
```

```
          Type: PKTS (2)
          Length: 4
Field (22/25): DESTINATION_MAC
          Type: DESTINATION_MAC (80)
          Length: 6
Field (23/25): SRC_MAC
          Type: SRC_MAC (56)
          Length: 6
Field (24/25): DST_MAC
          Type: DST_MAC (57)
          Length: 6
Field (25/25): SOURCE_MAC
          Type: SOURCE_MAC (81)
          Length: 6
```

IPFIX

IPFIX is a standardized protocol for exporting network flow information, that builds on the concepts of earlier flow protocols like NetFlow and enhances them with greater flexibility, extensibility, and support for modern network features. It was developed by the **Internet Engineering Task Force (IETF)** to provide a common format for exporting flow data from network devices for analysis, monitoring, and security purposes. IPFIX is designed to be more flexible and extensible than earlier versions of NetFlow, allowing for the export of a wide range of flow data attributes. It enables the export of flow data for comprehensive network analysis, monitoring, and security. Let us now learn more about IPFIX:

- **IPFIX protocol overview**: IPFIX is a protocol that enables network devices to export flow information to a collector for analysis and reporting. It builds upon the concepts of earlier versions of NetFlow while introducing improvements in terms of flexibility, extensibility, and support for different types of networks, including IPv6 and MPLS.

- **Key concepts**:

  o **Flow**: Similar to NetFlow, a flow in IPFIX represents a unidirectional sequence of packets with common attributes, such as source and destination IP addresses, ports, protocol, and more.

  o **Exporter**: The network device generating and exporting IPFIX records to a collector. It defines templates that specify the structure of exported flow records.

  o **Collector**: The server that receives IPFIX records from exporters, processes the data, and provides insights into network behavior.

- o **Template**: A crucial feature of IPFIX, templates define the structure of exported flow data records. They specify which attributes are included and their data types.

- o **Options template**: An extension of the basic template, options templates allow for the inclusion of optional attributes that are not always present in all flows.

- **IPFIX message structure**: IPFIX messages consist of a header, templates, and data records.

  - o **Header**:

    - ▪ **Version number**: The version of IPFIX protocol being used (for example, 10).

    - ▪ **Message length**: The length of the entire IPFIX message, including templates and data records.

    - ▪ **Export time**: The timestamp when the message was exported.

    - ▪ **Sequence number**: An incrementing value used to maintain message order.

    - ▪ **Observation domain ID**: An identifier for the domain or device exporting the flow data.

  - o **Template format**: Templates define the structure of flow data records and consist of the following elements:

    - ▪ **Template ID**: A unique identifier for the template.

    - ▪ **Field count**: The number of fields included in the template.

    - ▪ **Field type and length**: For each field, the type of attribute and its length.

  - o **Data record format**: Data records follow the structure defined by templates and include attributes specified in the templates. These attributes can include source IP, destination IP, ports, protocol, packet and byte counts, and more.

  - o **Option template format**: Options templates are used to define optional fields that might not be present in all flow records. They include attributes similar to regular templates but allow for greater flexibility.

- **IPFIX operation**:

  - o **Template definition**: Exporters define templates that describe the attributes to be included in flow data records and options templates for optional attributes.

  - o **Flow identification and aggregation**: Similar to other flow-based protocols, the exporter identifies flows, aggregates data, and updates counters.

o **Flow timeout and record generation**: Inactive flows or when the export timer triggers, flow data records are generated using the templates.

o **Record export**: Flow data records are encapsulated into IPFIX messages and transmitted to the collector using UDP.

o **Template management**: Collectors maintain a template cache and use templates to parse and interpret flow data records.

o **Collection and analysis**: The collector extracts and processes flow data records based on templates, providing detailed network analysis and insights.

Advantages of IPFIX

IPFIX offers a standardized, flexible, and extensible approach to exporting flow data. Its support for IPv6, MPLS, and optional attributes makes it suitable for diverse network environments.

Here we can see a couple of Wireshark dissected IPFIX protocol packets. In this example, a Mikrotik RB2011 (Firmware 7.11.2) with IP address 10.1.30.101 was configured to send packets to collector on 10.1.30.210 on port 2056 (which Wireshark labels as service omnisky). The first packet contains the templates and the second packet contains the data. Templates are normally exported periodically and could have their dedicated packets or can be mixed with data packets; normally, it is up to the vendor implementation. As you can see, IPFIX is very similar to NetFlow V9. Refer to the following:

```
No.     VLAN Time           Source              Destination
Protocol DST Port Length Info
    497        58.240001    10.1.30.101         10.1.30.210
CFLOW   omnisky  354     IPFIX flow ( 312 bytes) Obs-Domain-ID=   0 [Data-
Template:258,259]
```

The following frame describes a template packet for IPFIX, containing all the information used to decode the frames matching the template ID used in subsequent packets.

```
Frame 497: 354 bytes on wire (2832 bits), 354 bytes captured (2832 bits)
    Encapsulation type: Ethernet (1)
    Arrival Time: Oct 18, 2023 23:03:36.561494000 CEST
    [Time shift for this packet: 0.000000000 seconds]
    Epoch Time: 1697663016.661494000 seconds
    [Time delta from previous captured frame: 1.039578000 seconds]
    [Time delta from previous displayed frame: 1.040034000 seconds]
    [Time since reference or first frame: 58.240001000 seconds]
    Frame Number: 497
    Frame Length: 354 bytes (2832 bits)
```

```
    Capture Length: 354 bytes (2832 bits)
    [Frame is marked: False]
    [Frame is ignored: False]
    [Protocols in frame: eth:ethertype:ip:udp:cflow]
    [Coloring Rule Name: UDP]
    [Coloring Rule String: udp]
Ethernet II, Src: Routerbo_d8:3f:d7 (d4:ca:6d:d8:3f:d7), Dst:
HewlettP_15:9c:45 (2c:27:d7:15:9c:45)
    Destination: HewlettP_15:9c:45 (2c:27:d7:15:9c:45)
        [Destination (resolved): HewlettP_15:9c:45]
        [Destination OUI: 2c:27:d7 (Hewlett Packard)]
        [Destination OUI (resolved): Hewlett Packard]
        Address: HewlettP_15:9c:45 (2c:27:d7:15:9c:45)
        [Address (resolved): HewlettP_15:9c:45]
        [Address OUI: 2c:27:d7 (Hewlett Packard)]
        [Address OUI (resolved): Hewlett Packard]
        .... ..0. .... .... .... .... = LG bit: Globally unique address
(factory default)
        .... ..0. .... .... .... .... = LG bit: Globally unique address
(factory default)
        .... ...0 .... .... .... .... = IG bit: Individual address
(unicast)
        .... ...0 .... .... .... .... = IG bit: Individual address
(unicast)
    Source: Routerbo_d8:3f:d7 (d4:ca:6d:d8:3f:d7)
        [Source (resolved): Routerbo_d8:3f:d7]
        [Source OUI: d4:ca:6d (Routerboard.com)]
        [Source OUI (resolved): Routerboard.com]
        Address: Routerbo_d8:3f:d7 (d4:ca:6d:d8:3f:d7)
        [Address (resolved): Routerbo_d8:3f:d7]
        [Address OUI: d4:ca:6d (Routerboard.com)]
        [Address OUI (resolved): Routerboard.com]
        .... ..0. .... .... .... .... = LG bit: Globally unique address
(factory default)
        .... ..0. .... .... .... .... = LG bit: Globally unique address
(factory default)
        .... ...0 .... .... .... .... = IG bit: Individual address
(unicast)
        .... ...0 .... .... .... .... = IG bit: Individual address
(unicast)
    Type: IPv4 (0x0800)
Internet Protocol Version 4, Src: 10.1.30.101, Dst: 10.1.30.210
```

```
    0100 .... = Version: 4
    .... 0101 = Header Length: 20 bytes (5)
    Differentiated Services Field: 0x00 (DSCP: CS0, ECN: Not-ECT)
        0000 00.. = Differentiated Services Codepoint: Default (0)
        .... ..00 = Explicit Congestion Notification: Not ECN-Capable
Transport (0)
    Total Length: 340
    Identification: 0xb30a (45834)
    Flags: 0x0000
        0... .... .... .... = Reserved bit: Not set
        .0.. .... .... .... = Don't fragment: Not set
        ..0. .... .... .... = More fragments: Not set
    Fragment offset: 0
    Time to live: 255
    Protocol: UDP (17)
    Header checksum: 0xb655 [validation disabled]
    [Header checksum status: Unverified]
    Source: 10.1.30.101
    Source or Destination Address: 10.1.30.101
    [Source Host: 10.1.30.101]
    [Source or Destination Host: 10.1.30.101]
    Destination: 10.1.30.210
    Source or Destination Address: 10.1.30.210
    [Destination Host: 10.1.30.210]
    [Source or Destination Host: 10.1.30.210]
User Datagram Protocol, Src Port: omnisky (2056), Dst Port: omnisky (2056)
    Source Port: omnisky (2056)
    Destination Port: omnisky (2056)
    Source or Destination Port: omnisky (2056)
    Source or Destination Port: omnisky (2056)
    Length: 320
    [Checksum: [missing]]
    [Checksum Status: Not present]
    [Stream index: 0]
    [Timestamps]
        [Time since first frame: 58.240001000 seconds]
        [Time since previous frame: 1.040034000 seconds]
Cisco NetFlow/IPFIX
    Version: 10
    Length: 312
```

Note that, as previously described for NetFlow v9, here the timestamp of the flow export is computed in a similar but slightly different way, always considering the UNIX time epoch of 1/1/1970.

```
Timestamp: Oct 18, 2023 23:03:36.000000000 CEST
    ExportTime: 1697663016
FlowSequence: 56
Observation Domain Id: 0
Set 1 [id=2] (Data Template): 258,259
    FlowSet Id: Data Template (V10 [IPFIX]) (2)
    FlowSet Length: 296
    Template (Id = 258, Count = 37)
        Template Id: 258
        Field Count: 37
        Field (1/37): IP_PROTOCOL_VERSION
            0... .... .... .... = Pen provided: No
            .000 0000 0011 1100 = Type: IP_PROTOCOL_VERSION (60)
            Length: 1
        Field (2/37): FIRST_SWITCHED
            0... .... .... .... = Pen provided: No
            .000 0000 0001 0110 = Type: FIRST_SWITCHED (22)
            Length: 4
        Field (3/37): LAST_SWITCHED
            0... .... .... .... = Pen provided: No
            .000 0000 0001 0101 = Type: LAST_SWITCHED (21)
            Length: 4
        Field (4/37): systemInitTimeMilliseconds
            0... .... .... .... = Pen provided: No
            .000 0000 1010 0000 = Type: systemInitTimeMilliseconds
(160)
            Length: 8
```

Being a derivative of NetFlow v9, IPFIX shares a lot of field codes with NetFlow v9, but it also adds the **Private Enterprise Number** (**PEN**) for custom fields. The PEN numbers are registered with IANA by companies implementing flow exporters and their definitions are usually not public. The bit of PEN provided is 0 if it is an RFC described field, otherwise 1 and a PEN number field is also encoded in the field definition.

```
        Field (5/37): PKTS
            0... .... .... .... = Pen provided: No
            .000 0000 0000 0010 = Type: PKTS (2)
            Length: 4
        Field (6/37): BYTES
```

```
    0... .... .... .... = Pen provided: No
    .000 0000 0000 0001 = Type: BYTES (1)
    Length: 4
Field (7/37): L4_SRC_PORT
    0... .... .... .... = Pen provided: No
    .000 0000 0000 0111 = Type: L4_SRC_PORT (7)
    Length: 2
Field (8/37): L4_DST_PORT
    0... .... .... .... = Pen provided: No
    .000 0000 0000 1011 = Type: L4_DST_PORT (11)
    Length: 2
Field (9/37): INPUT_SNMP
    0... .... .... .... = Pen provided: No
    .000 0000 0000 1010 = Type: INPUT_SNMP (10)
    Length: 4
Field (10/37): OUTPUT_SNMP
    0... .... .... .... = Pen provided: No
    .000 0000 0000 1110 = Type: OUTPUT_SNMP (14)
    Length: 4
Field (11/37): PROTOCOL
    0... .... .... .... = Pen provided: No
    .000 0000 0000 0100 = Type: PROTOCOL (4)
    Length: 1
Field (12/37): IP_TOS
    0... .... .... .... = Pen provided: No
    .000 0000 0000 0101 = Type: IP_TOS (5)
    Length: 1
Field (13/37): TCP_FLAGS
    0... .... .... .... = Pen provided: No
    .000 0000 0000 0110 = Type: TCP_FLAGS (6)
    Length: 1
Field (14/37): DST_MAC
    0... .... .... .... = Pen provided: No
    .000 0000 0011 1001 = Type: DST_MAC (57)
    Length: 6
Field (15/37): DESTINATION_MAC
    0... .... .... .... = Pen provided: No
    .000 0000 0101 0000 = Type: DESTINATION_MAC (80)
    Length: 6
Field (16/37): SOURCE_MAC
```

```
                0... .... .... .... = Pen provided: No
                .000 0000 0101 0001 = Type: SOURCE_MAC (81)
                Length: 6
        Field (17/37): SRC_MAC
                0... .... .... .... = Pen provided: No
                .000 0000 0011 1000 = Type: SRC_MAC (56)
                Length: 6
        Field (18/37): IP_SRC_ADDR
                0... .... .... .... = Pen provided: No
                .000 0000 0000 1000 = Type: IP_SRC_ADDR (8)
                Length: 4
        Field (19/37): IP_DST_ADDR
                0... .... .... .... = Pen provided: No
                .000 0000 0000 1100 = Type: IP_DST_ADDR (12)
                Length: 4
        Field (20/37): IP_NEXT_HOP
                0... .... .... .... = Pen provided: No
                .000 0000 0000 1111 = Type: IP_NEXT_HOP (15)
                Length: 4
        Field (21/37): SRC_MASK
                0... .... .... .... = Pen provided: No
                .000 0000 0000 1001 = Type: SRC_MASK (9)
                Length: 1
        Field (22/37): DST_MASK
                0... .... .... .... = Pen provided: No
                .000 0000 0000 1101 = Type: DST_MASK (13)
                Length: 1
```

The following are some IPFIX specific fields that can be used by IPFIX decoders to provide further information about the flow.

```
        Field (23/37): IP_TTL
                0... .... .... .... = Pen provided: No
                .000 0000 1100 0000 = Type: IP_TTL (192)
                Length: 1
        Field (24/37): IS_MULTICAST
                0... .... .... .... = Pen provided: No
                .000 0000 1100 1110 = Type: IS_MULTICAST (206)
                Length: 1
        Field (25/37): IP_HEADER_LEN
                0... .... .... .... = Pen provided: No
                .000 0000 1011 1101 = Type: IP_HEADER_LEN (189)
```

```
            Length: 1
    Field (26/37): ipTotalLength
        0... .... .... .... = Pen provided: No
        .000 0000 1110 0000 = Type: ipTotalLength (224)
        Length: 8
    Field (27/37): UDP_LENGTH
        0... .... .... .... = Pen provided: No
        .000 0000 1100 1101 = Type: UDP_LENGTH (205)
        Length: 2
    Field (28/37): TCP_SEQ_NUM
        0... .... .... .... = Pen provided: No
        .000 0000 1011 1000 = Type: TCP_SEQ_NUM (184)
        Length: 4
    Field (29/37): TCP_ACK_NUM
        0... .... .... .... = Pen provided: No
        .000 0000 1011 1001 = Type: TCP_ACK_NUM (185)
        Length: 4
    Field (30/37): TCP_WINDOW_SIZE
        0... .... .... .... = Pen provided: No
        .000 0000 1011 1010 = Type: TCP_WINDOW_SIZE (186)
        Length: 2
```

Notice that, being an IETF standard and a general purpose exporting protocol, IPFIX is not
tied to TCP/UDP and ICMP only, but also supports details for other protocols like IGMP.

```
    Field (31/37): IGMP_TYPE
        0... .... .... .... = Pen provided: No
        .000 0000 0010 0001 = Type: IGMP_TYPE (33)
        Length: 1
    Field (32/37): ICMP_IPv4_TYPE
        0... .... .... .... = Pen provided: No
        .000 0000 1011 0000 = Type: ICMP_IPv4_TYPE (176)
        Length: 1
    Field (33/37): ICMP_IPv4_CODE
        0... .... .... .... = Pen provided: No
        .000 0000 1011 0001 = Type: ICMP_IPv4_CODE (177)
        Length: 1
    Field (34/37): postNATSourceIPv4Address
        0... .... .... .... = Pen provided: No
        .000 0000 1110 0001 = Type: postNATSourceIPv4Address (225)
        Length: 4
    Field (35/37): postNATDestinationIPv4Address
```

```
                    0... .... .... .... = Pen provided: No
                    .000 0000 1110 0010 = Type: postNATDestinationIPv4Address
(226)
                    Length: 4
              Field (36/37): postNAPTSourceTransportPort
                    0... .... .... .... = Pen provided: No
                    .000 0000 1110 0011 = Type: postNAPTSourceTransportPort
(227)
                    Length: 2
              Field (37/37): postNAPTDestinationTransportPort
                    0... .... .... .... = Pen provided: No
                    .000 0000 1110 0100 = Type:
postNAPTDestinationTransportPort (228)
                    Length: 2
         Template (Id = 259, Count = 34)
              Template Id: 259
              Field Count: 34
              Field (1/34): IP_PROTOCOL_VERSION
                    0... .... .... .... = Pen provided: No
                    .000 0000 0011 1100 = Type: IP_PROTOCOL_VERSION (60)
                    Length: 1
              Field (2/34): FIRST_SWITCHED
                    0... .... .... .... = Pen provided: No
                    .000 0000 0001 0110 = Type: FIRST_SWITCHED (22)
                    Length: 4
              Field (3/34): LAST_SWITCHED
                    0... .... .... .... = Pen provided: No
                    .000 0000 0001 0101 = Type: LAST_SWITCHED (21)
                    Length: 4
```

As seen before, IPFIX also considers the boot time of the exporter to compute the start and stop of the flow, which is reported in the two previous fields, **FIRST_SWITCHED** and **LAST_SWITCHED**.

```
              Field (4/34): systemInitTimeMilliseconds
                    0... .... .... .... = Pen provided: No
                    .000 0000 1010 0000 = Type: systemInitTimeMilliseconds
(160)
                    Length: 8
              Field (5/34): PKTS
                    0... .... .... .... = Pen provided: No
                    .000 0000 0000 0010 = Type: PKTS (2)
                    Length: 4
```

```
Field (6/34): BYTES
    0... .... .... .... = Pen provided: No
    .000 0000 0000 0001 = Type: BYTES (1)
    Length: 4
Field (7/34): L4_SRC_PORT
    0... .... .... .... = Pen provided: No
    .000 0000 0000 0111 = Type: L4_SRC_PORT (7)
    Length: 2
Field (8/34): L4_DST_PORT
    0... .... .... .... = Pen provided: No
    .000 0000 0000 1011 = Type: L4_DST_PORT (11)
    Length: 2
Field (9/34): INPUT_SNMP
    0... .... .... .... = Pen provided: No
    .000 0000 0000 1010 = Type: INPUT_SNMP (10)
    Length: 4
Field (10/34): OUTPUT_SNMP
    0... .... .... .... = Pen provided: No
    .000 0000 0000 1110 = Type: OUTPUT_SNMP (14)
    Length: 4
Field (11/34): PROTOCOL
    0... .... .... .... = Pen provided: No
    .000 0000 0000 0100 = Type: PROTOCOL (4)
    Length: 1
Field (12/34): IP_TOS
    0... .... .... .... = Pen provided: No
    .000 0000 0000 0101 = Type: IP_TOS (5)
    Length: 1
Field (13/34): TCP_FLAGS
    0... .... .... .... = Pen provided: No
    .000 0000 0000 0110 = Type: TCP_FLAGS (6)
    Length: 1
Field (14/34): DST_MAC
    0... .... .... .... = Pen provided: No
    .000 0000 0011 1001 = Type: DST_MAC (57)
    Length: 6
Field (15/34): DESTINATION_MAC
    0... .... .... .... = Pen provided: No
    .000 0000 0101 0000 = Type: DESTINATION_MAC (80)
    Length: 6
Field (16/34): SOURCE_MAC
```

```
        0... .... .... .... = Pen provided: No
        .000 0000 0101 0001 = Type: SOURCE_MAC (81)
        Length: 6
Field (17/34): SRC_MAC
        0... .... .... .... = Pen provided: No
        .000 0000 0011 1000 = Type: SRC_MAC (56)
        Length: 6
Field (18/34): IPV6_SRC_ADDR
        0... .... .... .... = Pen provided: No
        .000 0000 0001 1011 = Type: IPV6_SRC_ADDR (27)
        Length: 16
Field (19/34): IPV6_DST_ADDR
        0... .... .... .... = Pen provided: No
        .000 0000 0001 1100 = Type: IPV6_DST_ADDR (28)
        Length: 16
Field (20/34): IPV6_NEXT_HOP
        0... .... .... .... = Pen provided: No
        .000 0000 0011 1110 = Type: IPV6_NEXT_HOP (62)
        Length: 16
```

Note that the **MASK** fields normally are populated with values only if the flow exporter has a direct IP address on the interface that is part of the flow, otherwise it is quite difficult to obtain it.

```
Field (21/34): IPV6_SRC_MASK
        0... .... .... .... = Pen provided: No
        .000 0000 0001 1101 = Type: IPV6_SRC_MASK (29)
        Length: 1
Field (22/34): IPV6_DST_MASK
        0... .... .... .... = Pen provided: No
        .000 0000 0001 1110 = Type: IPV6_DST_MASK (30)
        Length: 1
Field (23/34): IP_TTL
        0... .... .... .... = Pen provided: No
        .000 0000 1100 0000 = Type: IP_TTL (192)
        Length: 1
Field (24/34): IS_MULTICAST
        0... .... .... .... = Pen provided: No
        .000 0000 1100 1110 = Type: IS_MULTICAST (206)
        Length: 1
Field (25/34): IP_HEADER_LEN
        0... .... .... .... = Pen provided: No
```

```
        .000 0000 1011 1101 = Type: IP_HEADER_LEN (189)
        Length: 1
Field (26/34): ipTotalLength
        0... .... .... .... = Pen provided: No
        .000 0000 1110 0000 = Type: ipTotalLength (224)
        Length: 8
Field (27/34): UDP_LENGTH
        0... .... .... .... = Pen provided: No
        .000 0000 1100 1101 = Type: UDP_LENGTH (205)
        Length: 2
```

It is interesting to see that, while NetFlow v5 provides only TCP flags information about TCP flows, IPFIX can be much more detailed with the information regarding TCP flows.

```
Field (28/34): TCP_SEQ_NUM
        0... .... .... .... = Pen provided: No
        .000 0000 1011 1000 = Type: TCP_SEQ_NUM (184)
        Length: 4
Field (29/34): TCP_ACK_NUM
        0... .... .... .... = Pen provided: No
        .000 0000 1011 1001 = Type: TCP_ACK_NUM (185)
        Length: 4
Field (30/34): TCP_WINDOW_SIZE
        0... .... .... .... = Pen provided: No
        .000 0000 1011 1010 = Type: TCP_WINDOW_SIZE (186)
        Length: 2
Field (31/34): IGMP_TYPE
        0... .... .... .... = Pen provided: No
        .000 0000 0010 0001 = Type: IGMP_TYPE (33)
        Length: 1
Field (32/34): ICMP_IPv6_TYPE
        0... .... .... .... = Pen provided: No
        .000 0000 1011 0010 = Type: ICMP_IPv6_TYPE (178)
        Length: 1
Field (33/34): ICMP_IPv6_CODE
        0... .... .... .... = Pen provided: No
        .000 0000 1011 0011 = Type: ICMP_IPv6_CODE (179)
        Length: 1
Field (34/34): FLOW_LABEL
        0... .... .... .... = Pen provided: No
        .000 0000 0001 1111 = Type: FLOW_LABEL (31)
        Length: 4
```

The following frame describes a data packet for IPFIX, encoding data using the previously received template IDs.

```
No.      VLAN Time           Source              Destination
Protocol DST Port Length Info
   528         59.279943      10.1.30.101         10.1.30.210
CFLOW    omnisky 178    IPFIX flow ( 136 bytes) Obs-Domain-ID=    0
[Data:258]

Frame 528: 178 bytes on wire (1424 bits), 178 bytes captured (1424 bits)
    Encapsulation type: Ethernet (1)
    Arrival Time: Oct 18, 2023 23:03:37.701436000 CEST
    [Time shift for this packet: 0.000000000 seconds]
    Epoch Time: 1697663017.701436000 seconds
    [Time delta from previous captured frame: 1.039644000 seconds]
    [Time delta from previous displayed frame: 1.039942000 seconds]
    [Time since reference or first frame: 59.279943000 seconds]
    Frame Number: 528
    Frame Length: 178 bytes (1424 bits)
    Capture Length: 178 bytes (1424 bits)
    [Frame is marked: False]
    [Frame is ignored: False]
    [Protocols in frame: eth:ethertype:ip:udp:cflow]
    [Coloring Rule Name: UDP]
    [Coloring Rule String: udp]
Ethernet II, Src: Routerbo_d8:3f:d7 (d4:ca:6d:d8:3f:d7), Dst:
HewlettP_15:9c:45 (2c:27:d7:15:9c:45)
    Destination: HewlettP_15:9c:45 (2c:27:d7:15:9c:45)
        [Destination (resolved): HewlettP_15:9c:45]
        [Destination OUI: 2c:27:d7 (Hewlett Packard)]
        [Destination OUI (resolved): Hewlett Packard]
        Address: HewlettP_15:9c:45 (2c:27:d7:15:9c:45)
        [Address (resolved): HewlettP_15:9c:45]
        [Address OUI: 2c:27:d7 (Hewlett Packard)]
        [Address OUI (resolved): Hewlett Packard]
        .... ..0. .... .... .... .... = LG bit: Globally unique address
(factory default)
        .... ..0. .... .... .... .... = LG bit: Globally unique address
(factory default)
        .... ...0 .... .... .... .... = IG bit: Individual address
(unicast)
        .... ...0 .... .... .... .... = IG bit: Individual address
(unicast)
```

Source: Routerbo_d8:3f:d7 (d4:ca:6d:d8:3f:d7)
    [Source (resolved): Routerbo_d8:3f:d7]
    [Source OUI: d4:ca:6d (Routerboard.com)]
    [Source OUI (resolved): Routerboard.com]
    Address: Routerbo_d8:3f:d7 (d4:ca:6d:d8:3f:d7)
    [Address (resolved): Routerbo_d8:3f:d7]
    [Address OUI: d4:ca:6d (Routerboard.com)]
    [Address OUI (resolved): Routerboard.com]
    .... ..0. .... = LG bit: Globally unique address
(factory default)
    .... ..0. .... = LG bit: Globally unique address
(factory default)
    ....0 .... = IG bit: Individual address
(unicast)
    ....0 .... = IG bit: Individual address
(unicast)
Type: IPv4 (0x0800)
Internet Protocol Version 4, Src: 10.1.30.101, Dst: 10.1.30.210
    0100 .... = Version: 4
    .... 0101 = Header Length: 20 bytes (5)
    Differentiated Services Field: 0x00 (DSCP: CS0, ECN: Not-ECT)
        0000 00.. = Differentiated Services Codepoint: Default (0)
        .... ..00 = Explicit Congestion Notification: Not ECN-Capable
Transport (0)
    Total Length: 164
    Identification: 0xb30b (45835)
    Flags: 0x0000
        0... .... = Reserved bit: Not set
        .0.. .... = Don't fragment: Not set
        ..0. .... = More fragments: Not set
    Fragment offset: 0
    Time to live: 255
    Protocol: UDP (17)
    Header checksum: 0xb704 [validation disabled]
    [Header checksum status: Unverified]
    Source: 10.1.30.101
    Source or Destination Address: 10.1.30.101
    [Source Host: 10.1.30.101]
    [Source or Destination Host: 10.1.30.101]
    Destination: 10.1.30.210
    Source or Destination Address: 10.1.30.210

```
    [Destination Host: 10.1.30.210]
    [Source or Destination Host: 10.1.30.210]
User Datagram Protocol, Src Port: omnisky (2056), Dst Port: omnisky (2056)
    Source Port: omnisky (2056)
    Destination Port: omnisky (2056)
    Source or Destination Port: omnisky (2056)
    Source or Destination Port: omnisky (2056)
    Length: 144
    [Checksum: [missing]]
    [Checksum Status: Not present]
    [Stream index: 0]
    [Timestamps]
        [Time since first frame: 59.279943000 seconds]
        [Time since previous frame: 1.039942000 seconds]
Cisco NetFlow/IPFIX
    Version: 10
    Length: 136
    Timestamp: Oct 18, 2023 23:03:37.000000000 CEST
        ExportTime: 1697663017
    FlowSequence: 56
    Observation Domain Id: 0
    Set 1 [id=258] (1 flows)
        FlowSet Id: (Data) (258)
        FlowSet Length: 120
        [Template Frame: 497]
        Flow 1
            IPVersion: 4
            [Duration: 0.000000000 seconds (switched)]
                StartTime: 346017.450000000 seconds
                EndTime: 346017.450000000 seconds
```

Note how the start and stop of the flow are reported. You get the system init time (which is based on the UNIX time epoch of 1/1/1970) and then the seconds after this value to understand the timestamp of the beginning and ending of the flow.

```
            System Init Time: Oct 14, 2023 22:56:23.941000000 CEST
            Packets: 1
            Octets: 190
            SrcPort: 5678
            DstPort: 5678
            InputInt: 218
            OutputInt: 0
```

```
Protocol: UDP (17)
IP ToS: 0x00
TCP Flags: 0x00
    00.. .... = Reserved: 0x0
    ..0. .... = URG: Not used
    ...0 .... = ACK: Not used
    .... 0... = PSH: Not used
    .... .0.. = RST: Not used
    .... ..0. = SYN: Not used
    .... ...0 = FIN: Not used
Post Destination Mac Address: Broadcast (ff:ff:ff:ff:ff:ff)
Destination Mac Address: Routerbo_d8:3f:d8 (d4:ca:6d:d8:3f:d8)
Post Source Mac Address: 00:00:00_00:00:00 (00:00:00:00:00:00)
Source Mac Address: Routerbo_a8:82:a6 (b8:69:f4:a8:82:a6)
SrcAddr: 10.1.61.2
DstAddr: 255.255.255.255
NextHop: 0.0.0.0
SrcMask: 0
DstMask: 0
IP TTL: 64
IsMulticast: 0x00
IP Header Length: 5
IP Total Length: 190
UDP Length: 170
TCP Sequence Number: 0
TCP Acknowledgement Number: 0
TCP Windows Size: 0
IGMP Type: 0
IPv4 ICMP Type: 0
IPv4 ICMP Code: 0
Post NAT Source IPv4 Address: 10.1.61.2
Post NAT Destination IPv4 Address: 255.255.255.255
Post NAPT Source Transport Port: 5678
Post NAPT Destination Transport Port: 5678
```

sFlow v5

sFlow is a network monitoring protocol that provides real-time visibility into network traffic by sampling packets and collecting statistics. **sFlow version 5 (sFlow v5)** is an enhancement of the sFlow protocol, designed to offer more comprehensive and flexible monitoring capabilities. sFlow v5 is an advanced network monitoring protocol that uses sampling and counter collection to provide real-time visibility into network traffic patterns. It allows network administrators to monitor and analyze network behavior without overwhelming the monitoring infrastructure. Let us now learn more about sFlow v5:

- **sFlow v5 protocol overview**: sFlow v5 is a protocol that allows network devices, such as switches and routers, to collect and send network traffic data to a monitoring station for analysis. Unlike traditional methods that involve capturing and storing all packets, sFlow uses a sampling approach to provide a representative view of network activity without overwhelming the monitoring infrastructure.

- **Key concepts**:
  - **Packet sampling**: sFlow captures a subset of packets passing through a network device, rather than capturing every packet. This approach helps reduce the load on both the network device and the monitoring infrastructure while still providing valuable insights.

  - **Counter sampling**: In addition to packet sampling, sFlow also collects counters that track various statistics about network flows, such as the number of packets and bytes transferred, for each sampled flow.

  - **sFlow agent**: The network device (switch, router, and so on.) that generates and sends sFlow data to a collector. The agent samples packets, collects counter information, and encapsulates data for transmission.

  - **sFlow collector**: The server or software application that receives and processes sFlow data from multiple agents. It performs analysis, reporting, and visualization of network traffic patterns.

- **sFlow v5 packet structure**: An sFlow v5 packet consists of header information, followed by a series of sampled packet data and counter samples.
  - **Header**:
    - **Version number**: 5 (indicating sFlow v5).
    - **Agent address**: The IP address of the sFlow agent that generated the packet.
    - **Sub-agent ID**: An identifier for different agent instances on the same device.
    - **Sequence number**: An incrementing value used for packet ordering and loss detection.
    - **System uptime**: Time in milliseconds since the device was booted.
    - **Sample count**: Number of samples in the packet.
  - **Sampled packet data**: For each packet sample, the following information is included:

- **Sequence number**: A unique identifier for the sample within the packet.

        - **Source ID**: An identifier for the source of the packet data.

        - **Sample rate**: The rate at which packets were sampled compared to the total number of packets.

        - **Packet data**: A snapshot of the sampled packet, including header and payload data.

    o **Counter samples**: Counter samples capture various statistics related to network flows, such as packet and byte counts, interface information, and more.

- **sFlow operation**:

    o **Sampling configuration**: Network administrators configure the sFlow agent on network devices to specify the sampling rate and other settings.

    o **Packet and counter sampling**: The sFlow agent samples incoming packets and collects counter information at the configured rate.

    o **Packet and counter encapsulation**: Sampled packet data and counter samples are encapsulated into sFlow v5 packets.

    o **Packet transmission**: The sFlow agent sends the encapsulated packets to the sFlow collector using UDP.

    o **Collection and analysis**: The collector receives sFlow packets, extracts sampled packet data and counter samples, and performs analysis, reporting, and visualization of network traffic patterns.

Advantages of sFlow v5

The advantages of sFlow v5 are as follows:

- **Reduced overhead**: The sampling approach reduces the load on both the network device and the monitoring infrastructure, allowing for efficient and scalable network monitoring.

- **Real-time insights**: sFlow provides real-time visibility into network traffic patterns, aiding in network troubleshooting, capacity planning, and security analysis.

- **Flexibility**: sFlow v5 offers flexibility in terms of the types of data collected, including packet samples and counter samples, providing a comprehensive view of network behavior.

There are several RFC related to the sFlow protocol. sFlow is an open standard network monitoring and sampling technology maintained by sFlow.org. Here are some key RFCs related to the sFlow protocol:

- **RFC 3176**:
  - ○ **Title**: sFlow: A Method for Monitoring Traffic in Switched and Routed Networks
  - ○ **URL**: RFC 3176

- **RFC 5353**:
  - ○ **Title: Endpoint Handlespace Redundancy Protocol (ENRP)**
  - ○ **URL**: RFC 5353
  - ○ **Note**: This RFC defines the registration of the sFlow standard data formats.

- **RFC 3177**:
  - ○ **Title**: IEEE 802.1X Authentication as a Network Access Layer Protocol
  - ○ **URL**: RFC 3177
  - ○ **Note**: This RFC mentions sFlow in the context of monitoring IEEE 802.1X authentication traffic.

Here we can see a Wireshark dissected sFlow V5 protocol packet. In this example, an HP Procurve 2610-24 switch (Firmware R.11.25) with IP Address 10.1.30.9 was configured to send packets to collector on 10.1.30.210 on port 6343 (which Wireshark labels as service InFlow). The packet contains several information: several counters for interfaces and also a flow between SRC IP 10.1.20.21 and multicast address 224.0.0.18 for a **Virtual Router Redundancy Protocol (VRRP)** packet it saw:

```
No.      VLAN Time             Source               Destination
Protocol DST Port Length Info
    12       22.213469       10.1.30.9            10.1.30.210
sFlow    sflow    734     V5, agent 10.1.30.9, sub-agent ID 0, seq 4184078, 4
samples

Frame 12: 734 bytes on wire (5872 bits), 734 bytes captured (5872 bits)
    Encapsulation type: Ethernet (1)
    Arrival Time: Oct 18, 2023 23:11:27.260772000 CEST
    [Time shift for this packet: 0.000000000 seconds]
    Epoch Time: 1697663487.260772000 seconds
    [Time delta from previous captured frame: 1.999618000 seconds]
    [Time delta from previous displayed frame: 1.999618000 seconds]
    [Time since reference or first frame: 22.213469000 seconds]
    Frame Number: 12
    Frame Length: 734 bytes (5872 bits)
    Capture Length: 734 bytes (5872 bits)
    [Frame is marked: False]
    [Frame is ignored: False]
```

    [Protocols in frame:
eth:ethertype:ip:udp:sflow:eth:ethertype:ip:vrrp:vssmonitoring]
    [Coloring Rule Name: Routing]
    [Coloring Rule String: hsrp || eigrp || ospf || bgp || cdp || vrrp ||
carp || gvrp || igmp || ismp]
Ethernet II, Src: ProCurve_38:e7:c0 (00:25:61:38:e7:c0), Dst:
HewlettP_15:9c:45 (2c:27:d7:15:9c:45)
    Destination: HewlettP_15:9c:45 (2c:27:d7:15:9c:45)
        [Destination (resolved): HewlettP_15:9c:45]
        [Destination OUI: 2c:27:d7 (Hewlet- Packard)]
        [Destination OUI (resolved): Hewlett Packard]
        Address: HewlettP_15:9c:45 (2c:27:d7:15:9c:45)
        [Address (resolved): HewlettP_15:9c:45]
        [Address OUI: 2c:27:d7 (Hewlett Packard)]
        [Address OUI (resolved): Hewlett Packard]
        .... ..0. .... = LG bit: Globally unique address
(factory default)
        .... ..0. .... = LG bit: Globally unique address
(factory default)
        ....0 .... = IG bit: Individual address
(unicast)
        ....0 .... = IG bit: Individual address
(unicast)
    Source: ProCurve_38:e7:c0 (00:25:61:38:e7:c0)
        [Source (resolved): ProCurve_38:e7:c0]
        [Source OUI: 00:25:61 (ProCurve Networking b]
        [Source OUI (resolved): ProCurve Networking by HP]
        Address: ProCurve_38:e7:c0 (00:25:61:38:e7:c0)
        [Address (resolved): ProCurve_38:e7:c0]
        [Address OUI: 00:25:61 (ProCurve Networking b]
        [Address OUI (resolved): ProCurve Networking by HP]
        .... ..0. .... = LG bit: Globally unique address
(factory default)
        .... ..0. .... = LG bit: Globally unique address
(factory default)
        ....0 .... = IG bit: Individual address
(unicast)
        ....0 .... = IG bit: Individual address
(unicast)
    Type: IPv4 (0x0800)
Internet Protocol Version 4, Src: 10.1.30.9, Dst: 10.1.30.210
    0100 .... = Version: 4

```
    .... 0101 = Header Length: 20 bytes (5)
    Differentiated Services Field: 0x00 (DSCP: CS0, ECN: Not-ECT)
        0000 00.. = Differentiated Services Codepoint: Default (0)
        .... ..00 = Explicit Congestion Notification: Not ECN-Capable
Transport (0)
    Total Length: 720
    Identification: 0x29bd (10685)
    Flags: 0x0000
        0... .... .... .... = Reserved bit: Not set
        .0.. .... .... .... = Don't fragment: Not set
        ..0. .... .... .... = More fragments: Not set
    Fragment offset: 0
    Time to live: 64
    Protocol: UDP (17)
    Header checksum: 0xfd83 [validation disabled]
    [Header checksum status: Unverified]
    Source: 10.1.30.9
    Source or Destination Address: 10.1.30.9
    [Source Host: 10.1.30.9]
    [Source or Destination Host: 10.1.30.9]
    Destination: 10.1.30.210
    Source or Destination Address: 10.1.30.210
    [Destination Host: 10.1.30.210]
    [Source or Destination Host: 10.1.30.210]
```

Here begins the sFlow packet data:

```
User Datagram Protocol, Src Port: blackjack (1025), Dst Port: sflow (6343)
    Source Port: blackjack (1025)
    Destination Port: sflow (6343)
    Source or Destination Port: blackjack (1025)
    Source or Destination Port: sflow (6343)
    Length: 700
    Checksum: 0x4f80 [unverified]
    [Checksum Status: Unverified]
    [Stream index: 0]
    [Timestamps]
        [Time since first frame: 22.213469000 seconds]
        [Time since previous frame: 1.999618000 seconds]
InMon sFlow
    Datagram version: 5
    Agent address type: IPv4 (1)
```

```
        Agent address: 10.1.30.9
        Sub-agent ID: 0
        Sequence number: 4184078
```

As you see, the sFlow protocol also relies on system uptime for computing flows timestamps.

```
        SysUptime: 1892 days, 8 hours, 35 minutes, 58 seconds (163499758s)
        NumSamples: 4
        Flow sample, seq 2664459
            0000 0000 0000 0000 0000 .... .... .... = Enterprise: standard
sFlow (0)
            .... .... .... .... .... 0000 0000 0001 = sFlow sample type: Flow
sample (1)
            Sample length (byte): 128
            Sequence number: 2664459
            0000 0000 .... .... .... .... .... .... = Source ID class: 0
            .... .... 0000 0000 0000 0000 0001 1010 = Index: 26
            Sampling rate: 1 out of 20 packets
            Sample pool: 769031139 total packets
            Dropped packets: 35552031
            Input interface (ifIndex): 26
            Output interface: 0x3fffffff
                00.. .... .... .... .... .... .... .... = Output interface
format: ifindex (0)
                ..11 1111 1111 1111 1111 1111 1111 1111 = Output interface
value: 1073741823
```

As you will see, the information provided by sFlow is similar to NetFlow and IPFIX, but more tied to Layer 2 of the ISO/OSI stack, mostly relating to switching.

```
        Flow record: 1
        Raw packet header
            0000 0000 0000 0000 0000 .... .... .... = Enterprise: standard
sFlow (0)
                Format: Raw packet header (1)
                Flow data length (byte): 88
                Header protocol: Ethernet (1)
                Frame Length: 78
                Payload removed: 8
                Original packet length: 72
                Header of sampled packet:
01005e00000120000 5e000102080045e00038b7e80000ff70…
                    Ethernet II, Src: IETF-VRRP-VRID_02 (00:00:5e:00:01:02),
```

```
Dst: IPv4mcast_12 (01:00:5e:00:00:12)
                    Destination: IPv4mcast_12 (01:00:5e:00:00:12)
                        [Destination (resolved): IPv4mcast_12]
                        [Destination OUI: 01:00:5e]
                        Address: IPv4mcast_12 (01:00:5e:00:00:12)
                        [Address (resolved): IPv4mcast_12]
                        [Address OUI: 01:00:5e]
                        .... ..0. .... .... .... .... = LG bit: Globally
unique address (factory default)
                        .... ..0. .... .... .... .... = LG bit: Globally
unique address (factory default)
                        .... ...1 .... .... .... .... = IG bit: Group
address (multicast/broadcast)
                        .... ...1 .... .... .... .... = IG bit: Group
address (multicast/broadcast)
                    Source: IETF-VRRP-VRID_02 (00:00:5e:00:01:02)
                        [Source (resolved): IETF-VRRP-VRID_02]
                        [Source OUI: 00:00:5e (ICANN, IANA Departmen]
                        [Source OUI (resolved): ICANN, IANA Department]
                        Address: IETF-VRRP-VRID_02 (00:00:5e:00:01:02)
                        [Address (resolved): IETF-VRRP-VRID_02]
                        [Address OUI: 00:00:5e (ICANN, IANA Departmen]
                        [Address OUI (resolved): ICANN, IANA Department]
                        .... ..0. .... .... .... .... = LG bit: Globally
unique address (factory default)
                        .... ..0. .... .... .... .... = LG bit: Globally
unique address (factory default)
                        .... ...0 .... .... .... .... = IG bit: Individual
address (unicast)
                        .... ...0 .... .... .... .... = IG bit: Individual
address (unicast)
```

Some fields are common, like protocol, source and destination IP.

```
                    Type: IPv4 (0x0800)
            Internet Protocol Version 4, Src: 10.1.20.21, Dst:
224.0.0.18
                    0100 .... = Version: 4
                    .... 0101 = Header Length: 20 bytes (5)
                    Differentiated Services Field: 0xe0 (DSCP: CS7, ECN:
Not-ECT)
                        1110 00.. = Differentiated Services Codepoint:
Class Selector 7 (56)
```

```
                    .... ..00 = Explicit Congestion Notification: Not
ECN-Capable Transport (0)
                    Total Length: 56
                    Identification: 0xb7e8 (47080)
                    Flags: 0x0000
                        0... .... .... .... = Reserved bit: Not set
                        .0.. .... .... .... = Don't fragment: Not set
                        ..0. .... .... .... = More fragments: Not set
                    Fragment offset: 0
                    Time to live: 255
                    Protocol: VRRP (112)
                    Header checksum: 0x0465 [validation disabled]
                    [Header checksum status: Unverified]
                    Source: 10.1.20.21
                    Source or Destination Address: 10.1.20.21
                    [Source Host: 10.1.20.21]
                    [Source or Destination Host: 10.1.20.21]
                    Destination: 224.0.0.18
                    Source or Destination Address: 224.0.0.18
                    [Destination Host: 224.0.0.18]
                    [Source or Destination Host: 224.0.0.18]
```

While some others deep dive into Layer 2 details like the ones regarding VRRP.

```
                    Virtual Router Redundancy Protocol
                    Version 2, Packet type 1 (Advertisement)
                        0010 .... = VRRP protocol version: 2
                        .... 0001 = VRRP packet type: Advertisement (1)
                    Virtual Rtr ID: 2
                    Priority: 0 (Current Master has stopped participating
in VRRP)
                    Addr Count: 7
                    Auth Type: No Authentication (0)
                    Adver Int: 1
                    Checksum: 0x14dd [correct]
                    [Checksum Status: Good]
                    IP Address: 62.57.96.212
                    IP Address: 4.53.57.4
                    IP Address: 156.97.156.136
                    IP Address: 214.104.243.39
                    IP Address: 184.150.206.141
                    IP Address: 68.218.35.178
```

```
              IP Address: 74.41.177.124
    Counters sample, seq 557290
        0000 0000 0000 0000 0000 .... .... .... = Enterprise: standard
sFlow (0)
        .... .... .... .... .... 0000 0000 0010 = sFlow sample type:
Counters sample (2)
        Sample length (byte): 168
        Sequence number: 557290
        0000 0000 .... .... .... .... .... .... = Source ID type: 0
        .... .... 0000 0000 0000 0000 0000 0010 = Source ID index: 2
        Counters records: 2
        Generic interface counters
            0000 0000 0000 0000 0000 .... .... .... = Enterprise: standard
sFlow (0)
            .... .... .... .... .... 0000 0000 0001 = Format: Generic
interface counters (1)
            Flow data length (byte): 88
```

We also see the **Interface** identifiers, still relaying on the SNMP values, and the physical duplex status and the **Up** or **Down** status of the interface.

```
            Interface index: 2
            Interface Type: 6
            Interface Speed: 100000000
            Interface Direction: Full-Duplex (1)
            .... .... .... .... .... .... .... ...1 = IfAdminStatus: Up
            .... .... .... .... .... .... .... ..1. = IfOperStatus: Up
            Input Octets: 37600768
            Input Packets: 0
            Input Multicast Packets: 0
            Input Broadcast Packets: 587512
            Input Discarded Packets: 0
            Input Errors: 0
            Input Unknown Protocol Packets: 0
            Output Octets: 331348498
            Output Packets: 0
            Output Multicast Packets: 4674684
            Output Broadcast Packets: 0
            Output Discarded Packets: 0
            Output Errors: 0
            Promiscuous Mode: 0
        Ethernet interface counters
```

```
                0000 0000 0000 0000 0000 .... .... .... = Enterprise: standard
sFlow (0)
                .... .... .... .... .... 0000 0000 0010 = Format: Ethernet
interface counters (2)
                Flow data length (byte): 52
                Alignment Errors: 0
```

We even have more details regarding the Layer 2 counters.

```
                FCS Errors: 0
                Single Collision Frames: 0
                Multiple Collision Frames: 0
                SQE Test Errors: 0
                Deferred Transmissions: 0
                Late Collisions: 0
                Excessive Collisions: 0
                Internal Mac Transmit Errors: 0
                Carrier Sense Errors: 1
                Frame Too Longs: 0
                Internal Mac Receive Errors: 0
                Symbol Errors: 0
    Counters sample, seq 558052
        0000 0000 0000 0000 0000 .... .... .... = Enterprise: standard
sFlow (0)
        .... .... .... .... .... 0000 0000 0010 = sFlow sample type:
Counters sample (2)
        Sample length (byte): 168
        Sequence number: 558052
        0000 0000 .... .... .... .... .... .... = Source ID type: 0
        .... .... 0000 0000 0000 0000 0000 0100 = Source ID index: 4
        Counters records: 2
        Generic interface counters
            0000 0000 0000 0000 0000 .... .... .... = Enterprise: standard
sFlow (0)
            .... .... .... .... .... 0000 0000 0001 = Format: Generic
interface counters (1)
                Flow data length (byte): 88
                Interface index: 4
                Interface Type: 6
                Interface Speed: 100000000
                Interface Direction: Full-Duplex (1)
                .... .... .... .... .... .... .... ...1 = IfAdminStatus: Up
```

```
        .... .... .... .... .... .... .... ..1. = IfOperStatus: Up
        Input Octets: 37840554
        Input Packets: 2799
        Input Multicast Packets: 0
        Input Broadcast Packets: 587015
        Input Discarded Packets: 0
        Input Errors: 0
        Input Unknown Protocol Packets: 0
        Output Octets: 333014837
        Output Packets: 5113
        Output Multicast Packets: 4668343
        Output Broadcast Packets: 0
        Output Discarded Packets: 0
        Output Errors: 0
        Promiscuous Mode: 0
    Ethernet interface counters
        0000 0000 0000 0000 0000 .... .... .... = Enterprise: standard
sFlow (0)
        .... .... .... .... .... 0000 0000 0010 = Format: Ethernet
interface counters (2)
        Flow data length (byte): 52
```

It even goes deeper relating to the switching interface counting input/output/broadcast/multicast and other packets.

```
        Alignment Errors: 0
        FCS Errors: 0
        Single Collision Frames: 0
        Multiple Collision Frames: 0
        SQE Test Errors: 0
        Deferred Transmissions: 0
        Late Collisions: 0
        Excessive Collisions: 0
        Internal Mac Transmit Errors: 0
        Carrier Sense Errors: 1
        Frame Too Longs: 0
        Internal Mac Receive Errors: 0
        Symbol Errors: 0
    Counters sample, seq 557479
        0000 0000 0000 0000 0000 .... .... .... = Enterprise: standard
sFlow (0)
        .... .... .... .... .... 0000 0000 0010 = sFlow sample type:
```

```
Counters sample (2)
        Sample length (byte): 168
        Sequence number: 557479
        0000 0000 .... .... .... .... .... .... = Source ID type: 0
        .... .... 0000 0000 0000 0000 0001 1001 = Source ID index: 25
        Counters records: 2
        Generic interface counters
            0000 0000 0000 0000 0000 .... .... .... = Enterprise: standard
sFlow (0)
            .... .... .... .... .... 0000 0000 0001 = Format: Generic
interface counters (1)
            Flow data length (byte): 88
            Interface index: 25
            Interface Type: 6
            Interface Speed: 100000000
            Interface Direction: Full-Duplex (1)
            .... .... .... .... .... .... .... ...1 = IfAdminStatus: Up
            .... .... .... .... .... .... .... ..0. = IfOperStatus: Down
            Input Octets: 0
            Input Packets: 0
            Input Multicast Packets: 0
            Input Broadcast Packets: 0
            Input Discarded Packets: 0
            Input Errors: 0
            Input Unknown Protocol Packets: 0
            Output Octets: 0
            Output Packets: 0
            Output Multicast Packets: 0
            Output Broadcast Packets: 0
            Output Discarded Packets: 0
            Output Errors: 0
            Promiscuous Mode: 0
        Ethernet interface counters
            0000 0000 0000 0000 0000 .... .... .... = Enterprise: standard
sFlow (0)
            .... .... .... .... .... 0000 0000 0010 = Format: Ethernet
interface counters (2)
            Flow data length (byte): 52
            Alignment Errors: 0
            FCS Errors: 0
```

```
Single Collision Frames: 0
Multiple Collision Frames: 0
SQE Test Errors: 0
Deferred Transmissions: 0
Late Collisions: 0
Excessive Collisions: 0
Internal Mac Transmit Errors: 0
Carrier Sense Errors: 0
Frame Too Longs: 0
Internal Mac Receive Errors: 0
Symbol Errors: 0
```

Differences between fixed and dynamic flow protocols

Fixed and dynamic network flow protocols refer to different approaches for capturing and analyzing network traffic flows. Here are the key differences between the two:

- **Definition of flow fields**:

  o **Fixed network flow protocols**: Define a fixed set of fields for each flow, including source and destination IP addresses, ports, protocol, and so on.

  o **Dynamic network flow protocols**: Allow for the flexible definition of flow fields based on the specific needs or characteristics of the network traffic.

- **Flexibility in flow field definitions**:

  o **Fixed network flow protocols**: Have predefined and static flow field definitions, limiting the ability to customize or modify the fields being collected.

  o **Dynamic network flow protocols**: Enable dynamic creation and modification of flow field definitions, allowing for a tailored approach to capture specific attributes and metadata about network traffic.

- **Template-based vs. schema less approach**:

  o **Fixed network flow protocols**: Typically use a template-based approach for defining flow records, with a specific format and structure that remains constant.

  o **Dynamic network flow protocols**: Often adopt a schema less or semi-structured approach, allowing for variable-length encoding and more adaptable data representation.

- **Overhead and efficiency**:
  - ○ **Fixed network flow protocols**: May have a higher overhead due to the fixed structure and potential inclusion of unnecessary fields for certain use cases.
  - ○ **Dynamic network flow protocols**: Tend to be more efficient in terms of overhead since they allow for more selective and targeted capture of flow information.

- **Ease of modification and evolution**:
  - ○ **Fixed network flow protocols**: Changes or additions to flow fields require updates to the protocol specifications and potentially widespread device/software updates.
  - ○ **Dynamic network flow protocols**: Allow for easier modification and evolution of flow field definitions without requiring changes to the underlying protocol specifications.

- **Suitability for diverse use cases**:
  - ○ **Fixed network flow protocols**: May be well-suited for standard use cases where a predefined set of flow attributes suffices.
  - ○ **Dynamic network flow protocols**: Better suited for diverse use cases where specific flow attributes need to be captured based on the requirements of the monitoring application or analysis.

Both fixed and dynamic network flow protocols have their own set of advantages and disadvantages based on their design and use cases. Here is a comparison of the advantages and disadvantages of using fixed and dynamic network flow protocols.

The advantages of fixed network flow protocols are:

- **Simplicity and standardization**: Fixed network flow protocols have a standardized structure and well-defined flow fields, making them easier to implement and interpret.

- **Predictability**: The fixed structure ensures that the format and order of flow fields are predictable, simplifying parsing and analysis.

- **Interoperability**: Due to their standardized nature, fixed network flow protocols facilitate interoperability across different devices and software systems.

- **Resource efficiency**: Fixed network flow protocols may have lower processing and memory requirements since the structure is fixed and well-known.

The disadvantages of fixed network flow protocols are:

- **Limited flexibility**: The predefined flow field structure can be limiting for capturing additional or customized attributes specific to certain use cases.

- **Potentially high overhead**: Including unnecessary or irrelevant flow fields in every flow record can lead to higher data volume and increased storage and transmission overhead.

- **Difficulties in evolution**: Modifying or extending the flow field definitions requires changes to the protocol specifications, potentially hindering protocol evolution and widespread adoption of new features.

The advantages of dynamic network flow protocols are:

- **Flexibility and customization**: Dynamic network flow protocols allow for the flexible definition and collection of flow fields based on specific requirements, providing adaptability to diverse use cases.

- **Efficiency and reduced overhead**: Dynamic protocols can tailor the flow field definitions to capture only relevant information, reducing data volume and minimizing storage and transmission overhead.

- **Adaptability to evolving needs**: These protocols enable easy modification and evolution of flow field definitions to accommodate changes in network traffic patterns and monitoring requirements.

- **Enhanced data relevance**: By capturing only relevant attributes, dynamic protocols can provide more focused and meaningful flow records for analysis.

The disadvantages of dynamic network flow protocols are:

- **Complexity**: The dynamic and flexible nature of these protocols can introduce complexity in implementation, parsing, and analysis due to variable-length encoding and dynamic field definitions.

- **Potential for interpretation issues**: Different implementations may define flow fields differently, leading to potential interpretation issues or discrepancies in the captured data.

- **Possible interoperability challenges**: The lack of a standardized, fixed structure may pose challenges for interoperability across diverse network devices and software systems.

In summary, the choice between using fixed or dynamic network flow protocols depends on the specific monitoring requirements, the level of flexibility needed, and considerations related to standardization, resource efficiency, and future adaptability. Fixed protocols offer simplicity and standardization, while dynamic protocols provide flexibility and customization to better meet evolving monitoring needs. The decision should be based on a careful evaluation of these advantages and disadvantages in the context of the intended use cases.

Now let us understand the advantages and disadvantages of sampled and unsampled network flow protocols.

Sampled flow protocols capture and analyse a subset or sample of network traffic rather than processing every packet. This subset is determined by a defined sampling rate. Its advantages are:

- **Reduced overhead**: Sampling reduces the amount of data to be processed and transmitted, lowering resource overhead on network devices and collectors.

- **Scalability**: Suitable for high-speed networks where processing every packet is resource-intensive, enabling flow monitoring at scale.

- **Resource efficiency**: Reduces CPU and memory usage on network devices, making it feasible to monitor high-speed links without affecting performance.

The disadvantages are:

- **Loss of granularity**: Sampling sacrifices detail and granularity, potentially missing important information about specific flows and patterns.

- **Less accurate analysis**: Analysis based on sampled data may not accurately represent the entire network behaviour, limiting the precision of certain analytical results.

Unsampled flow protocols analyse every packet in the network, generating flow records for each individual packet or flow. The advantages are:

- **Detailed insight**: Provides a comprehensive and accurate view of network traffic, offering detailed information about every flow.

- **Accurate analysis**: Offers precise analysis and understanding of network behavior, aiding in anomaly detection, troubleshooting, and security monitoring.

- **Granular data**: Enables monitoring of individual flows, which is vital for specific use cases such as application performance monitoring.

The disadvantages are:

- **Resource intensive**: Processing every packet consumes significant CPU and memory resources on network devices and collectors, limiting scalability and efficiency.

- **Increased overhead**: Generates a large volume of flow records, leading to higher bandwidth consumption for exporting flow data to collectors.

Let us now compare both:

- **Accuracy and granularity**:
  - **Sampled**: Provides a less granular view, potentially missing fine-grained details.
  - **Unsampled**: Offers a detailed and accurate view of network traffic.

- **Resource utilization**:
  - o **Sampled**: Reduces resource overhead and is more scalable for high-speed networks.
  - o **Unsampled**: Demands higher resource utilization, limiting scalability.

- **Use cases**:
  - o **Sampled**: Suited for high-speed networks, where monitoring every packet is impractical due to resource constraints.
  - o **Unsampled**: Ideal when precise and detailed analysis of network behaviour is necessary, even with resource-intensive processing.

- **Trade-off**:
  - o The choice between sampled and unsampled flow protocols involves a trade-off between resource efficiency and data accuracy/granularity.

In summary, sampled flow protocols are efficient for resource-constrained high-speed networks, providing a balance between resource utilization and visibility. Unsampled flow protocols offer detailed and accurate insights at the cost of higher resource usage, making them suitable for in-depth analysis and troubleshooting in environments where resource limitations are less critical.

Conclusion

Although this looks like a mess, it is easier than you think. Normally, if you do not make use of IPv6 and are not planning to use it, there is nothing bad in using NetFlow v5 from your routers/firewalls and so on. You do not have so many choices from your switches other than sFlow if they support it, although there are also other solutions. However, if you are planning for the future, definitely go for IPFIX . It could seem complex, but it is not. The choice between sampled and unsampled is not very difficult; sometimes it is forced by implementations of vendors (some vendors provide only sampled protocols), and sometimes you must analyze 800Gbit/s network trunks and going sampled is the only way. However, if you do not have to struggle with this, go unsampled! As usual, you need to find the best fit for your use case, and it must match your requirements without struggling with the devices to avoid possible disruptions. The sense of the Wireshark outputs is to let you understand both the complexity of the exporting process, and the decoding process in order to let you make better choices.

In the next chapter, we will discuss network topologies and physical/logical implementation differences, and this will give you further hints to better understand which parts of the network make more sense to monitor and in which way.

## CHAPTER 3

Network Topologies

Introduction

This chapter will discuss the different types of networks, logical and physical network topologies and cloud infrastructures. We will dive from simple **Local Area Networks** (**LANs**) to more complex **Virtual Private Cloud** (**VPC**) and **Software-Defined Networking** (**SDNs**), which are becoming increasingly common nowadays. It is important to understand the different logical and physical designs to understand better how and where it makes sense to improve network visibility. Moreover, a rational design gives more understanding of how the data flow inside the network should happen and the basis for the physical network design, keeping in mind all requirements regarding throughput, sizing, and redundancy.

Structure

In this chapter, we will discuss the following topics:

- Computer network
- Logical and physical design
- Main components of a computer network
- Making cloud providers networks
- VPC
- Placing network probes

Objectives

By the end of this chapter, the reader will have learned basic concepts of networking, differences between physical and logical designs, terms and acronyms commonly used in the industry, and an overview of what these technologies do. This is needed to better understand how to monitor a complex network successfully by understanding possible blind points.

Computer network

A computer network is a set of interconnected computers and devices that communicate with each other to share resources, information, and services. For the newcomers of networking, without adding the boredom of standards definition, the OSI model defines seven layers of networking, with Layer 2 (data link) handling MAC addressing and Layer 3 (network) managing IP routing. Networks can vary in size and complexity, ranging from small local networks within a home or office, to large global networks such as the Internet. Here are some key components and characteristics of computer networks:

- **Nodes**: Nodes are the individual devices connected to the network, including computers, servers, printers, routers, switches, and other devices capable of sending or receiving data.

- **Links and connections**: Links represent the physical or logical connections between nodes. Physical connections can include wired (for example, Ethernet cables) or wireless (such as, Wi-Fi) links. Logical connections are established through network protocols and addresses.

- **Topologies**: Network topologies define the physical or logical layout of nodes and links in a network. Common topologies include star, bus, ring, and mesh. The choice of topology affects factors such as scalability, fault tolerance, and ease of management.

- **Networking devices**: Devices that facilitate communication and data transfer within a network include routers, switches, hubs, access points, and gateways (routers, firewalls, and so on). These devices play specific roles in directing traffic, managing connections, and providing access to other networks.

- **Protocols**: Networking protocols define the rules and conventions for communication between devices on a network. TCP/IP is a fundamental protocol suite widely used in computer networks, including the Internet. Nowadays, TCP/IP networks are the de facto standard.

- **Addressing**: Devices on a network are assigned unique addresses, such as IP addresses, to identify and communicate with each other. Addressing ensures that data is routed to the correct destination.

- **LANs and WANs**: LANs connect devices within a limited geographic area, like a home, office, or campus. **Wide area networks (WANs)** span larger distances, connecting LANs across cities, countries, or continents.

- **Security measures**: Network security is crucial to protect against unauthorized access, data breaches, and other security threats. Security measures include firewalls, encryption, authentication, and intrusion detection systems.

- **Scalability**: Network scalability refers to the ability of a network to accommodate growth and additional devices. Scalable networks can expand to meet the changing needs of users and organizations.

- **Bandwidth and data transmission**: Bandwidth refers to the capacity of a network to transmit data. High-bandwidth networks can handle larger amounts of data, leading to faster and more efficient communication.

- **Network management**: Network management involves tasks such as monitoring network performance, configuring devices, troubleshooting issues, and ensuring the overall reliability of the network.

Computer networks are essential for facilitating communication, collaboration, and resource sharing in modern environments. They form the backbone of various applications, services, and technologies that drive the digital interconnected world, becoming a need for any company competing on whatever market.

Logical and physical design

Understanding the logical and physical designs of a network infrastructure is a very important piece of information that helps designers, security engineers, and analysts do their jobs. As a simple example, a logical design might specify three VLANs for departments; physically, this could mean configuring a switch with VLAN tags and connecting it to a router.

A network infrastructure could be as easy as a single switch with workstations and a router/firewall for the most straightforward designs. On the other hand, it could also have dozens of racks with redundant 100Gb switch per rack, multiple spanning trees, hundreds of VLANs, VXLANs to transport L2 VLANs over routing devices, with logical and physical firewalls separating different layers. Trying to converge physical and logical designs would be impractical and messy, so it is an excellent idea to keep them separate for both readability and flow understanding.

Main components of a computer network

The main components in terms of devices in a network infrastructure are:

- **Layer 2**: Hubs

- **Layer 2**: Switches
- **Layer 2**: Access Points
- **Layer 3**: Routers/Firewalls

Network hubs were used until the end of the '90s to interconnect at Layer 2 servers, workstations and clients, creating LANs. They are Layer 2 devices, and, despite being extremely easy to deploy, they had some big issues such as:

- Network speeds were limited to a minimum of 10Mbps and maximum 100Mbps, but due to their way of working, easily saturated.

- The working mechanism of a hub is that all ports get all the traffic and lots of systems sending data simultaneously created collisions. Therefore, it was necessary to retransmit data often.

- A security issue is that if all ports get all the traffic, a workstation can also get traffic that was sent to a server and try to do MITM or eavesdrop.

Because of these major issues, network hubs were replaced by network switches. A network switch is a fundamental networking device used to connect multiple devices within a LAN and facilitate communication between them. Unlike a hub, which simply broadcasts data to all connected devices, a switch is more intelligent. It makes data forwarding decisions based on the destination MAC addresses of the devices connected to it. Here are the key features and functions of a network switch:

- **Port connectivity**: A network switch typically has multiple ports (Ethernet ports) to connect devices such as computers, printers, servers, and other networking equipment. Ports can range from a few to several dozen, depending on the switch's capacity.

- **Switching fabric**: The switching fabric is the internal architecture of the switch that enables it to forward data between connected devices. Modern switches use high-speed switching fabrics to handle data traffic efficiently.

- **MAC address learning**: Switches learn and store the MAC addresses of devices connected to their ports. This information is used to build a MAC address table, allowing the switch to make forwarding decisions based on MAC addresses.

- **Forwarding and filtering**: When a device sends data to another device within the same network, the switch uses its MAC address table to determine the appropriate port for forwarding the data. This process reduces unnecessary network traffic by directing data only to the intended recipient.

- **Broadcast and multicast handling**: Unlike hubs, switches do not blindly broadcast data to all connected devices. Instead, they selectively forward data to the specific port where the target device is located. This reduces network congestion and improves efficiency.

- **Collision domain separation**: Switches create individual collision domains for each port, reducing the likelihood of data collisions that can occur in shared media environments. This enhances the overall performance of the network.

- **VLAN support**: Many switches support **Virtual LANs (VLANs)**, allowing network administrators to segment a physical network into multiple logical networks. VLANs help enhance network security and management. Think of it as a switch partitioning method.

- **Power over Ethernet**: Some switches are equipped with **Power over Ethernet (PoE)** capabilities, providing electrical power to connected devices such as IP cameras, VoIP phones, and wireless access points through the Ethernet cable itself.

- **QoS**: QoS features in switches enable the prioritization of certain types of network traffic. This ensures that critical applications, such as voice and video, receive higher priority for bandwidth.

- **Managed vs. unmanaged switches**: Unmanaged switches are plug-and-play devices that operate without user configuration. Managed switches offer additional features such as VLAN support, QoS configuration, and remote management capabilities.

- **Management interfaces**: Managed switches typically have web-based interfaces or command-line interfaces for configuration and management. This allows network administrators to customize settings and monitor switch performance.

- **Redundancy and link aggregation**: Some switches support redundancy features, allowing for failovers, in case of a hardware or link failure. Link aggregation enables the grouping of multiple physical links to increase bandwidth and provide redundancy.

Network switches are foundational to local area networks, providing the essential connectivity and intelligence needed for efficient and secure data transmission within a network. They come in various sizes and configurations to accommodate the specific requirements of different network environments. Most switches are Layer 2 devices, although some models can be configured to allow Inter-VLAN routing or do **Open Shortest Path First (OSPF)** or even **Border Gateway Protocol (BGP)** routing, but this blurs the line with dedicated Layer 3 routers. It is a good practice to separate Layer 2 and Layer 3 devices and let them perform the tasks they were designed for. Mixing functionalities, although in some cases could be allowed, can create difficult-to-understand topologies, single points of failure, and further problems when troubleshooting

An **Access Point (AP)** is a networking device that allows Wi-Fi-enabled devices to connect to a wired network using Wi-Fi. It acts as a bridge between wired and wireless networks, facilitating wireless communication between devices and the existing wired infrastructure. Here is a brief description of an access point:

- **Function**: The primary function of an access point is to provide wireless connectivity to devices within its coverage area. It serves as a central communication hub for Wi-Fi-enabled devices, such as laptops, smartphones, tablets, and other wireless clients.

- **Connection to the network**: Access points are typically connected to a wired network, often through an Ethernet cable. This connection allows them to access resources on the wired network and extend network connectivity to wireless devices.

- **Wireless standards**: Access points adhere to wireless standards, such as IEEE 802.11, which define the protocols for wireless communication. Common standards include 802.11a, 802.11b, 802.11g, 802.11n, 802.11ac, and 802.11ax (Wi-Fi 6).

- **Service set identifier**: Access points broadcast a **service set identifier** (SSID), which is a unique name that identifies the wireless network. Wi-Fi-enabled devices use the SSID to identify and connect to the desired network.

- **Security features**: Access points incorporate security features to protect wireless communication. Common security protocols include **Wired Equivalent Privacy (WEP)**, **Wi-Fi Protected Access (WPA)**, and WPA2/WPA3, which provide encryption and authentication.

- **Coverage area**: The coverage area of an access point is determined by factors such as its transmit power, antenna design, and environmental conditions. Multiple access points may be deployed to create an overlapping network for seamless coverage in larger areas.

- **Roaming support**: Access points support roaming, allowing devices to seamlessly switch from one access point to another as they move within the coverage area. This ensures uninterrupted connectivity for mobile devices.

- **Management and configuration**: Access points are managed and configured through web-based interfaces or centralized network management systems. Network administrators use these interfaces to set security parameters, monitor performance, and manage access policies.

- **Mesh networking**: In some scenarios, access points support mesh networking, allowing them to wirelessly connect to each other. This can be useful in extending coverage to areas where running Ethernet cables is impractical.

- **Integration with other network devices**: Access points often work in conjunction with routers, switches, and other networking devices to form a comprehensive network infrastructure. They play a crucial role in providing connectivity to devices in both home and enterprise environments.

Access points are integral components of modern wireless networks, enabling the proliferation of Wi-Fi connectivity in homes, offices, public spaces, and various other environments. They play a vital role in providing wireless access to the Internet and local network resources. Depending on their configuration, they could be both Layer 2 or Layer 3 devices.

Moving to Layer 3 devices, we have routers and firewalls (and often, they converge in a single physical or virtual device). A network router is a fundamental device in computer networking that connects different networks and directs data traffic between them. It operates at the OSI model's network layer (Layer 3) and is a key component in both home and enterprise networking environments. Here are the key features and functions of a network router:

- **Connectivity between networks**: Routers facilitate communication between different networks. This could involve connecting a LAN to the Internet or linking multiple LANs within an enterprise.

- **Routing**: The core function of a router is to decide where to send data packets based on network addresses. It uses routing tables and algorithms to determine the most efficient path for data to reach its destination.

- **IP addressing**: Routers use IP addresses to identify devices on a network. They assign and manage IP addresses for devices within their local network and enable communication between devices on different networks.

- **NAT**: Routers often implement NAT to allow multiple devices within a local network to share a single public IP address. NAT helps conserve the limited pool of public IP addresses and adds a layer of security by hiding internal network details.

- **Firewall functionality**: Many routers include firewall capabilities to control incoming and outgoing network traffic. This helps protect the network from unauthorized access and potential security threats.

- **Wireless routing**: Wireless routers incorporate Wi-Fi technology, allowing devices to connect to the network wirelessly. They typically have integrated wireless access points to provide Wi-Fi connectivity.

- **LAN and WAN ports**: Routers have multiple ports to connect to local devices within a LAN, and often at least one port for connecting to a WAN, such as the Internet. WAN ports are usually labeled for connections to cable or DSL modems.

- **Dynamic Host Configuration Protocol**: Routers can act as **Dynamic Host Configuration Protocol** (**DHCP**) servers, automatically assigning IP addresses to devices within the local network. This simplifies the process of connecting new devices to the network.

- **QoS**: Some routers support QoS features, allowing for prioritization of certain types of traffic. This is particularly useful in ensuring optimal performance for time-sensitive applications like VoIP or video streaming.

- **VLANs**: Enterprise-grade routers may support VLANs, allowing the segmentation of a physical network into multiple virtual networks. This enhances network security and management.

- **Management interfaces**: Routers are configured and managed through web-based interfaces or command-line interfaces. Users can access these interfaces to set up routing tables, configure security settings, and manage other features.

- **Logging and monitoring**: Routers often have logging and monitoring capabilities to track network activity, identify potential issues, and generate reports on network performance.

Network routers are critical in directing data traffic across networks, ensuring efficient and secure communication. They are a cornerstone of modern networking infrastructure, enabling connectivity in homes, businesses, and the Internet.

In the following *Figure 3.1*, we can see one of the simplest network designs, although very widely spread in small companies:

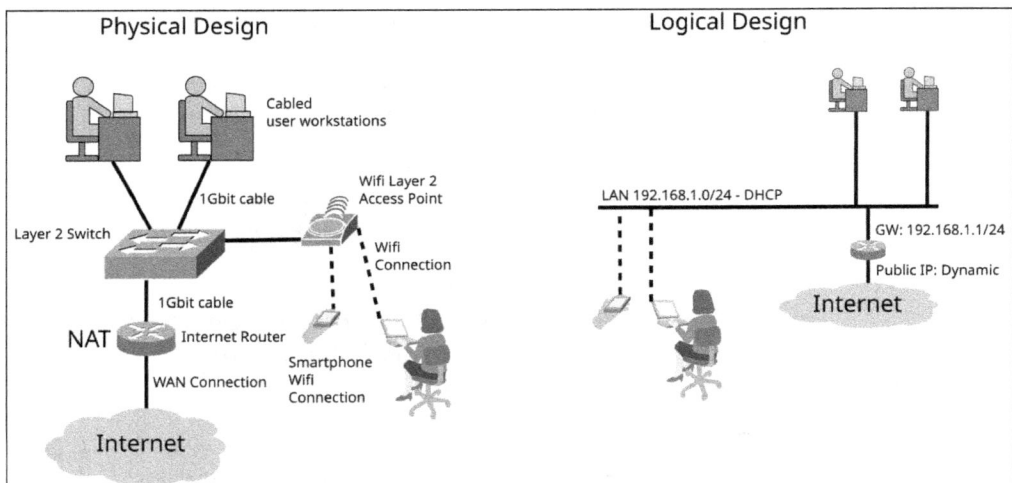

Figure 3.1: Simple physical and logical design

LAN

A LAN is a network of interconnected computers and devices within a limited geographic area, such as a home, office building, or campus. LANs are designed to facilitate communication and resource sharing among connected devices. Here are the key characteristics and components of a LAN:

- **Geographical scope**: LANs cover a relatively small geographic area, typically confined to a single building or a group of nearby buildings. They are ideal for connecting devices within close proximity.

- **Topologies**: Common LAN topologies include star, bus, ring, and mesh. The choice of topology depends on factors such as cost, scalability, and fault tolerance.

- **Networking devices**: Devices within a LAN are connected by networking hardware, including switches, routers, access points, and hubs. Switches are particularly common in modern LANs for efficient data forwarding.

- **Computers and end devices**: Computers, laptops, workstations, and servers are the primary end devices connected to a LAN. These devices communicate with each other and share resources, such as files and printers.

- **Network Interface Cards**: Each device on a LAN is equipped with a **Network Interface Card** (**NIC**) that enables it to connect to the network. NICs can be integrated into the device's motherboard or added as separate hardware.

- **Ethernet cabling**: LANs commonly use Ethernet cables (Cat5e, Cat6, and so on) for wired connections. Ethernet is a widely adopted standard for local area networking and provides reliable, high-speed data transmission.

- **Wireless LANs**: Wireless LANs utilize Wi-Fi technology, allowing devices to connect to the network without needing physical cables. WLANs are especially prevalent in modern environments, providing flexibility and mobility.

- **Networking protocols**: LANs use networking protocols such as TCP/IP to enable communication between devices. TCP/IP is the foundation of the Internet and is widely used in LANs.

- **IP addressing**: Devices on a LAN are assigned IP addresses to identify and communicate with each other. IP addresses can be dynamically assigned using DHCP or configured statically.

- **Subnetting**: Larger LANs may use subnetting to divide the network into smaller logical segments. Subnetting helps manage network traffic, enhance security, and simplify network administration.

- **File and printer sharing**: LANs enable resource sharing, including sharing files and printers among connected devices. This facilitates collaboration and enhances productivity in a local environment.

- **Security measures**: LANs implement security measures to protect against unauthorized access and data breaches. This can include firewalls, intrusion detection systems, and encryption protocols.

- **Gateway**: A gateway serves as an entry and exit point for data entering or leaving the LAN. It provides connectivity to other networks, such as the Internet or other LANs.

- **Switching and broadcasting**: Switches are used to manage data traffic within a LAN, directing data only to the specific device for which it is intended. Broadcasting is the process of sending data to all devices on the network.

- **LAN management**: LANs are typically managed using network management tools and protocols. These tools help monitor network performance, troubleshoot issues, and configure network devices.

LANs are crucial in local communication, resource sharing, and collaboration. They are fundamental to businesses, educational institutions, and homes, providing the foundation for local networking and connectivity. The simplest LAN can be created by using a hub or a simple switch and can grow to cover an entire building with redundancy using multiple switches, fiber channel connections, and spanning-tree protocol (to protect from loops). However, it is always a Layer 2 infrastructure local to a place (although using protocols such as VXLAN, it could be transported over L3 devices, even on the Internet).

WAN

A WAN is a type of computer network that spans a large geographical area, connecting multiple smaller networks or LANs. WANs are designed to facilitate communication and data exchange between devices and systems over long distances, often using various telecommunication technologies. Here are the key characteristics and components of a WAN:

- **Geographical scope**: WANs cover a broad geographical area, which can range from a city to a country or even span the entire globe. They enable connectivity between widely dispersed locations.

- **Network infrastructure**: WANs utilize a combination of public and private networking infrastructure. This can include leased lines, satellite links, fiber-optic cables, and other telecommunications technologies.

- **Connectivity between LANs**: The primary purpose of a WAN is to connect and interconnect LANs located in different geographic locations. This enables organizations to establish a unified network infrastructure despite physical distance.

- **Internet connectivity**: WANs often leverage the Internet as a means of connecting remote locations. This can involve the use of **virtual private networks** (**VPN**s) to create secure communication channels over the public Internet.

- **High data transfer rates**: WANs are designed to support high data transfer rates, although the actual speed may vary depending on the specific technologies used and the distance between connected locations.

- **Point-to-point and multipoint connections**: WANs support both point-to-point connections, where two locations are directly linked, as well as multipoint connections, where multiple locations are interconnected through a central hub or a mesh network.

- **WAN devices**: Routers and switches play a crucial role in WANs, facilitating the routing and forwarding of data between different networks. Modems, bridges, and other networking devices may also be employed.

- **Public and private connectivity**: WANs can include both public connections, such as the Internet, and private connections, such as leased lines or dedicated circuits. The choice depends on factors such as security requirements, bandwidth needs, and cost considerations.

- **Reliability and redundancy**: WANs often incorporate redundancy measures to ensure reliability. Multiple connections, backup routes, and failover mechanisms are employed to minimize downtime in case of a network failure.

- **Protocols**: WANs use various networking protocols to ensure compatibility and communication between different devices and networks. Common protocols include TCP/IP, **Multiprotocol Label Switching** (**MPLS**), and others.

- **QoS**: QoS features in WANs enable prioritization of specific types of traffic, ensuring that critical applications receive the necessary bandwidth and performance.

- **Managed services**: Many organizations opt for managed WAN services provided by telecommunications carriers. These services can include dedicated lines, MPLS connections, and other solutions tailored to specific business needs.

WANs are essential for connecting remote offices, data centers, and branch locations, enabling seamless communication and data sharing across diverse geographic locations. One of the most used (and still in use) technologies for WANs is the MPLS, that created a sort of **virtual VPN** between different branches of the same company using a Telco provided and managed VPN based on packet labelling. MPLS labels packets for faster routing across WANs, often used in provider networks for reliability.

Just think how important the most famous WAN (the Internet) was during the COVID-19 period; it allowed businesses and companies to keep working even with such a pandemic situation!

VXLAN

Virtual Extensible LAN (**VXLAN**), is a network virtualization technology that extends **Layer 2** (**L2**) network segments over an existing **Layer 3** (**L3**) infrastructure. Basically, VXLAN wraps Layer 2 frames in UDP packets, like putting a letter in an envelope, sent over Layer 3 networks. VXLAN is designed to address the scalability limitations of traditional VLANs by allowing the creation of large-scale, multi-tenant networks in virtualized and cloud environments. Here is a description of VXLAN and its key features:

- **Overlay network**: VXLAN creates an overlay network on top of an existing IP network, typically a Layer 3 infrastructure. This overlay allows for the creation of logical Layer 2 networks that can span across data centres, making it suitable for cloud and virtualized environments.

- **Encapsulation**: VXLAN encapsulates Layer 2 frames within UDP packets. This encapsulation allows these frames to traverse Layer 3 networks without relying on a specific underlying physical infrastructure.

- **Segmentation and tenant isolation**: VXLAN uses a 24-bit **VXLAN Network Identifier** (**VNI**) to provide segmentation and isolation. Each VNI represents a unique virtual network, allowing multiple tenants or applications to share the same physical infrastructure while maintaining logical separation.

- **Support for large-scale environments**: VXLAN addresses the limitations of traditional VLANs, which are restricted to 4,096 unique VLAN IDs. With a 24-bit VNI, VXLAN supports over 16 million unique network identifiers, enabling the creation of large-scale virtual networks.

- **Multicast or unicast transport**: VXLAN can use either multicast or unicast as the transport mechanism for encapsulated packets. Multicast is often used for broadcast and unknown unicast traffic, while unicast can be more scalable and more straightforward to implement in some environments.

- **Compatibility with existing networks**: VXLAN operates independently of the underlying physical network and can be deployed on existing IP networks. This allows organizations to introduce VXLAN gradually without requiring a complete network overhaul.

- **VXLAN Tunnel Endpoint**: **VXLAN Tunnel Endpoint** (**VTEP**) are devices that participate in VXLAN and serve as endpoints for VXLAN tunnels. VTEPs encapsulate and decapsulate VXLAN packets, ensuring the logical Layer 2 frames reach their intended destination across the Layer 3 network.

- **Integration with network virtualization platforms**: VXLAN is often used with network virtualization platforms and SDN solutions. It plays a crucial role in creating scalable and agile virtual network environments.

- **Use cases**: VXLAN is commonly employed in data centres and cloud environments where there is a need for scalable and isolated network segments. It is particularly beneficial for supporting virtual machine mobility, allowing VMs to move across physical hosts and data centres while maintaining network connectivity.

- **IETF standardization**: VXLAN is standardized by the Internet **Engineering Task Force** (**IETF**) in RFC 7348. This standardization ensures interoperability and facilitates the widespread adoption of VXLAN across different networking equipment and software.

VXLAN is a widely adopted technology for creating scalable, flexible, and isolated network overlays in modern data centers and cloud environments. Its ability to address the limitations of traditional VLANs makes it a key component in building agile and dynamic network architectures.

VPN

A VPN is a technology that allows for secure and encrypted communication over an untrusted network, such as the Internet. It creates a private and secure connection between the user's device and a remote server, enabling the user to access the Internet or a private network as if they were directly connected to the server. Here are the key components and characteristics of a VPN:

- **Secure connection**: The primary purpose of a VPN is to create a secure and encrypted connection, often referred to as a **tunnel**, between the user's device (client) and a VPN server. This encryption helps protect data from interception and unauthorized access.

- **Encryption protocols**: VPNs use various encryption protocols to secure data during transmission. Standard protocols include OpenVPN, L2TP/IPsec, IKEv2/IPsec, and SSTP. The protocol choice depends on security requirements, compatibility, and performance.

- **Authentication**: VPNs use authentication mechanisms to verify the identity of users and ensure that only authorized individuals can establish a connection. This can involve username and password authentication, digital certificates, or other methods.

- **Remote access and site-to-site VPNs**: VPNs can be classified into two main types:
    - **Remote access VPN**: Allows individual users to connect to a private network over the Internet remotely.
    - **Site-to-site VPN**: Connects entire networks or multiple branch offices, creating a secure connection between different locations.

- **Tunneling protocols**: VPNs employ tunneling protocols to encapsulate and protect data as it travels over the Internet. These protocols establish a secure connection and define how data is encapsulated, transmitted, and decrypted at the destination.

- **Access to restricted resources**: VPNs enable users to access resources on a private network or the Internet as if they were physically present at the location of the VPN server. This is particularly useful for remote workers who need access to company resources securely.

- **Bypassing geo-restrictions**: VPNs can bypass geographical restrictions imposed by content providers or governments. By connecting to a server in a different location, users can appear to be accessing the Internet from that location.

- **Privacy and anonymity**: VPNs enhance user privacy by masking their IP address and encrypting their Internet traffic. This makes it more challenging for third parties, such as hackers or advertisers, to monitor online activities.

- **Public Wi-Fi security**: VPNs are commonly used to secure Internet connections when using public Wi-Fi networks. By encrypting data, VPNs protect users from potential threats and eavesdrop on unsecured public networks.

- **Client software and configurations**: VPNs typically require client software on the user's device, which establishes and manages the VPN connection. Users may also need to configure connection settings, such as the VPN server address and authentication details.

- **Split tunneling**: Some VPNs offer split tunneling, allowing users to direct only specific traffic through the VPN while allowing other traffic to access the Internet directly. This can optimize bandwidth usage.

- **Corporate VPNs**: Many organizations implement corporate VPNs to provide secure remote access for employees. Corporate VPNs often include additional security measures, such as multi-factor authentication and centralized management.

VPNs are versatile tools that serve multiple purposes, from ensuring secure remote access to protecting user privacy and enabling access to geo-restricted content. They have become increasingly prevalent in today's interconnected and privacy-conscious digital environment. Again, just think how important VPN technology was during COVID-19; it allowed businesses and companies to keep on working!

DMZ/frontend/backend network

A **Demilitarized Zone** (**DMZ**) in the context of computer networks is a special network segment that acts as a buffer zone between an organization's internal network and an external, untrusted network, usually the Internet. The primary purpose of a DMZ is to provide an additional layer of security by isolating certain services or systems from the internal network. Usually, it is a separate Layer 2 LAN dedicated to this purpose, connected to the rest of the network infrastructure by a firewall interface.

The key characteristics of a DMZ include:

- **Isolation**: The DMZ is a segregated network that separates external-facing services from the internal network. This isolation helps contain and mitigate the impact of potential security breaches.

- **Security perimeter**: The DMZ serves as a security perimeter where services that need to be accessible from the Internet are placed. Examples include web servers, email servers, and public-facing application servers.

- **Firewall protection**: Firewalls are deployed at the boundaries of the DMZ to control and monitor traffic between the external network, the DMZ, and the internal network. Access control rules are typically configured to restrict unauthorized access.

- **Multi-tiered architecture**: In a typical DMZ setup, there might be multiple layers of security, often referred to as a multi-tiered architecture. For example, a DMZ might have a frontend web server tier, an application server tier, and a backend database tier, each with its own level of security.

- **Proxy servers and reverse proxies**: Proxy servers and reverse proxies are commonly used in the DMZ to enhance security. Proxies can filter and inspect incoming traffic before allowing it to reach internal services, adding an extra layer of protection.

- **Intrusion detection and prevention systems**: Security devices, such as **intrusion detection and prevention systems (IDPS)**, may be deployed within the DMZ to monitor and analyze network traffic for potential security threats.

- **Logging and monitoring**: The DMZ is closely monitored, and logs are often generated to track and analyze activities within the zone. This helps identify and respond to security incidents.

The concept of a DMZ is a fundamental part of network security best practices, helping organizations protect their internal assets from external threats. By carefully controlling and monitoring traffic in and out of the DMZ, organizations can balance making certain services accessible to the outside world and maintaining the security of their internal network.

In computer network infrastructure, the terms **backend** and **frontend** are often used to describe different layers or components of the overall architecture. Let us now explore each.

Frontend network infrastructure

Its features are as follows:

- The frontend network infrastructure refers to the network components and configurations that directly interact with users and handle their requests.

- **Web servers**: Frontend networks commonly involve web servers hosting user interface components, web pages, and static content. These servers respond to user requests initiated from web browsers.

- **Load balancers**: Load balancers distribute incoming network traffic across multiple web servers to ensure an even load distribution, improve responsiveness, and enhance fault tolerance.

- **Content delivery networks**: CDN may be part of the frontend infrastructure to optimize the delivery of static assets (like images, scripts, and stylesheets) by caching them at strategic locations closer to end-users.

- **Firewalls and security measures**: Security is crucial for the frontend network. Firewalls and other security measures are implemented to protect against common web-based threats such as DDoS attacks and unauthorized access.

Backend network infrastructure

Its features are as follows:

- The backend network infrastructure focuses on the servers and services responsible for processing business logic, managing databases, and handling other computational tasks.

- **Application servers**: Backend networks include servers that execute an application's server-side logic. These servers process user requests, interact with databases, and perform various computations.

- **Databases**: Backend infrastructure often involves databases for storing and retrieving data. These databases could be relational (for example, MySQL, PostgreSQL) or NoSQL (such as, MongoDB, Cassandra) depending on the application's requirements.

- **Internal communication**: Communication occurs between different backend services. This may involve protocols like HTTP/HTTPS apart from others, message queues, or other communication methods to ensure coordination and data exchange between various components.

- **Authentication and authorization services**: Backend networks often include services responsible for user authentication and authorization, ensuring that only authorized users can access specific resources.

- **Security measures**: Similar to the front end, security is a critical consideration in the backend network. Firewalls, intrusion detection/prevention systems, and encryption mechanisms are employed to protect sensitive data and services.

Communication between frontend and backend

The frontend and backend components communicate over the network using protocols such as HTTP/HTTPS. API play a crucial role in facilitating this communication, allowing the front end to request and receive data from the backend.

In summary, the frontend and backend network infrastructures work together to deliver a complete and functional web application. The frontend handles user interactions and interfaces, while the back end manages the underlying logic, data processing, and storage. Effective communication between the two is essential for a seamless and responsive user experience.

The terms DMZ and frontend network are related but refer to different concepts within the context of network architecture. Let us now clarify the differences between the two.

Demilitarized Zone

A DMZ is a network segment that is isolated from both an organization's internal network and the external, untrusted network (typically the Internet). It acts as a buffer zone, providing an additional layer of security.

Services that need to be accessible from the Internet, such as web servers, email servers, or application servers, are placed in a DMZ. The DMZ is designed to contain and mitigate the impact of potential security breaches by separating these external-facing services from the internal network.

The DMZ is often protected by firewalls, intrusion detection/prevention systems, and other security measures to control and monitor traffic between the internal network, the DMZ, and the external network.

Frontend network

The frontend network refers to the network infrastructure directly interacting with users and handling their requests. It includes components responsible for presenting the user interface and managing user interactions.

In a web application context, the frontend network typically involves web servers, load balancers, CDNs, and other components that deliver the user interface elements to end-users' devices.

The frontend network optimizes user experience, ensures responsiveness, and delivers static and dynamic content to users' browsers.

Key differences

The key differences between DMZ and frontend network are as follows:

- **Scope and purpose**

    o The DMZ is a specific network segment designed to provide a secure zone for external-facing services, protecting the internal network from potential external threats.

    o The frontend network is a broader concept encompassing the network infrastructure responsible for handling user interactions, delivering content, and managing the user interface. It may include components both within and outside the DMZ.

- **Placement of services**

    o In a DMZ, services like web or application servers needing external accessibility are placed.

    o The frontend network includes components responsible for delivering the user interface, which may or may not be within the DMZ. Depending on the architecture, the frontend components can exist both in the DMZ and the internal network.

- **Security measures**

    o The DMZ is heavily fortified with security measures such as firewalls to control and monitor traffic between different zones.

    o While security is also crucial in the frontend network, it may not have the same level of isolation and security measures as a dedicated DMZ.

In summary, a DMZ is a specific network segment designed for security purposes, while the frontend network encompasses the broader infrastructure responsible for user interactions and content delivery. While they may overlap in some cases, they serve different roles in the overall network architecture.

In the following *Figure 3.2*, we can see an example of both physical and logical designs of a frontend/backend/DMZ network:

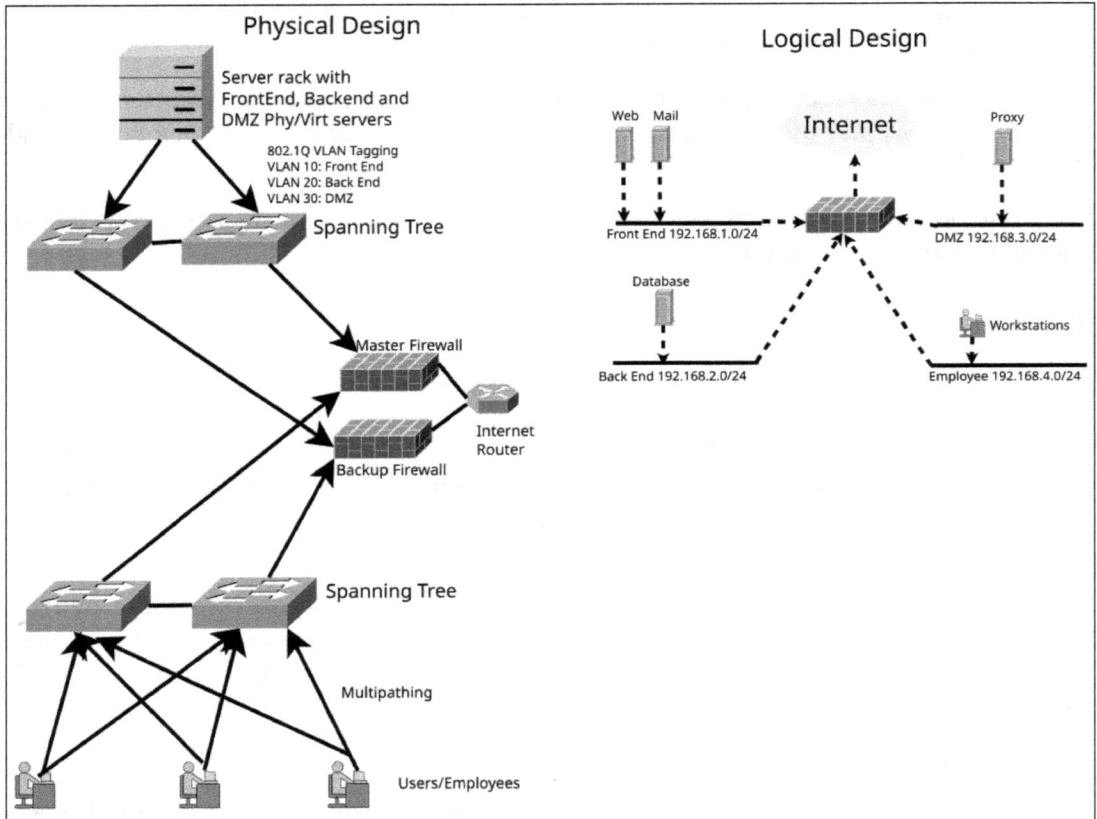

Figure 3.2: A frontend/backend/DMZ network infrastructure

SDN

A SDN is an innovative approach to network management and configuration that separates the control plane (which makes decisions about where to send traffic) from the data plane (which actually forwards the traffic). This separation is achieved using software-based controllers or APIs that communicate with the underlying hardware infrastructure and direct traffic on the network. Controllers like OpenDaylight and **Open Network Operating System** (**ONOS**), as simple open-source examples, enable centralized management and make use of OpenFlow for traffic control.

The key components and characteristics of a SDN include:

- **SDN controller**
    - The SDN controller is the brain of the SDN architecture. It acts as a central intelligence that decides where network traffic should be sent based on the overall network policies and conditions.
    - Controllers are typically implemented as software applications that run on commodity hardware. They communicate with switches and routers using standardized protocols like OpenFlow.

- **Control plane and data plane separation**
    - In traditional networking, the control plane and data plane are tightly integrated into network devices. SDN separates these two planes, allowing for more flexible and centralized control over network behavior.
    - The control plane, residing in the SDN controller, makes decisions about routing and traffic flow, while the data plane, implemented in network devices, is responsible for forwarding packets based on these decisions.

- **OpenFlow protocol**
    - OpenFlow is a standardized communication protocol (but not the only one) that enables communication between the SDN controller and the network devices (such as switches and routers) in the data plane.
    - It allows the controller to dynamically adjust the behavior of network devices, such as changing routing rules or updating access control policies.

- **Programmability**
    - SDN allows network administrators and developers to program the behavior of the network using software. This programmability enables the creation of custom network policies and the adaptation of the network to changing requirements.

- **Dynamic network provisioning**
    - SDN enables dynamic provisioning of network resources. It allows for the automatic allocation and reallocation of bandwidth, prioritization of traffic, and adjustment of network configurations based on application or user needs.

- **Centralized network management**
    - The centralized control provided by SDN allows for easier management and configuration of network resources. Changes can be made globally and applied consistently across the network, reducing the need for device-specific configurations.

- **Flexibility and adaptability**

  - o SDN architectures are highly flexible and adaptable to changing network conditions. This makes them well-suited for dynamic and scalable environments, such as data centers and cloud computing platforms.

- **Network automation**

  - o SDN facilitates network automation by allowing administrators to automate repetitive tasks and configurations. Automation can improve efficiency, reduce human errors, and accelerate the deployment of new services.

- **Enhanced network visibility**

  - o SDN provides enhanced visibility into network traffic and performance. Network administrators can gain real-time insights and analytics to monitor and troubleshoot network issues more effectively. Often, SDN provides options to enable flow-data export in some standard protocols, such as sFlow (for Layer 2 devices) or IPFIX (for Layer 3 devices).

SDN has gained popularity for its ability to provide greater agility, scalability, and efficiency in network management. However, in several cases, it still lacks interoperability between different network device vendors, so you will typically find one vendor shops deploying this type of technology in most places. It is particularly beneficial in environments where rapid changes, dynamic resource allocation, and centralized control are essential, such as in cloud computing, data centers, and modern enterprise networks.

Making cloud provider networks

The network infrastructure of a cloud provider is a complex and highly sophisticated environment designed to deliver scalable, reliable, and secure cloud services to users and organizations. The specifics can vary among different cloud providers, but here are some common elements and features of a typical cloud provider's network infrastructure:

- **Global data centers**

  - o Cloud providers operate multiple data centers strategically located around the world. These data centers house the physical hardware and infrastructure necessary for running cloud services.

  - o Geographical distribution allows users to deploy resources closer to their end-users, reducing latency and improving performance.

- **Virtualization**

  - o Cloud providers extensively use virtualization technologies to create **virtual machines** (**VM**) or containers from physical servers. This allows for efficient resource utilization and dynamic scaling based on demand.

- **Networking hardware**
    - High-performance networking hardware, including routers, switches, and load balancers, form the backbone of a cloud provider's network infrastructure.
    - High-speed, redundant connections between data centers and within data centers are essential for reliable and low-latency communication.

- **Software-defined networking**:
    - Cloud providers often implement SDN to manage and optimize network traffic dynamically. SDN allows for programmable and automated network configuration, improving flexibility and scalability.

- **Content delivery networks**
    - Cloud providers may integrate CDN to cache and deliver static content, reducing latency and improving the performance of web applications globally.

- **Edge computing**
    - Some cloud providers leverage edge computing, deploying resources closer to end-users or devices. This helps reduce latency for applications that require real-time processing like IoT or streaming.

- **Security measures**
    - Robust security measures, including firewalls, intrusion detection and prevention systems, and encryption, are integrated into the network infrastructure to protect against cyber threats.
    - VPC or similar constructs provide customers with isolated and secure environments within the cloud.

- **Load balancing**
    - Load balancers distribute incoming traffic across multiple servers to ensure optimal resource utilization and improve the availability and responsiveness of applications.

- **Identity and access management**
    - **Identity and access management** (**IAM**) systems control user access to cloud resources. **Role-based access control** (**RBAC**) mechanisms define permissions, ensuring that users have the appropriate level of access based on their roles.

- **Monitoring and analytics**
    - Cloud providers implement extensive monitoring and analytics tools to track their infrastructure's performance, availability, and security. This includes tools for logging, real-time analytics, and alerting.

- **Hybrid and multi-cloud connectivity**
  - Cloud providers offer services and solutions for connecting on-premises data centers to the cloud, enabling hybrid cloud architectures. Additionally, they may facilitate connectivity between different cloud providers for multi-cloud deployments.

- **APIs and orchestration**
  - Cloud providers expose API to allow users to programmatically manage and orchestrate resources. Orchestration tools enable automation and the creation of complex, interconnected services.

- **Scalability and elasticity**
  - Cloud infrastructure is designed to be highly scalable and elastic, allowing users to scale resources up or down based on demand. This scalability is a key feature of cloud computing.

Understanding and effectively managing this complex network infrastructure is crucial for cloud providers to deliver reliable, performant, and secure customer services. It enables users to deploy and manage applications without significant investment in physical infrastructure and allows for rapid innovation and adaptation to changing business needs.

VPC

A VPC is a cloud computing infrastructure that provides a private network in the cloud. It allows users to create and manage their own isolated virtual networks within a public cloud environment. The concept of a VPC is often associated with **Infrastructure as a Service (IaaS)** providers, such as **Amazon Web Services (AWS)**, Microsoft Azure, and **Google Cloud Platform (GCP)**.

The features of a VPC are as follows:

- **Isolation**: A VPC provides isolation and separation of resources from other users in the cloud. This isolation is achieved through network-level segmentation, allowing users to have their own private space within the larger cloud infrastructure.

- **Customization**: Users can customize the VPC to meet their specific requirements. This includes defining IP address ranges, configuring subnets, and setting up routing tables to control traffic flow between different VPC components.

- **Security**: VPCs typically include security features such as network **access control lists (ACL)**, security groups, and firewalls to control and monitor traffic. These features help users implement security policies to protect their applications and data.

- **Scalability**: VPCs are designed to be scalable, allowing users to add or remove resources as their needs change easily. This scalability is crucial for handling varying workloads and ensuring the infrastructure can adapt to the evolving demands.

- **Connectivity**: VPCs often provide options for connecting to on-premises data centers or other cloud environments. This can be achieved through dedicated connections (for example, Direct Connect in AWS) or VPN connections.

- **Resource management**: Users can manage various cloud resources within their VPC, including virtual machines, storage, and other services. This allows for efficient resource allocation and utilization.

- **High availability**: VPCs are designed to provide high availability for applications and services. This is often achieved by distributing resources across multiple availability zones or regions, reducing the risk of downtime due to hardware failures or other issues.

Typically, a VPC is split into a frontend subnet and a backend subnet, separated by an SDN-provided firewall. Overall, a VPC offers organizations a way to harness the benefits of cloud computing while maintaining control, security, and customization over their network infrastructure. It is a flexible and scalable solution that caters to the diverse needs of different businesses and applications.

In the following *Figure 3.3*, we can see an example of a logical design of a VPC. The physical design is up to the delivery infrastructure of the chosen provider, so we cannot decide it or describe it:

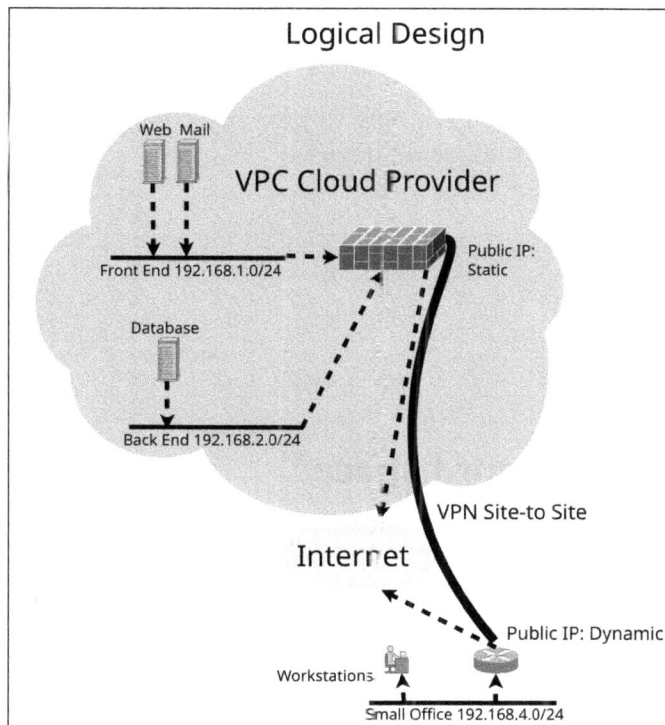

Figure 3.3: *The logical design of a VPC*

Placing network probes

This is where the logical and physical network designs come in handy. If you must decide where to monitor the network, it is essential to understand the logical and physical designs well. The logical design helps us to understand (based on the logical data flow) where the network probe should be placed in order to analyze the traffic, but only by viewing the physical design, we understand how to effectively make the deployment (which switches port, which LANs, and so on). It also depends on which type of probe we are going to deploy.

If we must deploy an IPS solution, its best placement would ideally be behind the inside network of a firewall, so everything reaching the firewall could be analysed. But if we are willing to have an in-depth view of what is happening on the whole network infrastructure by means of using flow-data analysis, we should enable it on most devices supporting it (most flow-data collectors can do some form of data-deduplication).

Conclusion

Understanding the network that we will analyze is the first step to understanding how it works, its potential, caveats, and dark spots. As we have seen in the previous chapter, Layer 3 devices can obtain better results (in terms of network visibility). However, when it is impossible or impractical to use a Layer 3 device, Layer 2 devices can at least provide some helpful information.

In the following chapters, we will see how to properly configure flow-data export from most Layer 2, Layer 3, and virtualization devices.

Join our book's Discord space

Join the book's Discord Workspace for Latest updates, Offers, Tech happenings around the world, New Release and Sessions with the Authors:

https://discord.bpbonline.com

CHAPTER 4

Implementing Flow Export on Layer 2 Devices

Introduction

As we all know, Layer 2 (data link) operates using physical network addresses and it is commonly used in network switches. In typical Ethernet networks, the physical network address is the MAC address. In this chapter, we will examine our options for catching network flows from Layer 2 devices. Catching traffic flows at this level can give us unprecedented network visibility and allow us to see traffic that could not even cross a router or a firewall, giving a clearer idea of what is really happening in the company's internal network.

Structure

In this chapter, we will discuss the following topics:

- Catching network flows on the Layer 2
- Importance of sFlow
- Configuring sFlow on a Cisco SG350 switch
- Configuring sFlow on an HP switch
- Configuring sFlow on a Huawei switch
- Standard way to get flows from anywhere

Objectives

The chapter will guide the reader to implement flow data export on the most widespread Layer 2 devices (switches and access points) from most vendors on the market. It will also describe a solution to get NetFlow/IPFIX data from a switch using port mirroring.

Catching network flows on Layer 2

As mentioned, it is beneficial to catch flows on Layer 2 devices such as switches and access points. Tracking flows at this level can allow us to detect actual traffic patterns, and security violations. We can get real traffic patterns since we can see what happens on devices on the same Layer 2, even if it is spread on different devices by means of 802.1Q trunking, and it allows us to identify security violations that would otherwise go unnoticed, probably for months. Think of something like this: someone goes into the data centre (or in an office) and connects a device like a Raspberry Pi with a cellular 4G modem shield (or any other unauthorized device) and Kali Linux for Raspberry. They keep it hidden under the floating floor, under the desktop, or in the switch closet on the floor. Or, even better, without cabling, it is just being joined to your (hacked) wireless network and sending data outside the 4G modem. Data exfiltration or remote unauthorized access at its finest levels, bypassing any firewall or security measure. How long would it take to detect it without any form of traffic control?

Importance of sFlow

The sFlow protocol comes to the rescue in the case of Layer 2 devices. While sFlow dominates Layer 2 flow export, some devices support alternatives like NetFlow Lite, though these are less common. Although sFlow is a sampled protocol, it allows us to retain visibility on the L2 part of the network. sFlow normally uses statistical sampling (for example, capturing 1 out of every 128 packets) to monitor traffic efficiently, reducing device load while providing visibility into Layer 2 activity. Sampling has its own reasons since L2 devices such as switches and access points usually need to move speedily, with much more data than a router or a firewall; just think about 100 Gb switches. So, in this case, sampling makes sense, probably not giving us the exact terms of the flow (how many bytes, how many packets and so on), but it shows us that there is actual communication between device A from a particular source IP, source port, to (un)known device B to a specific destination IP and destination port, using a specified protocol.

In our previously described scenario, a bad device like the Raspberry Pi could *phone home* by means of using OpenVPN via a 4G modem (where *home* could be an anonymous server anywhere on the Internet) and from there scan all local unprotected workstations sharing the precious company data between themselves for different users (remember, we are on the *protected* inside part of the network) and exfiltrate data like a champ.

Catching these flows between the unknown device and the workstations could give to the security team a good hint about what is happening.

Nowadays, most managed Layer 2 switches implement the sFlow protocol, although in some cases it could need a license to be enabled.

It would be impractical to report all possible configurations for all different vendors. Still, in most cases, you probably will need to specify the destination IPv4 address of the flow collector and the destination port for it, probably with the desired sampling rate if the device allows it. Some devices for some vendors could also request to specify on which network port the sFlow protocol should be enabled. As a rule of thumb, the lower the sampling (for example, 1/128 would mean taking 1 packet out of 128), the higher the CPU switch usage (1/1024 would mean taking 1 packet out of 1024). It always depends on the network load and on the specific network area and impact. If you have a lower sampling on the core switch, it could probably slow down the entire network. Maybe on the core, having a higher sampling and a lower sampling on the peripheral switches is preferable. It is up to the complexity of the physical network. Enabling sFlow or port mirroring may increase switch CPU and bandwidth usage, particularly in high-traffic environments; normally this increment is around 5-10% of CPU, but it is a good practice to monitor performance post-configuration.

Configuring sFlow export on a Cisco SG350 switch

In this example, we will configure sFlow export to a collector on a Cisco SG350. The sFlow collector will be listening to IP 10.1.30.220's address on port 6343. Let us now go over the following steps:

1. **Access the switch**: Connect to the Cisco SG350 switch using SSH or a console cable and terminal emulation software like PuTTY or SecureCRT.

2. **Enter privileged EXEC mode**: Log in with appropriate credentials, and then enter privileged EXEC mode by typing:

   ```
   enable
   ```

3. **Enter global configuration mode**: Once in privileged EXEC mode, enter global configuration mode:

   ```
   configure terminal
   ```

4. **Enable sFlow**: Enable sFlow on the switch.

   ```
   sflow enable
   ```

5. **Set the sFlow agent IP address**: Configure the IP address for the sFlow agent. Replace **X.X.X.X** with the IP address of the switch:

   ```
   sflow agent ip X.X.X.X
   ```

6. **Set the sFlow collector**: Configure the IP address and port of the sFlow collector. Replace **10.1.30.220** with the IP address of your collector and **6343** with the port number it listens on:

   ```
   sflow collector 10.1.30.220 port 6343
   ```

7. **Configure sFlow sampling rate (optional)**: You can optionally configure the sFlow sampling rate. The default is usually 1-in-256 packets. To set a different rate (for example, 1-in-128 packets), use the following command:

   ```
   sflow sampling-rate 128
   ```

8. **Configure sFlow polling interval (optional)**: You can also configure the sFlow polling interval. The default is usually 30 seconds. To set a different interval (for example, 60 seconds), use the following command:

   ```
   sflow polling-interval 60
   ```

9. **Exit configuration mode**: After configuring sFlow, exit global configuration mode:

   ```
   end
   ```

10. **Save configuration**: Save the configuration changes to ensure they persist across reboots:

    ```
    write memory
    ```

11. **Verify configuration**: Verify the sFlow configuration to ensure it is correctly set up by using the following command. It should display the configured parameters, including the agent IP address, collector IP address, and sampling rate:

    ```
    show sflow
    ```

12. **Exit**: Once you have verified the configuration, you can exit the terminal session:

    ```
    Exit
    ```

Configuring sFlow export on an HP switch

Configuring sFlow export to a collector on an HP switch involves several steps. Always check the documentation that comes with your device model; they have a wide spectrum of different devices and steps could be different. The sFlow collector will be listening to IP 10.1.30.220's address on port 6343. For the configuration, follow the given steps:

1. **Access the switch**: First, ensure you can access the HP switch through SSH, Telnet, or the web interface.

2. **Enter configuration mode**: Once logged in, enter privileged mode by typing:

   ```
   enable
   ```

   Then, enter configuration mode:

   ```
   configure terminal
   ```

3. **Enable sFlow**: Enable sFlow on the switch.

   ```
   sflow enable
   ```

4. **Configure sFlow sampling**: Set the sampling rate. This determines what fraction of packets will be sampled. For example, to sample 1 out of every 512 packets:

   ```
   sflow sample 512
   ```

5. **Configure sFlow polling interval**: Set the polling interval. This determines how often counter samples will be sent. For example, to poll every 30 seconds:

   ```
   sflow polling-interval 30
   ```

6. **Specify the sFlow collector**: Define the sFlow collector's IP address and port number. Assuming the collector's IP is 10.1.30.220 and port is 6343:

   ```
   sflow collector 1 ip 10.1.30.220 udp-port 6343
   ```

7. **Enable sFlow on interfaces**: Enable sFlow on interfaces that you want to monitor. You can enable it globally or on specific interfaces. For example, to enable sFlow on all interfaces:

   ```
   interface all
   sflow enable
   ```

8. **Verify configuration**: Verify your configuration settings:

   ```
   show sflow
   ```

9. **Exit configuration mode and save changes**: After verifying the configuration, exit configuration mode and save the changes:

   ```
   exit
   write memory
   ```

Configuring sFlow export on an Huawei switch

Configuring sFlow export to a collector on a Huawei switch involves several steps. Always check the documentation that comes with your device model. There is a wide spectrum of different devices, and the steps could be different. The sFlow collector will be listening to IP 10.1.30.220's address on port 6343. Follow the given steps:

1. **Access the switch**: Connect to the switch using a terminal emulator or SSH client. Log in with administrative credentials.

2. **Enter system view**: Switch to system view by typing:

   ```
   system-view
   ```

3. **Enable sFlow**: Enable sFlow globally on the switch:

   ```
   sflow enable
   ```

4. **Configure sFlow agent**: Define the sFlow agent, specifying the IP address and port of the collector:

```
sflow agent ip <IP_address_of_switch>
sflow agent collector 1 <IP_address_of_collector> <port_number>
```

For our case, it would be:

```
sflow agent ip 10.1.30.1
sflow agent collector 1 10.1.30.220 6343
```

5. **Configure sampling rate**: Define the sampling rate. This determines how frequently sFlow samples packets:

```
sflow agent sampling-rate <value>
```

Replace `<value>` with the desired sampling rate. For example:

```
sflow agent sampling-rate 4096
```

6. **Configure polling interval**: Define the polling interval. This determines how often the sFlow agent sends samples to the collector:

```
sflow agent polling-interval <value>
```

Replace `<value>` with the desired polling interval. For example:

```
sflow agent polling-interval 30
```

7. **Configure interface sampling**: Enable sFlow sampling on specific interfaces (optional):

```
interface <interface_type> <interface_number>
sflow enable
```

Replace `<interface_type>` and `<interface_number>` with the appropriate interface type and number. For example:

```
interface GigabitEthernet 1/0/1
sflow enable
```

8. **Save configuration**: Save the configuration changes:

```
Save
```

9. **Exit configuration mode**: Exit system view and return to the user view:

```
quit
```

10. **Verify configuration**: Verify that the sFlow configuration is correct:

```
display sflow configuration
```

Standard way to get flows from anywhere

While sFlow is widely supported, some scenarios require alternative methods, such as port mirroring coupled with tools converting mirrored traffic to network flows, especially for devices lacking native flow export. There are softwares that can take raw traffic as input, capturing all packets and grouping them in flows for export to a collector; one noticeable example is softflowd (**https://github.com/irino/softflowd**). The raw traffic as input can be provided to softflowd by means of a mirrored port of a switch, like an uplink.

There is another feature on practically all managed switches that allows traffic incoming/outgoing on a specific port(s) to be replicated on another switch port, eventually connected to a traffic analyzer. This feature is called port mirroring. Port mirroring, also known as **Switched Port Analyzer** (**SPAN**) or **Remote Switched Port Analyzer** (**RSPAN**), is commonly found in network switches, including Layer 2 switches. Port mirroring allows the switch to copy the traffic from one or more source ports and send it to a designated destination port for analysis, monitoring, or troubleshooting purposes.

Here is a basic overview of how port mirroring works on Layer 2 switches:

- **Source ports**: These are the ports from which you want to copy the network traffic. Source ports are typically selected based on specific criteria, such as monitoring a particular device, VLAN, or network segment.

- **Destination port**: This is the port to which the mirrored traffic is sent. The destination port is connected to a monitoring device, such as a network analyzer, packet sniffer, or **intrusion detection system** (**IDS**).

- **Configuration**: To enable port mirroring, you need to configure the switch. The specific steps may vary depending on the switch model and vendor. Typically, you will identify the source ports and specify the destination port.

Types of port mirroring

There are different types of port mirroring, such as:

- **Local port mirroring**: In local port mirroring (SPAN), the source and destination ports are on the same switch. We will use this for our solution.

- **Remote port mirroring**: Remote port mirroring (RSPAN) allows mirroring traffic from source ports on one switch to a destination port on another switch, enabling remote monitoring.

Use cases

Port mirroring is helpful for various purposes, including:

- **Network troubleshooting**: Analyzing network traffic for issues or anomalies.

- **Security monitoring**: Detecting and analyzing potential security threats.

- **Performance monitoring**: Monitoring bandwidth usage and identifying bottlenecks.

- **Packet capture**: Capturing packets for detailed analysis with tools like Wireshark.

Considerations

When implementing port mirroring, consider the potential impact on switch performance. Mirroring too much traffic can overload the switch's CPU and impact overall network performance.

The traffic is replicated in a raw way, so there is still work to be done to get only the flows, but there is a nice and free solution that allows us to get NetFlow v5, NetFlow v9 or IPFIX flows from a mirrored switch port. The solution is software that runs on UNIX platforms, that can take its input from a network interface, analyze the traffic on it, and can export NetFlow traffic on another one, and it is an open-source software called softflow. Although it is freely available on the Internet, there are several forks, some implementing VLAN traffic analysis, some implementing IPFIX . The most complete and tested version can be downloaded from BPB's GIT repository at the URL **https://github.com/bpbpublications/ Mastering-Network-Flow-Traffic-Analysis.**

It can be easily run on Linux, FreeBSD, NetBSD and most widespread UNIX systems, so preparing a small UNIX box getting traffic and exporting flows for flow analysis is not difficult.

The typical softflowd workflow can be summarized in the following picture:

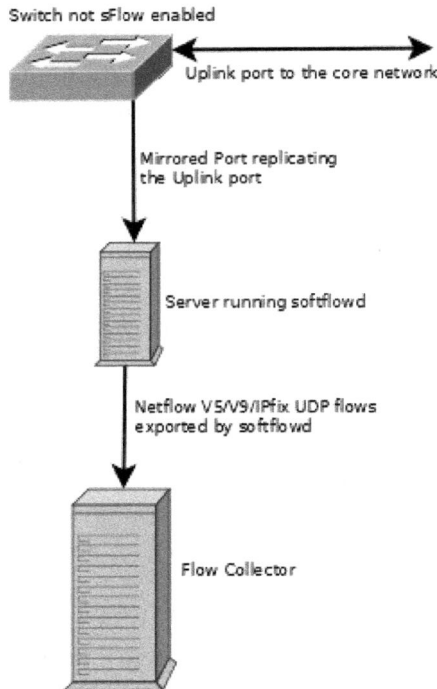

Figure 4.1: Softflowd workflow

Let us see how we can perform an installation on a Debian Linux system. Consider that probably most UNIX distributions already have the **softflowd** package available in their repositories; we just want to show how to build the most suitable version of it for our scopes.

The first thing is to obtain the software, so we will simply **git clone** a copy of it from the GIT repository using the following:

```
unixman@bld-deb11:~$ git clone https://github.com/bpbpublications/
Mastering-Network-Flow-Traffic-Analysis
Cloning into 'https://github.com/bpbpublications/Mastering-Network-Flow-
Traffic-Analysis'...
remote: Enumerating objects: 1344, done.
remote: Counting objects: 100% (46/46), done.
remote: Compressing objects: 100% (5/5), done.
remote: Total 1344 (delta 41), reused 41 (delta 41), pack-reused 1298 (from
2)
Receiving objects: 100% (1344/1344), 2.37 MiB | 2.83 MiB/s, done.
Resolving deltas: 100% (671/671), done.
```

Once cloned, you will have a **softflowd** in your UNIX system that will look like:

```
unixman@bld-deb11:~/build/prod/flower/softflowd$ ls
aclocal.m4      config.h.in      convtime.c   install-sh   Makefile
NetFlow9.c       softflowd.c       softflowd.sysconfig   treetype.h

closefrom.c     config.log       convtime.h   IPFIX.c      Makefile.in      README
softflowd.h      strlcat.c

collector.pl    config.status    daemon.c     LICENSE      mkinstalldirs
softflowctl.8    softflowd.h~      strlcpy.c

common.h        configure        freelist.c   log.c        NetFlow1.c
softflowctl.c    softflowd.init   sys-tree.h

config.h        configure.ac     freelist.h   log.h        NetFlow5.c
softflowd.8      softflowd.spec   TODO
```

You will need the **Berkeley Packet Filter** (**BPF**) development libraries on the build system. So, you will probably need to install the **libpcap-dev** or corresponding packages for your distribution.

Nonetheless, configuring the package is quite easy:

```
unixman@bld-deb11:~/build/prod/flower/softflowd$ ./configure --enable-nf9-vlan
checking for gcc... gcc
checking whether the C compiler works... yes
checking for C compiler default output file name... a.out
checking for suffix of executables...
checking whether we are cross compiling... no
checking for suffix of object files... o
checking whether we are using the GNU C compiler... yes
```

```
checking whether gcc accepts -g... yes
checking for gcc option to accept ISO C89... none needed
checking for a BSD-compatible install... /usr/bin/install -c
checking how to run the C preprocessor... gcc -E
checking for grep that handles long lines and -e... /usr/bin/grep
checking for egrep... /usr/bin/grep -E
checking for ANSI C header files... yes
checking for sys/types.h... yes
checking for sys/stat.h... yes
checking for stdlib.h... yes
checking for string.h... yes
checking for memory.h... yes
checking for strings.h... yes
checking for inttypes.h... yes
checking for stdint.h... yes
checking for unistd.h... yes
checking net/bpf.h usability... no
checking net/bpf.h presence... no
checking for net/bpf.h... no
checking pcap.h usability... yes
checking pcap.h presence... yes
checking for pcap.h... yes
checking pcap-bpf.h usability... yes
checking pcap-bpf.h presence... yes
checking for pcap-bpf.h... yes
checking sys/endian.h usability... no
checking sys/endian.h presence... no
checking for sys/endian.h... no
checking endian.h usability... yes
checking endian.h presence... yes
checking for endian.h... yes
checking for struct sockaddr.sa_len... no
checking for struct ip6_ext.ip6e_nxt... yes
checking for library containing daemon... none required
checking for library containing gethostbyname... none required
checking for library containing socket... none required
checking for pcap_open_live in -lpcap... yes
checking for closefrom... no
```

```
checking for daemon... yes
checking for setresuid... yes
checking for setreuid... yes
checking for setresgid... yes
checking for setgid... yes
checking for strlcpy... no
checking for strlcat... no
checking for strsep... yes
checking whether htobe64 is declared... yes
checking whether htonll is declared... no
checking for u_int64_t... yes
checking for int64_t... yes
checking for uint64_t... yes
checking for u_int32_t... yes
checking for int32_t... yes
checking for uint32_t... yes
checking for u_int16_t... yes
checking for int16_t... yes
checking for uint16_t... yes
checking for u_int8_t... yes
checking for int8_t... yes
checking for uint8_t... yes
checking size of char... 1
checking size of short int... 2
checking size of int... 4
checking size of long int... 8
checking size of long long int... 8
configure: creating ./config.status
config.status: creating Makefile
config.status: WARNING:  'Makefile.in' seems to ignore the --datarootdir
setting
config.status: creating config.h
config.status: config.h is unchanged
```

After that, the package is successfully configured. You can proceed with the build of it (it is standard C source, so probably any version of the **gcc** compiler should work flawlessly). You will also need the standard UNIX make utility. Refer to the following:

```
unixman@bld-deb11:~/build/prod/flower/softflowd$ make
gcc -g -O2 -DFLOW_SPLAY          -DEXPIRY_RB               -I.   -c -o
```

```
softflowd.o softflowd.c
gcc -g -O2 -DFLOW_SPLAY          -DEXPIRY_RB          -I.    -c -o log.o
log.c
gcc -g -O2 -DFLOW_SPLAY          -DEXPIRY_RB          -I.    -c -o
NetFlow1.o NetFlow1.c
       |    ^~~~~~~
gcc -g -O2 -DFLOW_SPLAY          -DEXPIRY_RB          -I.    -c -o
NetFlow5.o NetFlow5.c
gcc -g -O2 -DFLOW_SPLAY          -DEXPIRY_RB          -I.    -c -o
NetFlow9.o NetFlow9.c
gcc -g -O2 -DFLOW_SPLAY          -DEXPIRY_RB          -I.    -c -o
IPFIX.o IPFIX.c
gcc -g -O2 -DFLOW_SPLAY          -DEXPIRY_RB          -I.    -c -o
freelist.o freelist.c
gcc -g -O2 -DFLOW_SPLAY          -DEXPIRY_RB          -I.    -c -o
convtime.o convtime.c
gcc -g -O2 -DFLOW_SPLAY          -DEXPIRY_RB          -I.    -c -o
strlcpy.o strlcpy.c
gcc -g -O2 -DFLOW_SPLAY          -DEXPIRY_RB          -I.    -c -o
strlcat.o strlcat.c
gcc -g -O2 -DFLOW_SPLAY          -DEXPIRY_RB          -I.    -c -o
closefrom.o closefrom.c
gcc -g -O2 -DFLOW_SPLAY          -DEXPIRY_RB          -I.    -c -o
daemon.o daemon.c
gcc  -o softflowd softflowd.o log.o NetFlow1.o NetFlow5.o NetFlow9.o IPFIX.o
freelist.o convtime.o strlcpy.o strlcat.o closefrom.o daemon.o -lpcap
gcc -g -O2 -DFLOW_SPLAY          -DEXPIRY_RB          -I.    -c -o
softflowctl.o softflowctl.c
gcc  -o softflowctl softflowctl.o convtime.o strlcpy.o strlcat.o closefrom.o
daemon.o -lpcap
```

Despite some compiler warnings (mostly for deprecated UNIX C Library standards), the software was built successfully. We can just run it now to start collecting data:

```
unixman@bld-deb11:~/build/prod/flower/softflowd$ su root
Password:
root@bld-deb11:/home/unixman/build/prod/flower/softflowd# ./softflowd -i ens18
-n 10.1.30.210:2056 -v 10 -T vlan -6 -P udp
```

With this command line, we are instructing **softflowd** to analyze traffic on physical interface named ens18 and send IPFIX (also called NetFlow v10) to IP address 10.1.30.210 on port 2056 using the UDP protocol, and also to track IPv6 flows. In our examples, our flow collector will run on that IP address on the 2056 UDP port. Once flows reach the collector, tools like SolarWinds NTA or Fl0wer can analyze traffic patterns and detect anomalies.

When the process starts, it daemonizes itself, detaching from the shell where you started and continuing to work in the background.

You can check running it with the **-d** (do not daemonize) or by using the standard UNIX **ps** command:

```
root@bld-deb11:~# ps -efa
UID            PID     PPID  C STIME TTY          TIME CMD
root             1        0  0 Jan09 ?        00:00:04 /sbin/init
root             2        0  0 Jan09 ?        00:00:00 [kthreadd]
root             3        2  0 Jan09 ?        00:00:00 [rcu_gp]
root           396        1  0 Jan09 ?        00:00:01 /lib/systemd/systemd-
logind
root           403        1  0 Jan09 tty1     00:00:00 /sbin/agetty -o -p --
\u --noclear tty1 linux
root           407        1  0 Jan09 ?        00:00:00 sshd: /usr/sbin/sshd -D
[listener] 0 of 10-100 startups
root           890      407  0 09:25 ?        00:00:00 sshd: unixman [priv]
<Linux processes omitted for readability reasons>
root          4846     4324  0 10:13 pts/0    00:00:00 ./softflowd -i ens18 -n
10.1.30.210:2056 -v 10 -T vlan -6 -P udp
root          4847     4836  0 10:13 pts/2    00:00:00 ps -efa
```

We can also check if the flow packets are actually sent to our destination by simply using the standard **tcpdump** command:

```
root@bld-deb11:~# tcpdump -n -i ens18 udp port 2056
tcpdump: verbose output suppressed, use -v[v]... for full protocol decode
listening on ens18, link-type EN10MB (Ethernet), snapshot length 262144
bytes
10:17:30.916033 IP 10.1.20.206.2056 > 10.1.30.210.2056: UDP, length 252
10:17:31.817753 IP 10.1.20.206.2056 > 10.1.30.210.2056: UDP, length 216
10:17:31.818150 IP 10.1.20.206.2056 > 10.1.30.210.2056: UDP, length 484
10:17:31.956036 IP 10.1.20.206.2056 > 10.1.30.210.2056: UDP, length 312
10:17:32.334501 IP 10.1.20.206.2056 > 10.1.30.210.2056: UDP, length 288
```

Obviously, the best practice is to configure the UNIX system to start it at boot with a proper startup script. If you want to track more switches, you can connect one mirrored port per switch and run several instances of the **softflowd** software on each interface. In this way, you can have a single analyzing point for different switches that send all the flows to a single (or multiple collectors if you use the samplicator daemon, which is another UNIX software that can replicate UDP packets to different hosts) collector from where you can monitor all traffic on Layer 2 switches.

Conclusion

Obviously, properly configured switches with onboard sFlow v5 export capabilities are the more practical and manageable solution for analyzing traffic, but going the hard way with softflowd could also allow us to catch traffic where the Layer 2 network device cannot handle it. Just think about wireless access points connected to switches. Native sFlow on switches offers a practical solution for most networks, while port mirroring with softflowd provides flexibility for unsupported devices or specific use cases, such as monitoring wireless access points.

In the next chapter, we will analyze how Layer 3 devices can be configured to export flow data that we can use in our network analysis toolbox chain.

Join our book's Discord space

Join the book's Discord Workspace for Latest updates, Offers, Tech happenings around the world, New Release and Sessions with the Authors:

https://discord.bpbonline.com

CHAPTER 5
Implementing Flow Export on Layer 3 Devices

Introduction

In this chapter, we will examine our options for catching network flows from Layer 3 devices. Flow tracking technology was originally born on routers and was slowly adapted to work on most types of devices, as we have seen on Layer 2 devices and will see on other types of platforms. However, this is probably the most practical viewpoint for most network traffic.

Structure

In this chapter, we will discuss the following topics:

- Catching flows on Layer 3
- General considerations for the example configurations
- Configuring NetFlow V9 export on a Cisco 1721 router with IOS 12.1
- Configuring NetFlow V9 export on a Cisco 2800 router with IOS 12.3
- Configuring IPFIX export on a Cisco 887 router with IOS 15.4
- Configuring IPFIX export on a Cisco ASA firewall
- Configuring IPFIX export on a Cisco Firepower firewall

- Configuring IPFIX export on a Juniper SRX-100 firewall
- Configuring IPFIX export on a Juniper MX router
- Configuring NetFlow export on a Paloalto PA-500 firewall
- Configuring IPFIX export on a Mikrotik router
- Configuring NetFlow V9 export on a Huawei AR150 router
- Configuring NetFlow V9 export on a Huawei Eudemon 8000E-X firewall
- Configuring IPFIX export on a Fortinet FG-60 firewall
- Configuring IPFIX export on a SonicWALL firewall with SonicOS 7.0
- Configuring IPFIX export on a Sophos firewall
- Configuring IPFIX export on a Checkpoint firewall
- Configuring IPFIX export on a Watchguard firewall
- Configuring IPFIX export on a BigIP F5 Load Balancer

Objectives

The chapter will guide the reader to implement flow data export on most widespread Layer3 devices such as firewalls, routers, load balancers, wireless gateways from most vendors on the market. Obviously this chapter focuses on common devices; newer models (for example, Cisco IOS-XE routers) may require adjusted commands. As a rule of thumb, always check the documentation provided by the vendor.

Catching network flows on Layer 3

Flow technology was born on Layer 3 devices. NetFlow is a feature that was introduced on Cisco routers around 1996, and it provides the ability to collect IP network traffic as it enters or exits an interface. So, in the stack of the network infrastructure, Layer 3 devices (moving IP data flows inside and outside) are the best candidates and the most suitable to check for flow data. Almost any router, firewall, load balancer, and generic Layer 3 device provides this opportunity.

> **Tip: One important consideration, if you want to make good use of flow technology, you should reduce to minimum, the use of NAT. NAT alters IP addresses, making it harder to track original flow sources/destinations, thus reducing flow data accuracy. This would be ideally used (if public IP addresses are not available) only on the external interface of a firewall. NAT technology can be a life saver in certain cases, but should not be abused since it reduces performance and messes up the logics of network routing.**

General considerations for the example configurations

All the configurations provided here were tested on real devices, but as always, it is a good procedure to refer to the product documentation for your specific version to ensure accuracy. Please also note that the exact commands and syntax might vary depending on the version of the device firmware. All the examples configure the described device to send NetFlow or IPFIX data to a collector running on IP address 10.1.30.220 on UDP port 2056.

Configuring NetFlow v9 export on a Cisco 1721 router with IOS 12.1

To configure NetFlow v9 export on a Cisco 1721 router with IOS 12.1, follow the given steps:

1. **Access the Cisco 1721 router**: Connect to the Cisco 1721 router using a terminal emulator, console cable, or SSH.

2. **Enter global configuration mode**:
   ```
   enable
   configure terminal
   ```

3. **Enable NetFlow on the router**:
   ```
   ip flow-export source <interface>
   ip flow-export version 9
   ip flow-export destination 10.1.30.220 2056
   ```

   Replace `<interface>` with the actual interface you want to use as the source for NetFlow export. This is typically the interface facing the collector.

4. **Enable NetFlow on specific interfaces**: Apply NetFlow to specific interfaces you want to monitor. For example, to enable NetFlow on **interface FastEthernet0/0**:
   ```
   interface FastEthernet0/0
   ip flow ingress
   ```

5. **Set flow exporting parameters**: Configure additional parameters like the active and inactive timeout values:
   ```
   ip flow-cache timeout active 60
   ip flow-cache timeout inactive 15
   ```

6. **Save configuration and exit**:
   ```
   end
   write memory
   ```

   These commands save the configuration and exit from configuration mode.

Configuring NetFlow v9 export on a Cisco 2800 router with IOS 12.3

To configure NetFlow v9 export on a Cisco 2800 router with IOS 12.3, follow the given steps:

1. **Access the Cisco 2800 router**: Connect to the Cisco 2800 router using a terminal emulator, console cable, or SSH.

2. **Enter global configuration mode**:
   ```
   enable
   configure terminal
   ```

3. **Configure NetFlow version 9**:
   ```
   ip flow-export version 9
   ```

   This command sets the NetFlow export version to **version 9**.

4. **Set the NetFlow exporter**
   ```
   ip flow-export destination 10.1.30.220 2056
   ```

   This will send all NetFlow data to IP address 10.1.30.220 on 2056 UDP port.

5. **Configure flow monitoring on interfaces**: Apply NetFlow to specific interfaces you want to monitor. For example, to enable NetFlow on **interface GigabitEthernet0/0**:
   ```
   interface GigabitEthernet0/0
   ip flow ingress
   ```

6. **Set flow exporting parameters (optional)**:
   ```
   ip flow-cache timeout active 60
   ip flow-cache timeout inactive 15
   ```

   These commands set the active timeout to 1 minute and the inactive timeout to 15 minutes.

7. **Save configuration and exit**:
   ```
   end
   write memory
   ```

These commands save the configuration and exit from configuration mode.

Configuring IPFIX export on a Cisco 887 router with IOS 15.4

To configure IPFIX export on a Cisco 887 router with IOS 15.4, follow the given steps:

1. **Access the router**: Connect to the router either through the console port or via SSH/Telnet.

2. **Enter privileged EXEC mode:**
   `enable`

3. **Enter global configuration mode:**
   `configure terminal`

4. **Enable IPFIX on the router:**
   `ip flow-export version 10`

5. **Specify the IP address and port of the collector:**
   `ip flow-export destination 10.1.30.220 2056`

6. **Configure flow export template refresh rate (optional):** This step is optional and defines how often the router will send templates to the collector. The value is in seconds.
   `ip flow-export template refresh-rate 30`

7. **Configure interfaces for IPFIX:** Go to the interface configuration mode for each interface you want to monitor.
   `interface <interface-type> <interface-number>`

   Make sure to replace `<interface-type>` and `<interface-number>` with the specific values for your router.

8. **Enable IPFIX on the interface:**
   `ip flow ingress`

9. **Configure flow monitor (optional):** This step is optional and allows you to create a flow monitor for more granular control.
   `flow monitor <monitor-name>`
   `record NetFlow-original`

10. **Apply flow monitor to interface (optional):** If you created a flow monitor, apply it to the interface.
    `ip flow monitor <monitor-name> input`

11. **Exit interface configuration mode:**
    `exit`

12. **Exit configuration mode:**
    `exit`

13. **Save configuration:** Save the configuration to ensure changes persist after a reboot.
    `write memory`

14. **Verify configuration:** Check the configuration to ensure that everything is set up correctly.
    `show ip flow export`
    `show ip flow export statistics`

15. **Exit privileged EXEC mode:**
    `exit`

Configuring IPFIX export on a Cisco ASA firewall

To configure IPFIX export on a Cisco ASA firewall, follow these steps:

1. **Access the Cisco ASA**: Connect to the Cisco ASA device using a terminal emulator, SSH, or through the device's console port.

2. **Enter configuration mode**:

   ```
   enable
   configure terminal
   ```

3. **Enable NetFlow on the ASA**:

   ```
   flow-export destination inside 10.1.30.220 2056
   flow-export template timeout-rate 1
   ```

   Here,

   flow-export destination inside specifies that the flow records should be exported from the inside interface.

   10.1.30.220 is the IP address of the collector.

   2056 is the port number on which the collector listens for NetFlow records.

4. **Specify the flow record format (optional)**: You can configure the ASA to export a specific template for NetFlow records. This step is optional but can be useful for ensuring compatibility with the collector.

   ```
   flow-export template timeout-rate 1
   ```

   The **timeout-rate** option determines how often the template is exported in relation to data records. In this example, the template is exported once for every data record.

5. **Configure NetFlow version (optional)**: By default, the ASA uses NetFlow version 9. If your collector supports a different version, you can configure it explicitly:

   ```
   flow-export version 9
   ```

   This command sets the NetFlow export version to 9. If your collector supports a different version, adjust accordingly.

6. **Specify the traffic to monitor**: Specify the traffic you want to monitor using NetFlow. You can apply this to specific interfaces, subnets, or traffic types. Policy maps define traffic monitoring rules, linking access-lists to flow-export actions. For example, to enable NetFlow on the outside interface:

   ```
   access-list NetFlow-export extended permit ip any any
      class-map NetFlow-export-class
         match access-list NetFlow-export
   ```

```
policy-map global_policy
  class NetFlow-export-class
    flow-export event-type all destination 10.1.30.220
```

This example creates an access list allowing all IP traffic and associates it with a class map. The policy map then applies the NetFlow export to the specified destination IP.

7. **Apply the policy map to the interface**: Apply the policy map to the interface(s) where you want to monitor traffic:

    ```
    service-policy global_policy global
    ```

    This command applies the **global_policy** to the interface.

8. **Verify configuration**: Verify that the configuration is correct:

    ```
    show flow-export counters
    ```

    This command displays the NetFlow export counters, allowing you to verify that records are being sent to the collector.

9. **Save configuration**: Save the configuration to ensure it persists after a reboot:

    ```
    write memory
    ```

10. **Exit configuration mode**:

    ```
    exit
    ```

Configuring IPFIX export on a Cisco Firepower firewall

To configure IPFIX export on a Cisco Firepower firewall, follow the given steps (assuming you have the necessary administrative access to the firewall):

1. **Access the Cisco FMC**: Open a web browser and enter the IP address or hostname of your **Firepower Management Center (FMC)**.

2. **Login to FMC**: Enter your credentials to log in to the Firepower Management Center.

3. **Navigate to device management**: From the FMC dashboard, go to **Devices** or **System** (depending on your software version). Select the appropriate device (Firepower Threat Defense device) from the list.

4. **Configure IPFIX**: Under the selected device, go to **Platform Settings** or a similar section. Locate and select **Logging** or **Syslog** settings.

5. **Enable IPFIX**: Find the IPFIX section and enable it. Specify the collector IP address (10.1.30.220) and the export port (2056).

6. **Define IPFIX template**: Some Firepower versions require you to define an IPFIX template. If so, specify the necessary parameters such as flow fields, record format, and so on. The template defines the information that will be exported to the IPFIX collector.

7. **Apply and save configuration**: After configuring the IPFIX settings, save your changes.

8. **Deploy configuration**: Deploy the updated configuration to the Firepower device. This step is crucial to apply the changes.

9. **Verify configuration**: Confirm that the IPFIX configuration has been applied successfully. Check the status or logs for any errors or warnings related to IPFIX configuration.

Configuring IPFIX export on a Juniper SRX-100 firewall

Configuring IPFIX on a Juniper SRX100 involves several steps. IPFIX is a standardized protocol for exporting flow information from network devices to a collector. Here is a step-by-step guide for configuring IPFIX export to a collector with the IP address 10.1.30.220 and port 2056 on a Juniper SRX100:

1. **Access the device**: Connect to the Juniper SRX100 device using the **command line interface (CLI)** via SSH or the console.

2. **Enter operational mode**: Enter operational mode by typing:

   ```
   cli
   ```

3. **Configure IPFIX**: Enter configuration mode

   ```
   configure
   ```

4. **Specify IPFIX export parameters**: Configure the basic parameters for IPFIX export, including the destination IP address and port:

   ```
   set services flow-monitoring version-IPFIX template template1
   set services flow-monitoring version-IPFIX template template1
   ipv4-template
   set services flow-monitoring version-IPFIX template template1
   template-refresh-rate 10
   set services flow-monitoring version-IPFIX transport udp
   set services flow-monitoring version-IPFIX transport udp udp-port
   2056
   set services flow-monitoring version-IPFIX transport udp udp-
   source-port 4739
   ```

```
set services flow-monitoring version-IPFIX template template1
option-refresh-rate 10
```

In these commands:

template1 is the template name.

ipv4-template indicates that it is an IPv4 template.

template-refresh-rate sets the template refresh rate to 10 seconds.

transport udp specifies the transport protocol as UDP.

udp-port sets the destination UDP port to 2056.

udp-source-port sets the source UDP port to 4739.

5. **Specify the exporter**: Configure the exporter information, including the source address and template:

```
    set services flow-monitoring version-IPFIX template template1
option-refresh-rate 10
    set services flow-monitoring version-IPFIX template template1
option-scope-interfaces
    set services flow-monitoring version-IPFIX active-flow-timeout 60
    set services flow-monitoring version-IPFIX inactive-flow-timeout 60
    set services flow-monitoring version-IPFIX source-address 10.1.30.1
```

Here,

option-scope-interfaces includes interface information in the exported flow records.

active-flow-timeout and **inactive-flow-timeout** set the timeout values for active and inactive flows.

source-address is the IP address of the device exporting the flow records.

6. **Apply flow monitoring to interfaces**: Apply flow monitoring to the desired interfaces:

```
    set interfaces ge-0/0/0 unit 0 family inet sampling input
    set interfaces ge-0/0/0 unit 0 family inet sampling output
```

Replace **ge-0/0/0** with the actual interface you want to monitor.

7. **Commit the configuration**: Commit the configuration changes:
   ```
   commit
   ```

8. **Exit configuration mode**:
   ```
   exit
   ```

9. **Verify configuration**: Verify that the configuration is applied correctly by checking the status:
   ```
   show services flow-monitoring
   ```

Ensure that the output indicates that IPFIX is enabled and the templates are configured.

Configuring IPFIX export on a Juniper MX router

To configure IPFIX export on a Juniper MX router, follow these steps:

1. **Access the Juniper MX router**: Log in to the Juniper MX router using a terminal or SSH session.

2. **Enter configuration mode**: Access the configuration mode on the router by entering the following command:
   ```
   configure
   ```

3. **Configure IPFIX export profile**: Create an IPFIX export profile that specifies the collector's IP address and port. Assign a name to the profile, such as **IPFIX-export-profile**.

   ```
   set services flow-monitoring version-IPFIX export-profiles IPFIX-export-profile
   set services flow-monitoring version-IPFIX export-profiles IPFIX-export-profile local-address x.x.x.x
   set services flow-monitoring version-IPFIX export-profiles IPFIX-export-profile collector-address 10.1.30.220
   set services flow-monitoring version-IPFIX export-profiles IPFIX-export-profile collector-port 2056
   ```

   Replace **x.x.x.x** with the router's IP address.

4. **Configure flow monitoring for interfaces**: Enable flow monitoring for the specific interfaces that you want to export flows for.

   ```
   set interfaces ge-0/0/0 unit 0 family inet sampling input
   set interfaces ge-0/0/0 unit 0 family inet sampling output
   ```

   Replace **ge-0/0/0** with the actual interface name.

5. **Associate IPFIX export profile with flow monitoring**: Associate the previously configured IPFIX export profile with the flow monitoring configuration on the router.

   ```
   set services flow-monitoring version-IPFIX
   set services flow-monitoring version-IPFIX template refresh-rate 10
   set services flow-monitoring version-IPFIX template active-timeout 60
   set services flow-monitoring version-IPFIX template inactive-timeout 60
   set services flow-monitoring version-IPFIX template rate-limit 1000
   ```

6. **Commit the configuration**: Commit the changes to apply the configuration.

   ```
   Commit
   ```

7. **Verify configuration**: Verify that the configuration is applied correctly by checking the IPFIX export profile and flow monitoring status.

    ```
    show configuration services flow-monitoring
    show services flow-monitoring version-IPFIX
    ```

    Ensure that the collector address, port, and interface associations are correctly configured.

This configuration assumes that the Juniper MX router is running Junos OS with support for IPFIX.

Configuring NetFlow export on a Palo Alto PA-500 firewall

To configure NetFlow export on a Paloalto PA-500 firewall, follow these steps:

1. **Log in to the Palo Alto Device**: Access the Palo Alto firewall's web interface or use the CLI to log in.

2. **Configure NetFlow**: Navigate to the **Device** tab and select **Setup**. Under the **Management** section, click on **Logging and Reporting**. Click on **NetFlow**. Click the **Enable NetFlow** checkbox. Configure the following parameters:

    a. **NetFlow profile**:

        i.   Click on **Add** to create a new NetFlow profile.

        ii.   Set a name for the profile (for example, **NetFlow-Profile**).

        iii. Select the version as **IPFIX**.

        iv.   Set the **Collector** IP address to 10.1.30.220.

        v.   Set the **Port** to 2056.

    b. **Template refresh rate (minutes)**: Set the interval at which the template is sent to the collector.

    c. **Active timeout (seconds)**: Set the active flow timeout.

    d. **Inactive timeout (seconds)**: Set the inactive flow timeout.

3. **Apply NetFlow profile to interfaces**:

    a. Navigate to the **Network** tab and select **Interfaces**.

    b. Click on the interface to which you want to apply NetFlow.

    c. In the **Interface Management Profile** section, select the NetFlow profile you created (for example, **NetFlow-Profile**) from the drop-down menu.

4. **Commit changes**: Click on the **Commit** button to apply the changes.

5. **Verify configuration**: To verify that NetFlow is working, check the flow logs or use monitoring tools on your NetFlow collector.

To configure NetFlow export to IP address 10.1.30.210 on a **Palo Alto PA-500** via **CLI only**, follow these steps:

1. **Enter configuration mode**: Log in to the **PA-500** via SSH or console, then enter configuration mode:

   ```
   Configure
   ```

2. **Define the NetFlow server**: Set up the NetFlow collector with IP 10.1.30.220 and a specific UDP port (for example, 2056):

   ```
   set deviceconfig setting NetFlow collector ip 10.1.30.220 port 2056
   ```

3. **Configure the NetFlow template refresh rate**: Set the refresh rate (in seconds) and template timeout (in minutes). Adjust these values as needed:

   ```
   set deviceconfig setting NetFlow template-refresh-rate 30
   set deviceconfig setting NetFlow template-timeout-rate 5
   ```

4. **Enable NetFlow on the desired interface**: Determine which interface (for example, ethernet1/1) you want to monitor, then enable NetFlow on that interface:

   ```
   set network interface ethernet ethernet1/1 layer3 NetFlow-profile default
   ```

   Repeat this command for all interfaces that need NetFlow monitoring.

5. **Commit the configuration**: Apply the changes:

   ```
   commit
   ```

6. **Verify NetFlow configuration**: To verify that NetFlow is configured correctly, run:

   ```
   show NetFlow statistics
   ```

7. To ensure the configuration is applied to an interface, check:

   ```
   show interface ethernet1/1
   ```

8. **Optional debugging commands**: If NetFlow data is not being sent or received correctly:

   ```
   show NetFlow status
   show NetFlow template
   ```

Configuring IPFIX export on a MikroTik router

To configure IPFIX export on a Mikrotik router, follow these steps:

1. **Access RouterOS CLI**: Connect to the MikroTik router through SSH, Telnet, or directly through the console.

2. **Navigate to IPFIX configuration**: Enter the following command to access the IPFIX configuration section:

```
/ip IPFIX
```

3. **Set active flow timeout and cache time**: It is recommended to set the **active-flow-timeout** and **cache-timeout** parameters. These values control how long flows are kept in the cache. For example:

```
set active-flow-timeout=5m
set cache-timeout=1m
```

4. **Configure IPFIX export**: Enter the command to configure IPFIX export. Replace **<collector-IP>** with the actual IP address of your collector (10.1.30.220) and **<collector-port>** with the desired port (2056):

```
add name=exporter-1 target-addresses=<collector-IP> target-port=<collector-port>
```

5. **Enable IPFIX on interfaces**: To enable IPFIX on specific interfaces, use the following command. Replace **<interface>** with the name of the interface you want to monitor (for example, **ether1**):

```
/interface ethernet set <interface> IPFIX-template=exporter-1
```

6. **Verify configuration**: To verify the configuration, you can check the status and details of the IPFIX exporter:

```
/ip IPFIX print detail
```

7. **Save configuration**: Save the configuration to make the changes persistent across reboots:

```
/export compact file=your_config_backup
```

8. **Save the configuration**:

```
/save
```

Configuring NetFlow v9 export on a Huawei AR150 router

To configure NetFlow v9 export on a Huawei AR150 router, follow these steps:

1. **Access the router**: Connect to the Huawei AR150 router using a terminal emulator or SSH.

2. **Enter system view**: Enter system view to access the global configuration mode.
```
system-view
```

3. **Enable NetStream**: Enable the NetStream feature globally on the router.
```
Netstream
```

4. **Configure NetStream export**: Configure NetStream to export flow information to the specified collector IP address and port.

```
netstream export host 10.1.30.220 port 2056
```

5. **Specify export source interfaces**: Specify the interfaces from which the NetStream data will be exported. Replace `GigabitEthernet0/0/1` with the actual interface connected to the network.

```
interface GigabitEthernet0/0/1
netstream outbound
```

Repeat this step for each interface you want to monitor.

6. **Configure flow record**: Configure the flow record to define the fields to be included in the exported data. You can customize this based on your requirements.

```
netstream record flow-record ipv4 original-input
match ipv4 source-address
match ipv4 destination-address
match transport source-port
match transport destination-port
collect counter packets
collect counter bytes
collect interface input
```

7. **Apply flow record**: Apply the configured flow record to the interfaces.

```
interface GigabitEthernet0/0/1
netstream record ipv4 original-input
```

Repeat this step for each interface.

8. **Save configuration**: Save the configuration to ensure changes persist after a reboot.

```
save
```

9. **Verify configuration**: You can check the NetStream configuration to ensure it is applied correctly.

```
display netstream configuration
```

10. **Exit and logout**: Exit the configuration mode and logout from the router.

```
quit
```

Configuring NetFlow v9 export on a Huawei Eudemon 8000E-X firewall

To configure NetFlow v9 export on a Huawei Eudemon 8000E-X firewall, follow these steps:

1. **Connect to the Eudemon firewall**: Log in to the Eudemon firewall using a terminal or SSH session.

2. **Enter system view**: Enter system view to access the global configuration mode.

   `system-view`

3. **Create an IPFIX template**: Create a new IPFIX template to be used in the configuration:

   `flow IPFIX-template template-name TEMPLATE_NAME`

   Replace **TEMPLATE_NAME** with a meaningful name for your template.

4. **Configure IPFIX export parameters**: Configure the IPFIX export parameters for sending data to the collector:

   ```
   flow IPFIX-template TEMPLATE_NAME
    export version 10
    export collector COLLECTOR_ADDRESS COLLECTOR_PORT
    export source INTERFACE_TYPE INTERFACE_NUMBER
   ```

   Here,

   Replace **TEMPLATE_NAME** with the name of the template created in the 2nd step.

   Replace **COLLECTOR_ADDRESS** with the IP address of the collector (10.1.30.220 in your case).

   Replace **COLLECTOR_PORT** with the port number on which the collector is listening (2056 in your case).

   Replace **INTERFACE_TYPE** and **INTERFACE_NUMBER** with the appropriate interface type and number for the source interface.

5. **Apply the IPFIX template to the firewall policy**: After creating the Netstream configuration, it must be applied to a Firewall Policy.

   ```
   firewall policy POLICY_ID
    flow-export template TEMPLATE_NAME
    quit
   ```

   Here,

   Replace **POLICY_ID** with the ID of the firewall policy to which you want to apply the IPFIX template.

   Replace **TEMPLATE_NAME** with the name of the template created in the 2nd step.

6. **Save configuration**: Proceed with saving the configuration to make it permanent across reboots:

   `save`

7. **Verify configuration**: You can verify the IPFIX configuration using the following commands:

```
display IPFIX-template
display firewall policy POLICY_ID
```

Replace **POLICY_ID** with the ID of the firewall policy you configured.

8. **Exit system view**: Now that the configuration is completed, you can exit the system view mode.

```
quit
```

9. **Restart the firewall process (optional)**: If required, you can restart the firewall process to apply the changes immediately:

```
reset firewall
```

Configuring IPFIX export on a Fortinet FG-60 firewall

To configure IPFIX export on a Fortiner FG-60 firewall:

1. **Access the Fortinet web interface**: Log in to the Fortinet web interface using a web browser.

2. **Configure IPFIX**:

   a. Navigate to **System | Settings**.

   b. Under **Logging and Reporting**, click on **Settings**.

   c. In the **Settings** page, find the **IPFIX** section.

   d. Enable IPFIX by checking the **Enable IPFIX** box.

   e. Set the **IPFIX Collector** to 10.1.30.220.

   f. Set the **Collector Port** to 2056.

   g. Configure other IPFIX settings as needed.

3. **Apply IPFIX to security policies (optional)**:

   a. If you want to apply IPFIX to specific security policies, navigate to **Policy & Objects | IPv4 Policy**.

   b. Edit the security policy for which you want to enable IPFIX.

   c. Under the **Logging Options** section, enable **Log Allowed Traffic** and **Log Denied Traffic**.

   d. Save the configuration.

4. **Save configuration**: Click on the **Apply** button to save the IPFIX configuration.

5. **Verify configuration**: Verify that IPFIX is enabled and configured correctly:

    a. Navigate to **System | Settings | Status**.

    b. In the **System Information** section, check the status of IPFIX.

Please note that the screenshots and steps provided are based on Fortinet documentation for version 7.0. The web interface and configuration options may vary slightly depending on your Fortinet FortiOS version. Always refer to the official Fortinet documentation for your specific FortiOS version to ensure accurate configuration.

Configuring IPFIX export on a SonicWALL firewall with SonicOS 7.0

To configure IPFIX export on a SonicWall firewall with SonicOS 7.0, follow these steps:

1. **Login to SonicWall management interface**: Open a web browser and enter the IP address of your SonicWall device. Log in with your credentials.

2. **Navigate to the log settings**:

    a. In the SonicOS management interface, go to the **Manage** tab.

    b. Select **Log Settings** from the left-hand menu.

3. **Enable IPFIX**:

    a. Under the **Log Settings** page, find the **IPFIX** section.

    b. Enable IPFIX by toggling the switch to the **On** position.

4. **Configure IPFIX settings**:

    a. Once IPFIX is enabled, you should see options to configure the IPFIX settings.

    b. Enter the IP address of the collector in the **Server IP Address** field. In this case, enter **10.1.30.220**.

    c. Set the Server Port to **2056**.

5. **Choose template options**: SonicWall allows you to choose a predefined template or customize the template for exporting IPFIX records. Choose the appropriate option based on your requirements.

6. **Select interfaces to export**: Choose the network interfaces whose traffic you want to export as IPFIX records. This is typically done in the same section where you configure IPFIX settings.

7. **Save and apply changes**: After configuring the IPFIX settings, save the changes.

8. **Verify configuration**: Go back to the **Log Settings** page and confirm that IPFIX is still enabled, and the settings are correctly configured.

Please note that the steps outlined here are general and based on SonicOS 7.0. The exact steps might differ based on the specific model and firmware version of your SonicWall device. Refer to the SonicWall documentation or contact SonicWall support for model-specific instructions or any updates to the firmware.

Configuring IPFIX export on a Sophos firewall

To configure IPFIX export on a Sophos firewall, follow these steps:

1. **Login to Sophos XG firewall web interface**: Open a web browser and enter the IP address of your Sophos XG firewall. Log in with your administrative credentials.

2. **Navigate to Log & Report Settings**: In the Sophos XG firewall web interface, go to **Log & Report** in the left-hand menu.

3. **Select the log settings**: Click on **Log Settings** under **Log & Report**.

4. **Configure IPFIX settings**: Scroll down to find the **IPFIX** section and enable IPFIX by toggling the switch to the **ON** position.

5. **Specify IPFIX collector settings**:

    a. Enter the IP address of the collector in the **Collector IP** field (10.1.30.220).

    b. Set the **Collector Port** to 2056.

6. **Choose protocol and template version**:

    a. Select the appropriate IPFIX protocol version. Common choices are 9 and 10.

    b. Choose the IPFIX template version. Version 10 is widely used.

7. **Configure export interval**: Set the **Export Interval** to define how often the Sophos XG firewall should export IPFIX records.

8. **Enable logging for specific traffic types (optional)**: You can choose to log specific types of traffic by toggling the corresponding switches (for example, **Enable Logging for UDP**, **Enable Logging for TCP**).

9. **Save and apply changes**: After configuring the IPFIX settings, scroll down and click on the **Save** button.

10. **Firewall rule configuration (if necessary)**: If there are restrictive firewall rules, ensure that traffic from the Sophos XG firewall to the IPFIX collector on port 2056 is allowed.

11. **Restart services (if necessary)**: In some cases, changes to IPFIX settings may require restarting the firewall or related services. Check the Sophos XG documentation for guidance on restarting services if needed.

Configuring IPFIX export on a Checkpoint firewall

To configure IPFIX export on a Checkpoint firewall, follow these steps:

1. **Log in to Checkpoint Management Server**: Access the Checkpoint Management Server, where the firewall configuration is managed.

2. **Open SmartDashboard**: Use the SmartDashboard application to configure the firewall settings.

3. **Navigate to the firewall object**:

   a. In the SmartDashboard, locate the firewall object for which you want to enable IPFIX.

   b. This is typically found in the **Objects** sidebar under **Network Objects**.

4. **Edit firewall object**: Right-click on the firewall object and select **Edit**.

5. **Enable NetFlow on the firewall object**:

   a. In the firewall object properties, go to the **Logs and Masters** tab.

   b. Enable **NetFlow** and select **IPFIX** as the NetFlow version.

6. **Configure IPFIX export parameters**: Click on the **IPFIX** tab (or similar) to access the IPFIX settings. Set the following parameters:

   a. **Collector IP Address**: Enter **10.1.30.220** as the IP address of the collector.

   b. **Collector Port**: Set the port to **2056** (or the desired port on the collector).

   c. **Export Interval**: Define the interval at which flow information is exported.

7. **Save changes**: Click **OK** or **Apply** to save the changes made to the firewall object.

8. **Install policy**: After making changes, install the policy to apply the new configuration to the firewall.

9. **Verify configuration**: Confirm that the IPFIX configuration is successfully applied by checking the firewall logs or using monitoring tools.

Note: The exact steps and terminology may vary slightly depending on the Checkpoint firewall version. Always refer to the official documentation for your specific version for the most accurate and up-to-date information.

Configuring IPFIX export on a WatchGuard firewall

To configure IPFIX export on a WatchGuard firewall, follow the given steps:

1. **Access the WatchGuard Web UI**: Open a web browser and enter the IP address of your WatchGuard firewall to access the Web UI.

2. **Login to the Web UI**: Enter your administrator credentials to log in to the WatchGuard Web UI.

3. **Navigate to Logging & Notification**: In the Web UI, go to **System** and then select **Logging & Notification**.

4. **Configure log settings**:

   a. Under the **Logging & Notification** section, click on **Log Settings**.

   b. Look for the **Settings** tab or a similar option.

5. **Enable flow reporting**:

   a. Locate the option for flow reporting or NetFlow, which may be under the **Proxy** or **Services** section.

   b. Enable flow reporting and choose the appropriate version (for example, IPFIX).

6. **Configure IPFIX settings**:

   a. Find the IPFIX settings or NetFlow configuration section.

   b. Enter the IP address of the collector (for example, 10.1.30.220) in the designated field.

7. **Specify collector port**: Enter the port number for the IPFIX collector (for example, 2056).

8. **Adjust flow timeout settings**: Set the flow timeout values according to your requirements. These values determine how long a flow is considered active before being exported.

9. **Save configuration**: After making the necessary changes, save the configuration.

10. **Verify configuration**: Verify the IPFIX configuration by checking the settings and ensuring that the collector IP address and port are correctly specified.

11. **Restart services**: In some cases, you may need to restart the services or the firewall for the changes to take effect. Check for a **Restart** or **Apply Changes** option in the Web UI.

Configuring IPFIX export on a BigIP F5 load balancer

To configure IPFIX export on a BigIP F5 load balancer, follow these steps:

1. **Access the F5 configuration utility**: Open a web browser and enter the management IP address of your F5 BigIP load balancer. Log in with your credentials.

2. **Navigate to the IPFIX configuration**: In the F5 configuration utility, go to **System** and then **Logs**.

3. **Create an IPFIX pool**:

    a. Click on **Configuration** and then **Local Traffic**.

    b. Under **Pools**, click **Create** to create a new pool.

    c. Configure the pool with a name (for example, **IPFIX_pool**) and add the IP addresses of the devices from which you want to collect flow data.

4. **Create an IPFIX iRule**:

    a. Go to **iRules** under **Local Traffic**.

    b. Click **Create** to create a new iRule.

    c. Provide a name (for example, **IPFIX_irule**) and add the following example iRule script:

```
when CLIENTSSL_HANDSHAKE {
    IPFIX::template add 256 4 8 4 4 2 2
}
```

    This iRule is a basic example, and you may need to adjust it based on your specific requirements and the version of F5 software you are using.

5. **Attach the iRule to the virtual server**:

    a. Go to **Local Traffic** and then **iRules**.

    b. Click on your iRule (for example, **IPFIX_irule**) and attach it to the appropriate Virtual Server.

6. **Configure the IPFIX exporter**:

    a. In the configuration utility, go to **System** and then **Logs**.

    b. Click on **Configuration** and select the **Remote Logging** tab.

    c. Click **Create** to create a new remote logging profile.

    d. Set the following parameters:

        i.   **Name**: Choose a name for the profile (for example, **IPFIX_exporter**).

       ii. **Remote High-Speed Log Servers**: Add the IP address and port (for example, 10.1.30.220:2056) of the IPFIX collector.

     iii. **Protocol**: Select **UDP** or **TCP** based on your collector's requirements.

     iv. **Facility**: Choose **local0** or another facility based on your syslog configuration.

    e. Click **Finished** to save the configuration.

7. **Apply the IPFIX exporter to the pool**:

    a. Go to **Local Traffic** and then **Pools**.

    b. Click on the pool you created (for example, **IPFIX_pool**).

    c. In the **Logging** section, select the **IPFIX_exporter** profile you created.

8. **Save and apply configuration**: After completing the preceding steps, click **Apply** or **Update** to save and apply the configuration changes.

9. **Verify configuration**: Test the configuration by generating traffic through the load balancer and checking if flow data is sent to the configured IPFIX collector.

Keep in mind that F5's interface and options might vary slightly depending on the software version. Refer to F5's official documentation for your specific version for more detailed and accurate instructions.

Conclusion

In this chapter, we have seen how to configure most widespread Layer 3 types of network devices to send flows to a named collector, and in the previous one, we have seen how to spot traffic flows on Layer 2 devices, too.

In the next chapter, we will see how to work on different devices; this can be necessary in different scenarios, like not on-premises network infrastructure or particularly important systems. However, if your network infrastructure is on-premise, the infrastructure itself can be self-monitoring itself, providing useful information to an intelligent collection system that can track down anomalies and unusual patterns. We will explore this further in subsequent chapters.

CHAPTER 6

Implementing Flow Export on Servers

Introduction

So far, we have seen how to exploit flow data exporting from Layer 2 devices to virtualization platforms. Basically, we covered the widest possible available options. However, in scenarios where we lack control over the infrastructure, such as cloud-based systems, obtaining flow data directly from network devices may not be feasible. Just think of cloud-based systems inside VPC that are isolated network environments in cloud platforms, and so on. Whatever your cloud provider is, chances are that you will not be allowed (to even ask) to collect flow data simply because the devices that see and manage network traffic are shared with several customers, and they will not give you the same for privacy reasons.

So, are we stuck? No. Not at all. It obviously depends on your organization and your available budget. There are many commercial alternatives available, such as nProbe or Flowmon Probe; however, we will focus on freely available alternatives. On one hand, this will give the benefit of not dealing with excessively high costs if you have a lot of hosts; on the other, this will provide you with the option to test if flow monitoring is what you really want for your cloud-based systems without investing a fortune.

Structure

In this chapter, we will discuss the following topics:

- Catching network flows on Microsoft Windows systems
- Catching network flows on Linux and UNIX systems

Objectives

By the end of this chapter, readers will learn to install and configure hsflowd and softflowd on Windows and Linux/UNIX systems, enabling flow data export from servers in cloud or unmanaged environments.

Catching network flows on Microsoft Windows systems

There are some open-source projects available around, but the one we are going to discuss is very interesting and also available for several different platforms. The software is an sFlow exporter called **host sFlow** (**hsflow**) and it is available with all sources at **https://sflow.net/index.php**.

The software is available both in source code form and as MSI packages, so it can be easily deployed using SCCM or other solutions like a GPO. The software can run from Windows XP to later versions, like Windows 2003, Windows 2008 and later.

The installation is very easy; it gets installed as a Windows Service, which starts automatically at boot.

Once you downloaded the MSI file, just click on it to run it (as Administrator) and start the installation, as shown in the following figure:

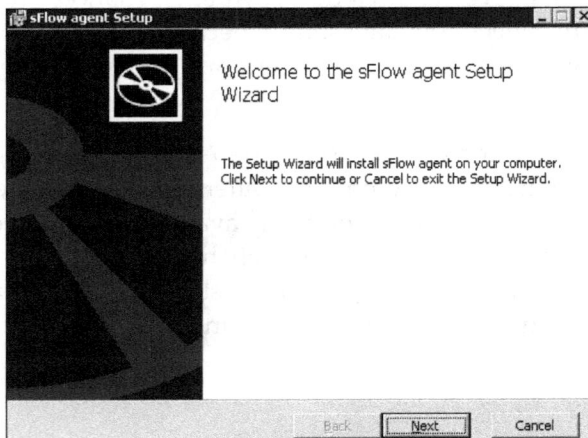

Figure 6.1: Installing the hsflowd agent

Evaluate the license terms and accept the license, clicking **Next** to proceed, as shown:

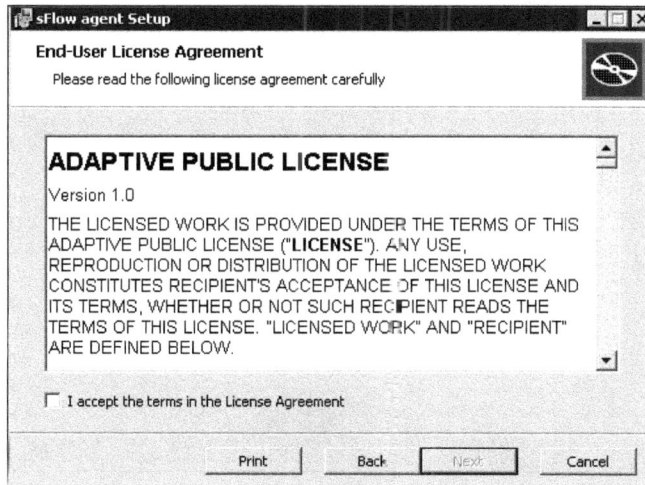

Figure 6.2: *Accepting the licensing terms*

Press **Next** to accept the destination folder, as shown:

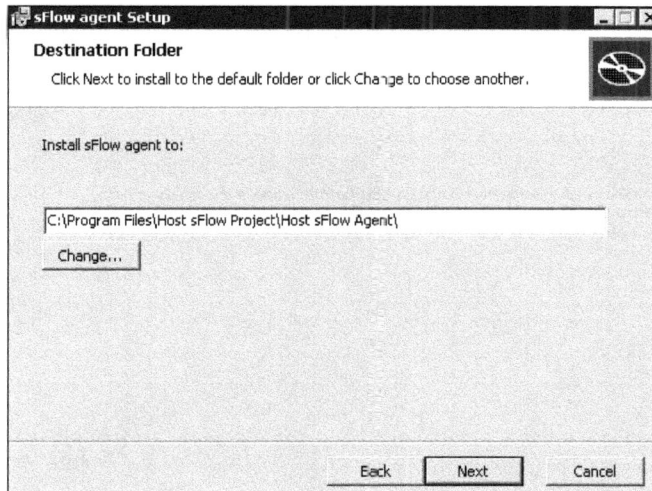

Figure 6.3: *Choose folder for installation*

In the following examples, we configure it to send flow data to the collector on IP 10.1.30.220 (the default UDP port for sFlow is 6343; if a different port is needed, it can be specified with two colons after the IP address, like 10.1.30.220:6343). Refer to the following figure:

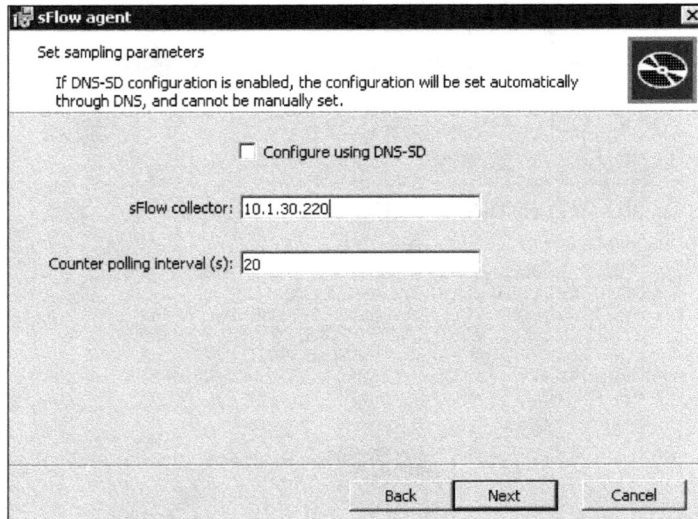

Figure 6.4: Choose IP address and port for sFlow collector

Once the parameters are setup, press **Install** and the installation will begin. If the installer fails, ensure administrative privileges and check event logs for errors:

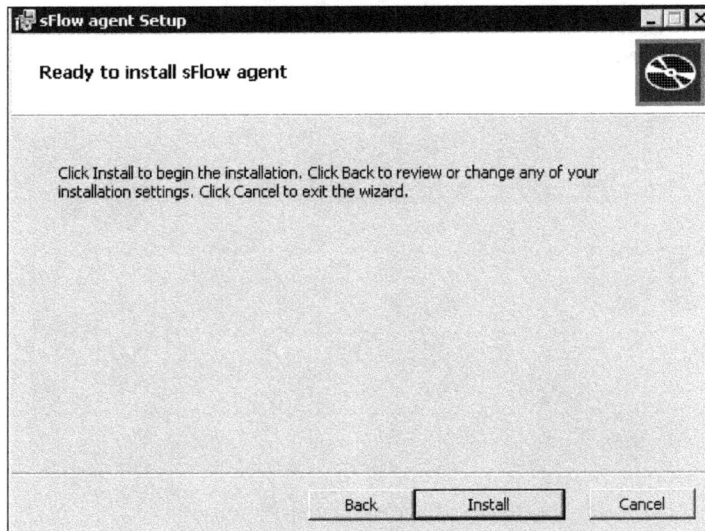

Figure 6.5: Start installation and configuration process

The files will be copied, the service will be set up, and the installation will be complete, as shown:

Figure 6.6: *Finish the installation*

We can check if the service is correctly running by checking on Windows Services and looking for the **Host sFlow Agent Properties**. It should be running with **Startup Type Automatic**, as shown:

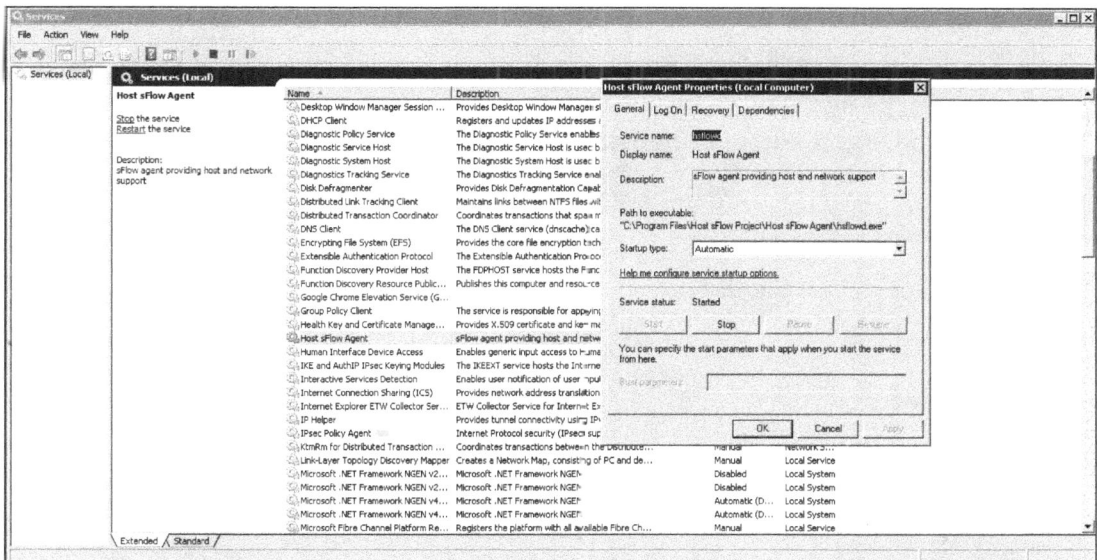

Figure 6.7: *Check that the service is running*

If we need to make changes to the configuration, we need to use the **regedit.exe** tool, perform the changes, and restart the service.

The key to look for is **HKLM\SYSTEM\CurrentControlSet\Services\hsflowd\ Parameters**, as shown:

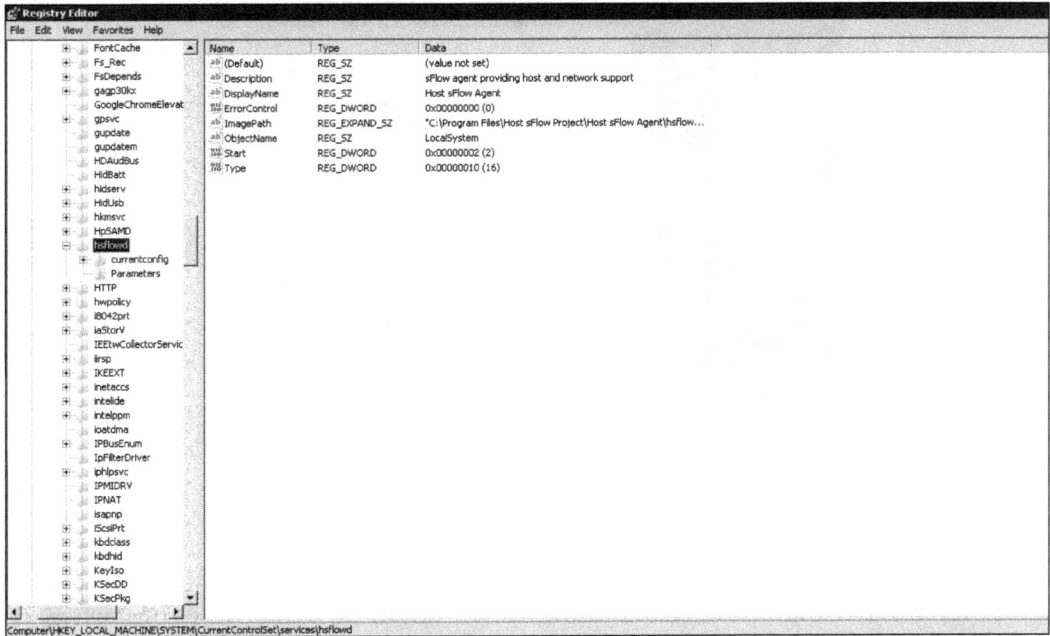

Figure 6.8: Changing parameters using regedit

As can be seen, the parameters for the IP address for the target are stored in the **Parameters** group of Registry Keys:

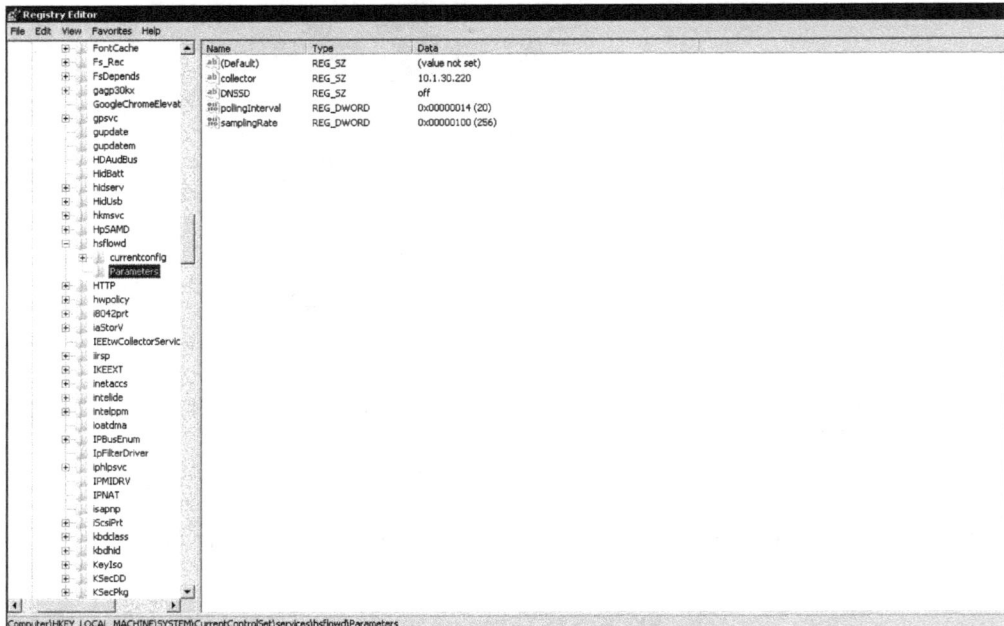

Figure 6.9: Checking current parameters from regedit

Catching network flows on Linux and UNIX systems

Having covered Windows, let us now explore flow capture on Linux and UNIX systems, which offer additional flexibility. Given its conception as a server-type operating system, Linux and UNIX platforms offer a wider choice of flow exporters. The above-described flow can be used and run to export flows using the sFlow protocol.

Pre-built binaries for various CentOS and Red Hat-derived versions are available on the **https://github.com/sflow/host-sflow/releases** path, and installation is very easy, like downloading it with **wget** and installing.

As example, for CentOS7 we could do (as root user):

```
# Download the package on the system
# wget https://github.com/sflow/host-sflow/releases/download/v2.0.53-1/
hsflowd-centos7-2.0.53-1.x86_64.rpm
# Install the package
# sudo rpm -i hsflowd-centos7-<latest>.x86_64.rpm
# Enable the service provided by the installed package
# sudo systemctl enable hsflowd
```

Then you adjust parameters in **/etc/hsflowd.conf** file setting something like:

```
sflow {
        collector { ip=10.1.30.210 udpport=6343}
        pcap { speed=1G-1T}
        tcp {}
system {}
}
```

The **tcp {}** parameter means to measure TCP round-trip-time/loss/jitter, the **speed=1G-1T** simply states to check all network interfaces. The **system {}** parameter sets up the monitoring of systemd cgroups.

All other Linux and Unix distributions installation and configuration steps are quite similar.

Alternatively, given that we are using a straight host (probably a VM), the Linux distribution provided and maintained version of softflowd should be fit for the job, unless we are using VLANs on the system; in that case, it would be better to use the specially crafted version described in *Chapter 4, Implementing Flow Export on Layer 2 Devices.*

On Debian 11, it is very straightforward. You just do (as root user):

```
# apt install softflowd
```

Then edit **/etc/softflowd/default.conf** which should look like:

```
# The interface softflowd listens on. You may also use "any" to listen
# on all interfaces. Mandatory.
interface='any'

# Further options for softflowd, see "man softflowd" for details.
# You should at least define a host and a port where the accounting
# datagrams should be sent to, e.g.
# options="-n 127.0.0.1:9995"
# You may override the control socket location (-c) if you really want to.
# Do not override the pid file location (-p).
options='-n 10.1.30.210:2056 -v 10'
```

On CentOS and other Red Hat-based distributions, you should probably look for a trusted RPM repository that provides pre-built packages to install or revert to building them yourself (the package source contains hooks to be used by **rpmbuild**).

In any case, the installation and the configuration of both hsflowd or softflowd should be performed by an experienced system administrator with root privileges on the system.

Conclusion

In this chapter, we have seen how to prepare host systems to export flow data to a collector. This is a bit against the philosophy of the NetFlow/IPFIX/sFlow working model, where the network is monitoring itself, but in some cases it is the only possible solution to receive traffic flows from systems, like these running on VPCs in cloud providers.

In the next chapters, we are going to show how to implement a flow collector and ingest its data on big-data platforms for analysis.

Join our book's Discord space

Join the book's Discord Workspace for Latest updates, Offers, Tech happenings around the world, New Release and Sessions with the Authors:

https://discord.bpbonline.com

## CHAPTER 7

Implementing Flow Export on Virtualization Platforms

Introduction

In this chapter, we will examine our options for catching network flows on hardware virtualization platforms. Nowadays, most computing stuff is running inside some form of VM or container inside a data center. Gone are the times when we had the luxury of having a dedicated physical machine for an application or a database.

Nonetheless, this does not impact our ability to capture the flows on the networks connecting them. Sometimes, capturing traffic at the L3 level is more than enough; sometimes, you need to delve into higher details; thus, you work at the virtualization platform level.

Structure

In this chapter, we will discuss the following topics:

- SDN and its importance in modern virtualization
- Open vSwitch
- Catching flows on VMware distributed virtual switches
- Catching flows on Proxmox VE 7.x/8.x
- Catching flows on Canonical MicroStack

Objectives

The chapter focuses on solutions for implementing flow export on virtualization systems like VMware and Proxmox, which can give you network visibility in traffic not crossing the network infrastructure (imagine traffic between different virtual machines on the same hypervisor).

SDN and its importance in modern virtualization

Software Defined Networking (SDN) is a modern networking architecture that decouples the control plane (the part that makes decisions about where traffic is sent) from the data plane (the part that actually forwards traffic to the selected destination). This separation allows network administrators to programmatically manage, configure, and optimize network resources, making networks more flexible and easier to manage.

The key concepts in SDN are as follows:

- **Control plane vs. data plane**:
  - **Control plane**: This is responsible for making decisions about where packets should be sent within the network. It handles routing protocols, network topology, and policies.
  - **Data plane**: Also known as the forwarding plane, this is responsible for the actual movement of packets based on the decisions made by the control plane.

- **SDN controller**: The SDN controller is the central component of the SDN architecture. It acts as the brain of the network, centralizing the control logic that was traditionally distributed across the devices in the network. The controller communicates with network devices using standardized protocols (like OpenFlow) to manage the flow of traffic.

- **Southbound APIs**: These are the communication protocols and interfaces between the SDN controller and the networking hardware (switches, routers, and so on). The most common protocol used is OpenFlow, but other protocols like NETCONF, **Border Gateway Protocol (BGP)**, and **Open vSwitch DataBase (OVSDB)** can also be used.

- **Northbound APIs**: These are the communication interfaces between the SDN controller and the applications running on top of the SDN environment. Northbound APIs allow network administrators to write programs that automate and optimize network behavior. These APIs enable applications to request and consume network services in a more abstracted manner.

- **Virtualization and abstraction**: SDN allows for network virtualization, where the physical infrastructure is abstracted and treated as a virtual network. This abstraction allows for greater flexibility in managing network resources and enables features like network slicing, which allows multiple virtual networks to run over a single physical network.

Let us now understand the working of SDN:

- **Decoupling control from data**: In traditional networking, each device (for example, a switch or router) has its own control plane, which decides how to forward traffic. In SDN, this decision-making process is moved to a centralized SDN controller. The controller has a global view of the network, enabling more efficient and holistic decision-making.

- **Centralized control**: The SDN controller uses its global view of the network to make intelligent decisions about traffic flow. It can dynamically adjust traffic paths, apply policies, and optimize network performance based on real-time network conditions.

- **Programmability**: Network administrators and applications can program the network behavior via the SDN controller. This programmability enables automation of complex tasks, such as load balancing, traffic engineering, and security enforcement. For example, if a particular path in the network becomes congested, the SDN controller can dynamically reroute traffic to less congested paths without manual intervention.

- **Communication via APIs**: The SDN controller communicates with the underlying network devices using southbound APIs. For example, through the OpenFlow protocol, the controller can instruct a switch on handling specific types of packets. Similarly, applications can interact with the SDN controller via northbound APIs to request network resources or monitor network performance.

- **Dynamic and adaptive networks**: One of the primary benefits of SDN is the ability to create dynamic, adaptive networks that can respond to changing conditions in real-time. For example, in a cloud environment, SDN can automatically provide new network resources as virtual machines are spun up or down, ensuring optimal performance and utilization of network resources.

Let us now understand SDN architecture:

- **Application layer**: This layer consists of applications that run on top of the SDN controller. These applications might include network monitoring tools, security applications, or services that automate network configurations. They interact with the SDN controller through northbound APIs.

- **Control layer**: The control layer is where the SDN controller resides. It acts as the intermediary between the applications in the application layer and the physical or virtual network devices in the infrastructure layer.

- **Infrastructure layer**: This layer includes physical and virtual network devices like switches, routers, and firewalls. The SDN controller controls the infrastructure layer and communicates with these devices via southbound APIs.

The benefits of SDN are as follows:

- **Flexibility**: SDN provides the ability to adapt the network dynamically based on current requirements. This flexibility is particularly valuable in environments like data centers, where traffic patterns can change rapidly.

- **Centralized management**: With a centralized control plane, SDN simplifies network management. Administrators can manage the entire network from a single point of control, which is more efficient than managing each device individually.

- **Cost efficiency**: By decoupling the control plane from the data plane, SDN allows the use of less expensive commodity hardware for network devices, reducing capital expenditure.

- **Enhanced security**: SDN provides the ability to enforce consistent security policies across the network. The centralized control plane can apply security policies dynamically, based on the overall state of the network.

- **Automation and orchestration**: SDN enables the automation of many network management tasks, reducing the likelihood of human error and increasing operational efficiency. For instance, network resources can be automatically provisioned or de-provisioned based on demand.

- **Scalability**: SDN can easily scale to manage large networks. The centralized nature of SDN makes it easier to add new devices, manage traffic, and enforce policies consistently across a growing network.

Some use cases of SDN are as follows:

- **Data centers**: SDN is widely used in data centers to manage and optimize network resources, automate provisioning, and improve security.

- **Cloud networking**: SDN helps cloud providers manage their networks more efficiently, enabling network slicing and multi-tenant isolation features.

- **WANs**: SDN is used in SD-WAN solutions to manage wide-area networks more flexibly and cost-effectively, optimizing traffic across multiple connections.

- **Security**: SDN can enforce dynamic security policies, segmenting the network in real-time to respond to threats or changing conditions.

The challenges of SDN are as follows:

- **Complexity**: While SDN simplifies network management in many ways, it can introduce complexity in terms of initial setup and integration with existing infrastructure.

- **Interoperability**: Ensuring that different vendors' SDN solutions work together can be challenging, as not all devices or software may fully support open standards like OpenFlow.

- **Security**: The centralized control plane in SDN can become a single point of failure or target for attacks (just try to think of the effects that a DDoS attack could have on it), so it is crucial to secure the controller and its communication channels.

SDN represents a paradigm shift in how networks are designed, managed, and optimized. By decoupling the control plane from the data plane and centralizing network management, SDN provides unprecedented flexibility, scalability, and efficiency, particularly in dynamic environments like data centers and cloud networks. While SDN introduces some new challenges, its benefits make it a powerful tool for modern network infrastructure.

That said, it appears immediately clear how network virtualization will coexist with server virtualization, whatever form of virtualization is chosen.

Some vendors, like Broadcom (formerly VMware), developed proprietary solutions like NSX, although other virtualization solutions (like Proxmox, OpenStack, and Docker) switched to using the open-source solution Open vSwitch.

Open vSwitch

Building on SDN's flexibility, Open vSwitch provides a practical implementation for virtualized networks. **Open vSwitch (OVS)** is a highly programmable, multilayer virtual switch (a switch operating across multiple network layers, handling both L2 and L3 traffic) widely used in SDN environments. It is designed to enable network automation through programmatic extensions while supporting standard management interfaces and protocols. OVS operates as a virtual switch within a virtualized environment (such as a hypervisor like KVM or Xen). It allows VM on a host to communicate with each other, as well as with the physical network, by managing and directing network traffic within the virtualized environment. OVS is designed to work across multiple virtualization platforms, including Linux-based systems, making it versatile for various deployment scenarios.

OVS is an open-source project, which means it is freely available and maintained by a community of developers. It is also integrated into many Linux distributions and supported by major cloud and virtualization platforms.

The key features of OVS are as follows:

- **Flow-based switching**: OVS uses a flow-based model where network traffic is categorized into flows. These flows are defined by a set of packet fields and actions, allowing for fine-grained control over how traffic is handled.

- **Support for SDN protocols**: OVS supports standard SDN protocols like OpenFlow. This enables the switch to interact with SDN controllers, such as OpenDaylight or ONOS, for centralized network management and control.

- **Advanced networking features**: OVS includes support for 802.1Q VLAN tagging (VLAN tagging isolates traffic between VMs on the same L2 broadcast domain)., QoS policies, ACL, network tunneling (for example, GRE, VXLAN), and other advanced networking features typically found in physical switches.

- **Programmability and automation**: OVS can be configured and managed programmatically through its command-line tools and APIs, allowing for high levels of automation in SDN environments.

- **Distributed switching**: When used in conjunction with an SDN controller, OVS can be part of a distributed virtual switch architecture, where multiple OVS instances are managed as a single logical switch across multiple hosts.

Let us now learn more about the use of OVS in SDN Networks:

- **Integration with SDN controllers**: In an SDN environment, OVS is typically controlled by an SDN controller using the OpenFlow protocol. The controller provides a centralized point of control, enabling administrators to manage the network through software rather than configuring each switch individually. The SDN controller communicates with OVS instances on various hosts, installing flow rules that dictate how traffic should be forwarded, dropped, or modified based on network policies.

- **Virtual networking in data centers**: OVS is extensively used in data centers to manage virtual network infrastructure. It allows for the creation of complex network topologies, such as overlays and tunnels, that connect VMs across different physical hosts, while maintaining isolation and security between tenants. It also supports dynamic network provisioning, where new network services can be deployed and scaled without requiring physical changes to the underlying infrastructure.

- **Network Function Virtualization (NFV)**: In NFV environments, OVS can be used to connect various **Virtual Network Functions** (**VNF**) such as firewalls, load balancers, and routers. By managing these connections programmatically, OVS allows for rapid deployment and reconfiguration of network services. OVS's ability to handle high-performance packet forwarding and provide detailed flow monitoring makes it ideal for NFV deployments.

- **Overlay networks**: OVS supports various tunneling protocols (for example, VXLAN, GRE) that enable the creation of overlay networks. These overlays allow for scalable network segmentation, where each tenant in a multi-tenant environment can have its isolated network, even if they share the same physical infrastructure. The SDN controller manages these tunnels, ensuring that traffic between tenants remains isolated and secure.

- **High availability and scalability**: In cloud environments, OVS can be used to create resilient, scalable networks that adapt to changing workloads. For example, OVS can be part of a network configuration that automatically adjusts to the addition or removal of VMs, maintaining consistent network performance and connectivity. Its ability to distribute traffic across multiple paths and handle failover scenarios contributes to the reliability of cloud-based services.

The benefits of using OVS in SDN are as follows:

- **Flexibility**: OVS's programmability allows for highly customized network configurations tailored to specific needs, making it adaptable to various use cases, from simple network segmentation to complex multi-tenant cloud environments.

- **Centralized management**: When integrated with an SDN controller, OVS allows for centralized network management, reducing the complexity of network operations and enabling rapid deployment of new services.

- **Cost efficiency**: Being open-source and designed to run on standard x86 hardware, OVS provides a cost-effective alternative to proprietary switching solutions, especially in large-scale virtualized environments.

- **High performance**: OVS is optimized for performance, with features like **Data Plane Development Kit (DPDK)** integration, which can significantly increase packet processing speeds, making it suitable for environments with high network traffic demands.

- **Interoperability**: OVS's support for standard protocols and integration with various virtualization platforms ensures that it can operate effectively in a wide range of environments, providing consistent performance and functionality.

OVS is a powerful tool in the SDN ecosystem, providing the flexibility, programmability, and advanced features necessary to build dynamic, efficient, and scalable virtual networks. Its ability to integrate with SDN controllers and support complex networking scenarios makes it an essential component in modern data centers, cloud environments, and NFV infrastructures. By leveraging OVS, organizations can achieve greater control over their network infrastructure, automate network management tasks, and improve overall network performance and reliability.

Besides OVS, container-based solutions (such as Docker and Kubernetes) make use of several alternatives, both commercial, opensource and hybrid solutions like:

- Project Calico (**https://tigera.io/project-calico**)

- Flannel (**https://github.com/flannel-io**)

Additionally, both OVS and Calico support NetFlow/IPFIX flow export!

Catching flows on VMware distributed virtual switches

VMware (now property of *Broadcom*) is one of the most used and well-known hardware virtualization platforms. Its virtualization capabilities go beyond CPU and server only and started including full network virtualization by means of their NSX solution. This SDN solution, due to its cost and complexity, is not yet so widespread and could be the topic of a book itself. What is certain is that VMware distributed virtual switches have been there with the capability to export IPFIX data since VMware and ESXi 5.1! So, configuring a **distributed virtual switch** (**DVS**) to send data to a NetFlow/IPFIX collector has become a quite easy activity.

The prerequisites are as follows:

- Ensure that you have administrative access to the vCenter Server.
- Verify that the DVS is created and configured.
- Ensure that your IPFIX collector is set up and ready to receive IPFIX data.

Let us now go over the following step-by-step configuration steps:

1. **Log in to vCenter Server**:
   a. Open a web browser and navigate to the vCenter Server URL.
   b. Log in with your administrative credentials.

2. **Navigate to Networking**:
   a. In the vSphere Client, click on the **Menu** icon and select **Networking**.
   b. In the left navigation pane, expand the data center where your Distributed Virtual Switch is located.
   c. Select the DVS you want to configure.

3. **Edit DVS settings**: Right-click on the DVS and select **Settings | Edit Settings**.

4. **Enable NetFlow**:
   a. In the **Edit Settings** window, navigate to the **Monitoring** section.
   b. Check the **Enable NetFlow** box.

5. **Configure NetFlow collector**:
   a. Still in the **Monitoring** section, you will see the **NetFlow** settings.
   b. Enter the Collector IP Address (for example, 10.1.30.210).
   c. Enter the **Collector Port** (for example, 2056).
   d. Optionally, you can set the **Observation Domain ID** and **Active Flow Timeout** (in seconds).

Refer to the following figure:

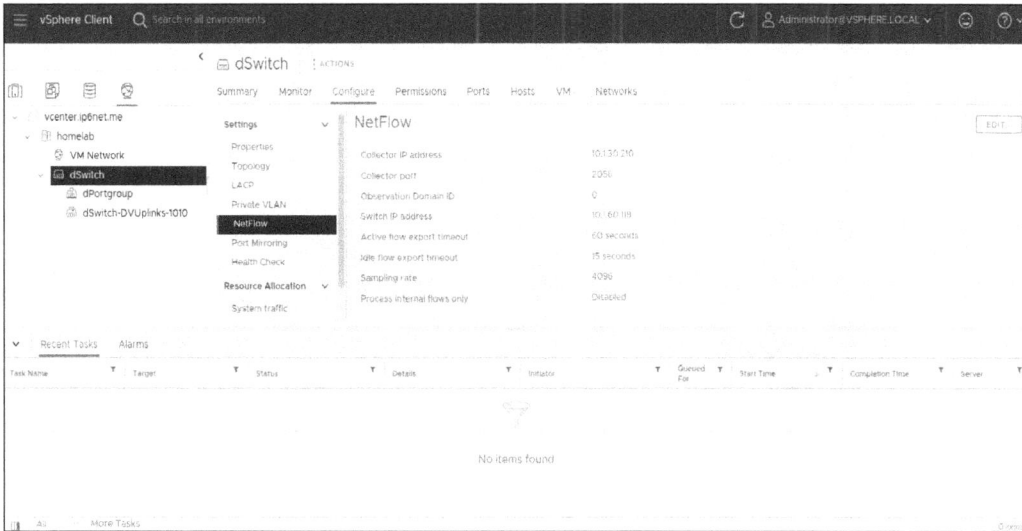

Figure 7.1: *Configuring NetFlow export on a DVS*

It is a common mistake to label IPFIX export as NetFlow by a lot of software vendors and VMware is no exception. What we are going to receive from our collector are actually IPFIX flow exports and not NetFlow ones.

6. In our example, we created two Linux VMs connected to a distributed vSwitch on VLAN 60, as shown:

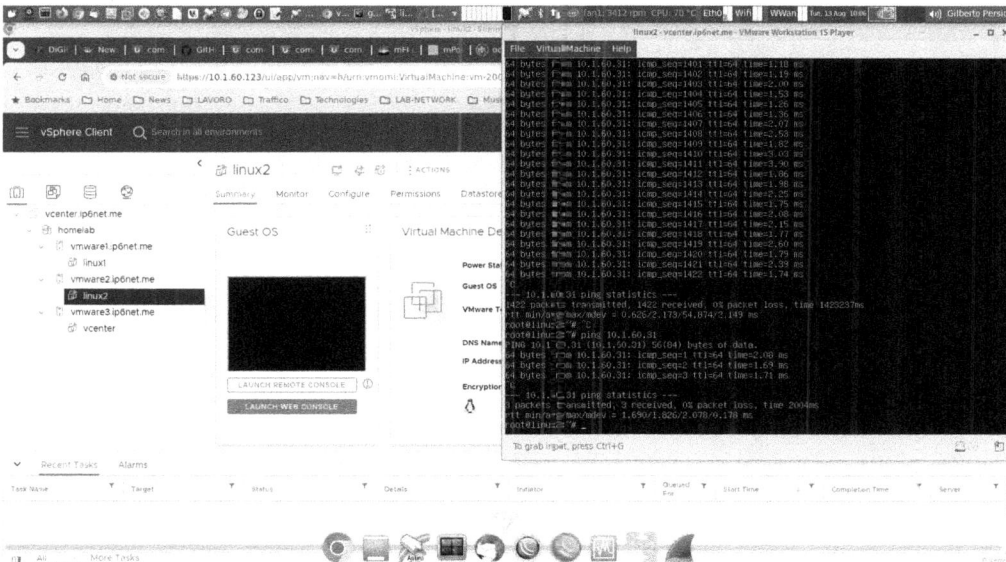

Figure 7.2: *Ensuring that the two VM can communicate using the DVS*

7. The two VM has IP 10.1.60.31 and 10.1.60.17 and they can ping each other by means of the distributed vSwitch. They run on 2 different ESXi nodes, so the packets need to get out of one node's physical interface to reach the other node's physical interface and back. Crossing the distributed vSwitch, flows are created, managed, forwarded and in the end, exported to our collector on IP 10.1.30.210 on port UDP 2056 as we previously configured. Refer to the following figure:

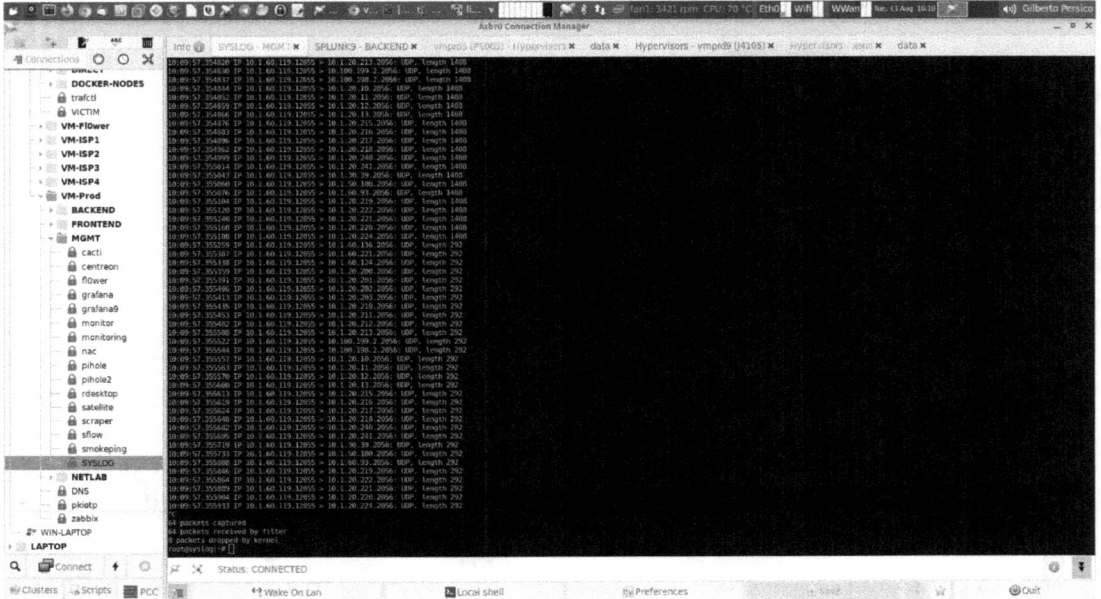

Figure 7.3: Ensuring that the DVS is correctly sending NetFlow packets for traffic between the two VMs

8. Here we see the NetFlow packets from the distributed vSwitch we created before and connected the VMs to. If we analyze the received packets, they are indeed not NetFlow packet, but IPFIX packets even containing undisclosed elements, as shown:

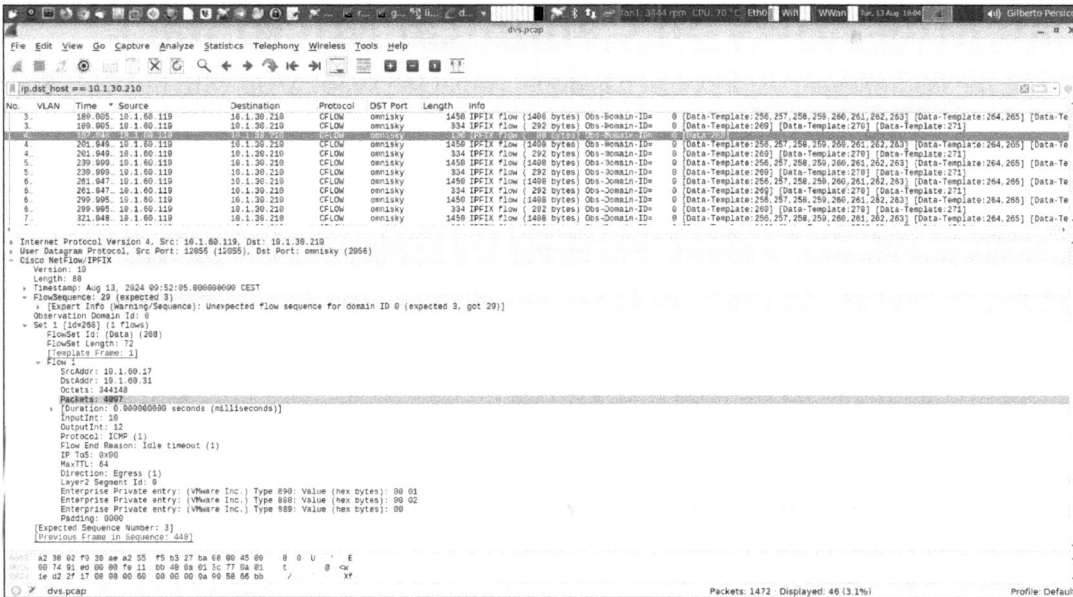

Figure 7.4: *Inspecting the NetFlow packets from the DVS*

They are marked under **Enterprise Private entry** rows in Wireshark and can contain custom data that the vendor could decide not to make public. Nonetheless, in our nice flow example, we see the ICMP traffic from 10.1 60.17 to 10.1.60.31 and all related info.

Catching flows on Proxmox VE 7.x/8.x

Proxmox is a very good hardware virtualization platform based on GNU Linux/Debian and uses KVM to its fullest to provide hardware virtualization. After Broadcom's acquisition of VMware and its removal of a free-tier version, in most use cases, Proxmox easily fills the leftover gap by VMware, and it is evolving into an enterprise solution. Using standard Linux Networking, we can easily monitor traffic using a software-based solution that will be described in *Chapter 6, Implementing Flow Export on Servers*, section *Catching network flows on Linux and UNIX systems*.

The solution (already seen in *Chapter 4, Implementing Flow Export on Layer 2 Devices*) makes use of a popular Linux software called **softflowd**, which performs the activity of analyzing and capturing flows incoming and outgoing from the operating system on the configured (or all) interfaces, and exporting the flows by means of NetFlow v5, v9 or IPFIX protocols.

By means of this solution, we can easily track all the traffic, both from VMs and from LXC Linux Containers.

This software, in your preferred variant, should be installed on all the nodes in the Proxmox cluster (or, generically, on all the nodes you could be interested in to analyze in/out traffic).

Catching flows on Canonical MicroStack

During the last few years, Canonical has done a great job keeping up with the OpenStack platform and community and created several interesting useful projects to run your private cloud on premises, like for example Canonical MicroStack or their own version of OpenStack. OpenStack, originally a derivative work from NASA Nebula and from Rackspace platform, is an open-source platform for providing and managing IaaS platforms. It is, for sure, a virtualization platform, but with a different concept. Normally, in a data center, you have the 2 big database machines in **high availability** (**HA**), a bunch of web servers, and that accounting platform; shortly, you manage each server (or VM once it is virtualized) singularly.

The cloud concept (on which IaaS platforms are based) is rather different. You do not have a special system to handle or to care. Imagine you are dealing with a herd of cows, and you do not have a special cow. They are brought to life by providing, managing, and removing the customer needs (like Amazon or Azure do). The IaaS manager creates templates of systems with standard capabilities (standard number of CPUs, standard memory size, standard storage) and so on.

The OpenStack orchestration software components will use a networking control plane to deal with its architecture of nodes (which the guest machines will never see) while the VMs will rely on the external networking to be reachable from and to reach the Internet.

A typical OpenStack farm could be built by dozens of hosts. The suggestion is to install softflowd on all the OpenStack nodes and also configure sFlow on the L2 switching side if available. In this way, you should be able to track all incoming and outgoing traffic into and out of the OpenStack infrastructure.

You can choose to monitor both the control plane to check what is really happening on your IaaS platform (and look for spurious or dangerous fake **Vxlan Tunnel EndPoints** or **VTEPs**) for VXLANs) or step further into details about what customer VMs are doing by means of monitoring also external networking because you have chosen to provide your customers an extra level of security. Based on standard Linux networking, we have the same monitoring capabilities already described in the previous paragraph about monitoring Proxmox; you will see in the succeeding chapter how to monitor the networking of a generic UNIX/Linux server. it is strongly advised to use the softflowd solution; it has a better trade-offs about CPU utilization, detail level, and provided info.

Conclusion

In this chapter, we have seen different concepts, from the SDN to Open vSwitch to virtualization, VMware, Proxmox, OpenStack, VXLAN, VTEPs, and so on. It seems to be a lot of stuff, but keep in mind just the important concepts and our target. We need to know how these infrastructures work because we want to have the best possible visibility on them. They run the core business of our company, so having aid in monitoring the infrastructure itself, is not a bad idea!

## CHAPTER 8

Ingesting Data into Clickhouse and Elasticsearch

Introduction

By this point, we have examined most of our opportunities to view network traffic from most of the datacenter. Routers, firewalls, switches, and virtualization platforms are hopefully all configured now to produce and send the flow data they can see over a network. But to make practical use of it, we need something to receive it, store it, and transform it in a helpful way. To explain in a better and more practical way, we opted for mostly open-source software due to their power and effectiveness.

Structure

In this chapter, we will discuss the following topics:

- Choosing and installing a flow collector
- Clickhouse
- Elasticsearch

Objectives

The chapter shows the user how to ingest raw flow data into more usable and structured analysis platforms like Elasticsearch and Clickhouse (open-source high-performance OLAP).

Choosing and installing a flow collector

To make practical use of the flows sent via network (using one of the protocols described in *Chapter 7, Implementing Flow Export on Virtualization Platforms*), we need software that receives them and stores them in a helpful way. This kind of software is called **flow collector**. There is plenty of choice, both in the commercial and the open-source licensed ones, and since it is written, we will make use of it throughout the book.

The software is a commercial one, but there is a free version that can be used for unlimited time. Its main limitations are that it will use just one of the cores available on your CPU and that is limited to NetFlow v1, NetFlow v5 and sFlow protocols, which are more than enough for the scope of this book.

The software is named Fl0wer and can be downloaded at **https://fl0wer.me/download/**

Fl0wer

Fl0wer is a NetFlow/IPFIX/sFlow collector and platform that was conceived for performance and features. Normally, it can handle the reception of tens of thousands of **flows per second (fps)** and store them in a convenient CSV way, for further ingestion in your favorite analytics platform, be it an OLAP like Clickhouse, a classical SQL database like MySQL, or big data analytic solutions like OpenSearch, Splunk or Elasticsearch. Ingestion job runs as a separate process, and the traffic flows can be digitally signed for non-repudiation on WORM storage.

There are several differences with other software, such as:

- Network probabilistic application recognition, which uses statistical methods to identify applications from flow patterns. Pre-classification of network traffic.
- Buildup of a flow matrix table.
- Pre-identification of traffic with network bad actors.
- Pre-identification of network scans, both horizontal and vertical.
- REST API for integration with other software.

Along with many others that you will be able to discover reading the provided manual. We will have the opportunity to see some of them throughout the other chapters of this book.

Installing Fl0wer and UDP samplicator

Fl0wer is very easy to install. Just choose your Linux distribution and download the appropriate package. As time of writing of this book, the following Linux distributions are supported:

- RedHat/CentOS 7.x, 8.x and 9.x
- Debian 8.x, 9.x, 10.x, 11.x, 12.x

The Fl0wer platform is split in 3 packages: the collector itself, the development environment (containing sources for all the open-source parts of the platform, including the Python GUI and CLI) and the **Run Time Environment (RTE)**, containing most used tools and a full Python runtime environment with all modules normally used by the GUI, CLI and data pumper. It is strongly suggested to install all of them on your collector machine. Once the platform specific package is downloaded, use the specific **dpkg** or **rpm** command to install it. During the installation, the fl0wer user and group are created (once started as root, the software will switch to fl0wer user for running), everything is installed in the **/opt/fl0wer** directory-tree and the following parameters must be set in **/etc/security/limits.conf** file:

```
*               -       nofile      131072
*               -       nproc       4096
*               -       stack       65536
*               -       memlock     unlimited
*               hard    rtprio      99
*               soft    rtprio      99
```

Proper configuration should be adjusted in **/opt/fl0wer/etc/fl0wer.conf** file for storage of data blocks, listening ports, and so on, for which the user manual is best fitted to check. A reboot of the system is suggested.

If you want to experiment with more than one flow collector, you can make use of the fine UDP samplicator software available at: **https://github.com/sleinen/samplicator**

In our examples, we will make use of the samplicator, so you should end up with something like this:

```
root@syslog:~# netstat -anp | grep -i udp
udp   0   0 0.0.0.0:2056    0.0.0.0:*    447/samplicate
udp   0   0 0.0.0.0:2057    0.0.0.0:*    27742/fl0werd
udp   0   0 0.0.0.0:6343    0.0.0.0:*    449/samplicate
udp   0   0 0.0.0.0:6344    0.0.0.0:*    27742/fl0werd
```

As you see, in our configuration, fl0werd is listening on UDP ports 2057 and UDP port 6344. The real ports to which we forward our traffic are UDP 2056 (NetFlow/IPFIX) and 6343 (sFlow V5), which are managed by the UDP samplicator with a command line like:

```
root@syslog:~# ps -efa | grep samplicate
root        447       1  0 Aug06 ?       06:14:12 /usr/local/bin/
samplicate -f -p 2056 -b 262144 -S -n 10.1.30.210/2057 10.1.60.136/2056
root        449       1  0 Aug06 ?       03:26:27 /usr/local/bin/
samplicate -f -p 6343 -b 262144 -S -n 10.1.30.210/6344 10.1.60.136/6343
```

If you noticed, all flow protocols are UDP based, thus you can configure the flow-receiver with an instance of the UDP samplicator, forwarding (with all original headers) the traffic flows to multiple flow-collectors.

So, the local installation of samplicate will forward incoming traffic to local port 2056 on two hosts: localhost on port 2057 and another host. The same will happen for port 6343. Since the content and the original headers are preserved, you are getting the flow traffic on both the Fl0wer installation and onto another host of our choice, but you can add as many as you want.

Clickhouse

Clickhouse is an open-source **Online Analytical Processing (OLAP)** database that was conceived and developed by *Yandex* (if you have never heard of them, imagine the Russian version of Google). An OLAP database is a specialized database optimized for fast, multidimensional analysis of large volumes of structured data to support complex queries and decision-making, though performance varies with workload and configuration.; at the cost of losing some features versus relational database, can be hundreds or thousands of times faster than a classical relational database when coming to searching or reporting. We will choose it because it scales very well, running from low-power Linux boxes like Intel J1900 based **System On a Chip (SOC)** to high performance server clusters, it is open-source, it is very well documented, there is commercial support and it is really, really fast.

An OLAP database is a type of database optimized for querying and reporting, rather than for transaction processing. It is designed to handle large amounts of data and support complex queries that are typical in data analysis and **business intelligence (BI)** applications. OLAP databases are used to discover patterns, trends, and insights into data by enabling fast, multi-dimensional analysis across large datasets.

The performance depends on the way an OLAP works and the drawback of Clickhouse (and most other OLAPs) is that the DELETE or ALTER operations are not possible once the data is stored (or better, is possible but have a very high cost in terms of performance). This is quite different from a traditional relational SQL environment such as MySQL (although there is even a MySQL compatibility mode in Clickhouse, so you can reuse it to rehost applications through it), which, to preserve its DELETE and ALTER capabilities, is forced to store data in a completely different way.

However, flow-traffic data is basically time-series data, which needs no modification. We just delete older blocks of data that we are no longer interested in, so it is a perfect fit for our analysis. Plus, all common SQL statements are available, so we can build and fine-tune all our queries, and they will always be very fast.

Ingesting data into Clickhouse

As previously stated, despite its core being written in C language, Fl0wer is also a platform that makes strong use of Python code, for its GUI and CLI environments and the flow pumper software. Yes, there is a Python script that can be run in the background, located in **/opt/fl0wer/flowpumper** named **pumper.py** that is already supporting multiple ingesting platforms like:

- Clickhouse
- MySQL
- Elasticsearch
- OpenSearch
- Syslog

So, if you check the script, you can provide the parameters for the database using command line options, or prepare a **pumper.ini** file to be stored inside the same directory of the script, something like:

```
root@syslog:/opt/fl0wer/flowpumper# cat pumper.ini
[main]
ch_server = 10.1.20.17
ch_port = 8123
ch_user = fl0wer
ch_password = fl0werr0x
my_server =
my_port =
my_user =
my_password =
elk_server =
elk_port =
elk_user =
elk_password =
elk_opensearch =
k_server =
k_port =
k_user =
k_password =
i_server =
i_port =
i_user =
i_password =
s_server =
s_port =
datapath = /opt/fl0wer/data/bricks/
nodelete =
```

Clearly, **ch_** parameters are related to Clickhouse, **my_** parameters are related to MySQL, **elk_** parameters are related to the **Elasticsearch stack** (**ELK**), **k_** parameters are related to Apache Kafka (future implementation), **i_** parameters are related to InfluxDB (future implementation) and **s_** parameters are related to syslog sending.

You can easily run it using the screen system tool to detach it from the running console and have it running in the background. It can ingest multiple different platforms at the same time.

Once run, you should see something like:

```
31/08/2024 19:09:03 Clickhouse - Processing flows file: /opt/fl0wer/data/
bricks/flowbrick-tid-3342849792-20240817-132200.csv

31/08/2024 19:09:04 Clickhouse - inserted flows data in Clickhouse, it took:
0.7160137337632477 seconds

31/08/2024 19:09:04 Clickhouse - flows processed from file: /opt/fl0wer/data/
bricks/flowbrick-tid-3342849792-20240817-132200.csv

31/08/2024 19:09:04 Removed file: /opt/fl0wer/data/bricks/flowbrick-
tid-3342849792-20240817-132200.csv

31/08/2024 19:09:04 Removed file: /opt/fl0wer/data/bricks/flowbrick-
tid-3342849792-20240817-132200.csv.sha256

31/08/2024 19:09:04 Clickhouse - Processing flows file: /opt/fl0wer/data/
bricks/flowbrick-tid-3342849792-20240817-132251.csv

31/08/2024 19:09:05 Clickhouse - inserted flows data in Clickhouse, it took:
0.9544245740398765 seconds

31/08/2024 19:09:05 Clickhouse - flows processed from file: /opt/fl0wer/data/
bricks/flowbrick-tid-3342849792-20240817-132251.csv

31/08/2024 19:09:05 Removed file: /opt/fl0wer/data/bricks/flowbrick-
tid-3342849792-20240817-132251.csv

31/08/2024 19:09:05 Removed file: /opt/fl0wer/data/bricks/flowbrick-
tid-3342849792-20240817-132251.csv.sha256

31/08/2024 19:09:05 Clickhouse - Processing flows file: /opt/fl0wer/data/
bricks/flowbrick-tid-3342849792-20240817-132404.csv

31/08/2024 19:09:05 Clickhouse - inserted flows data in Clickhouse, it took:
0.6483424119651318 seconds

31/08/2024 19:09:05 Clickhouse - flows processed from file: /opt/fl0wer/data/
bricks/flowbrick-tid-3342849792-20240817-132404.csv

31/08/2024 19:09:05 Removed file: /opt/fl0wer/data/bricks/flowbrick-
tid-3342849792-20240817-132404.csv

31/08/2024 19:09:05 Removed file: /opt/fl0wer/data/bricks/flowbrick-
tid-3342849792-20240817-132404.csv.sha256
```

If you want to check if real data is incoming, you just connect to the Clickhouse server and do something like:

```
[unixman@clickhouse ~]$ clickhouse-client
ClickHouse client version 24.7.3.42 (official build).
Connecting to localhost:9000 as user default.
Connected to ClickHouse server version 24.7.3.

Warnings:
 * Linux transparent hugepages are set to "always". Check /sys/kernel/mm/
transparent_hugepage/enabled

clickhouse.ip6net.me :) USE FLOWER;

USE FLOWER

Query id: 1a46d8b3-dd72-4459-8da4-a90ebeb74a77

Ok.

0 rows in set. Elapsed: 0.002 sec.

clickhouse.ip6net.me :) SELECT COUNT(*) FROM FLOWS;

SELECT COUNT(*)
FROM FLOWS

Query id: aef8307a-c6d1-419c-80d6-dc46655e2aff

     ┌──COUNT()─┐
1.   │ 83372000 │  -- 83.37 million
     └──────────┘

1 row in set. Elapsed: 0.010 sec.
```

As you can figure out, there are more than 83 million of flows stored for a 26 days period in the lab test network, which is probably more complex than a small company but much simpler than a real production datacenter. For these flows, the occupied disk space is around 2G, which is really peanuts compared to the space that would be used by a traditional SQL (non OLAP) database like Oracle or MySQL.

You can use DBeaver as a free and simple GUI tool to perform your queries from normal Windows clients, as shown:

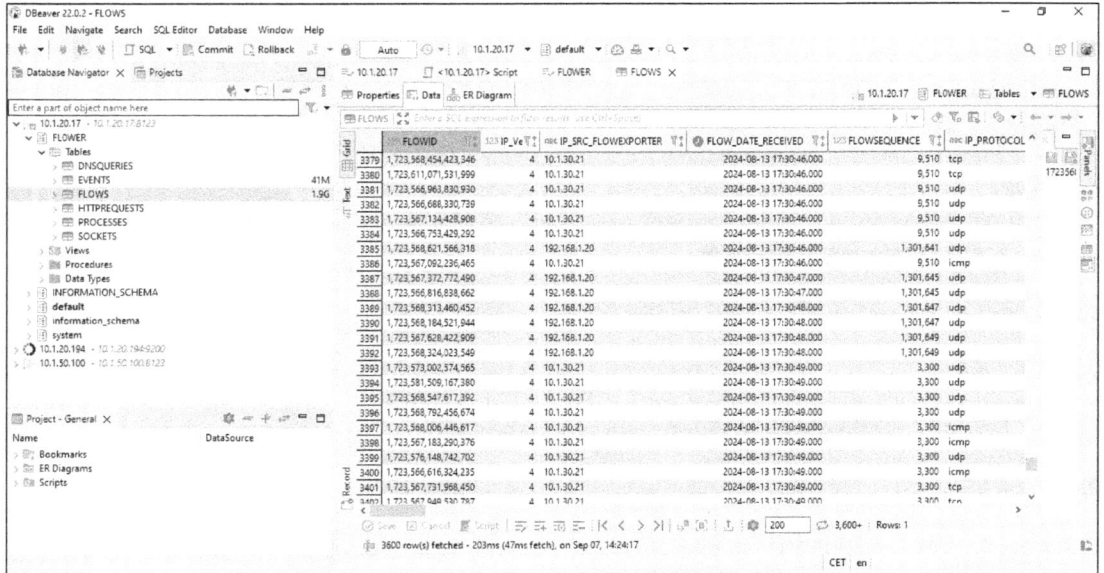

Figure 8.1: *Using DBeaver to browse FL0WER database on Clickhouse*

The database created has the name **FL0WER** and the most used tables are:

- **FLOWS**
- **EVENTS**

There are also other tables that will be used when the Agent is completed; by means of the **DESCRIBE** command, you can see the fields that are used:

```
clickhouse.ip6net.me :) describe FLOWS

DESCRIBE TABLE FLOWS

Query id: 5b0a2aa4-dd59-4921-8d47-65176e27b5d5
```

	name	type	default_type	default_expression	comment	codec_expression	ttl_expression
1.	FLOWID	UInt64					
2.	IP_Version	UInt8					
3.	IP_SRC_FLOWEXPORTER	String					
4.	FLOW_DATE_RECEIVED	DateTime					
5.	FLOWSEQUENCE	UInt64					
6.	IP_PROTOCOL	String					
7.	FLOW_START_DATE	DateTime					
8.	FLOW_END_DATE	DateTime					
9.	FLOW_BYTE_DELTA_COUNT	UInt64					
10.	FLOW_PACKET_DELTA_COUNT	UInt64					
11.	IP_CLASSOFSERVICE	UInt8					
12.	TCP_CONTROL_BITS	UInt8					

```
13. | IP_FLOW_DIRECTION | String   |        |        |        |        |        |
14. | NPAR              | String   |        |        |        |        |        |
15. | CATEGORY          | String   |        |        |        |        |        |
16. | SRC_PORT          | UInt16   |        |        |        |        |        |
17. | DST_PORT          | UInt16   |        |        |        |        |        |
18. | SRC_ADDRESS       | String   |        |        |        |        |        |
19. | DST_ADDRESS       | String   |        |        |        |        |        |
20. | XINFO             | String   |        |        |        |        |        |
21. | RULE              | String   |        |        |        |        |        |
22. | SRC_ORGANIZATION  | String   |        |        |        |        |        |
23. | SRC_ISP_AS        | String   |        |        |        |        |        |
24. | SRC_COUNTRYCODE   | String   |        |        |        |        |        |
25. | SRC_REGION        | String   |        |        |        |        |        |
26. | SRC_REGION_NAME   | String   |        |        |        |        |        |
27. | SRC_CITY          | String   |        |        |        |        |        |
28. | SRC_POSTALCODE    | String   |        |        |        |        |        |
29. | SRC_LONGITUDE     | Float64  |        |        |        |        |        |
30. | SRC_LATITUDE      | Float64  |        |        |        |        |        |
31. | SRC_AREACODE      | String   |        |        |        |        |        |
32. | SRC_TIMEZONE      | String   |        |        |        |        |        |
33. | DST_ORGANIZATION  | String   |        |        |        |        |        |
34. | DST_ISP_AS        | String   |        |        |        |        |        |
35. | DST_COUNTRYCODE   | String   |        |        |        |        |        |
36. | DST_REGION        | String   |        |        |        |        |        |
37. | DST_REGION_NAME   | String   |        |        |        |        |        |
38. | DST_CITY          | String   |        |        |        |        |        |
39. | DST_POSTALCODE    | String   |        |        |        |        |        |
40. | DST_LONGITUDE     | Float64  |        |        |        |        |        |
41. | DST_LATITUDE      | Float64  |        |        |        |        |        |
42. | DST_AREACODE      | String   |        |        |        |        |        |
43. | DST_TIMEZONE      | String   |        |        |        |        |        |
44. | SRC_FQDN          | String   |        |        |        |        |        |
45. | DST_FQDN          | String   |        |        |        |        |        |
46. | USERNAME          | String   |        |        |        |        |        |
47. | RISK_INDEX        | UInt16   |        |        |        |        |        |
48. | NEXTHOP_ADDRESS   | String   |        |        |        |        |        |
49. | BGP_SRC_AS        | String   |        |        |        |        |        |
50. | BGP_DST_AS        | String   |        |        |        |        |        |
51. | VLAN_SRC          | UInt32   |        |        |        |        |        |
52. | VLAN_DST          | UInt32   |        |        |        |        |        |
53. | NBAR              | String   |        |        |        |        |        |
54. | FWD_STATUS        | UInt8    |        |        |        |        |        |
55. | SNMP_IN           | UInt16   |        |        |        |        |        |
```

	name	type	default_type	default_expression	comment	codec_expression	ttl_expression
56.	SNMP_OUT	UInt16					
57.	PLATFORM	String					
58.	PROCESS	String					
59.	PID	UInt32					
60.	COMMAND	String					
61.	DNS_QUERY	String					
62.	HTTP_URL	String					
63.	HTTP_CODE	UInt16					
64.	USER_AGENT	String					
65.	srcPrefix	String					
66.	dstPrefix	String					
67.	srcZone	String					
68.	dstZone	String					
69.	outOfMatrix	String					
70.	BidirectionalFlow	String					
71.	IN_PKTS	UInt64					
72.	OUT_PKTS	UInt64					
73.	IN_BYTES	UInt64					
74.	OUT_BYTES	UInt64					

74 rows in set. Elapsed: 0.002 sec.

The **EVENTS** table is even simpler:

clickhouse.ip6net.me :) describe EVENTS

DESCRIBE TABLE EVENTS

Query id: 6d7fe92a-14fa-4419-bed8-853332bf3946

Connecting to database FLOWER at localhost:9000 as user default.
Connected to ClickHouse server version 24.7.3.

	name	type	default_type	default_expression	comment	codec_expression	ttl_expression
1.	EVENTID	UInt64					
2.	TIMESTAMP	DateTime					
3.	LEVEL	String					
4.	CATEGORY	String					
5.	SOURCE	String					
6.	MESSAGE	String					

6 rows in set. Elapsed: 0.007 sec.

This is exactly what you can find in the source of the **pumper.py** Python script, and this is what will be used for future product developments. However, you can alter these to fit your needs; it is advised to stick to these names, which are quite self-explanatory.

By having traffic-flows pumped constantly into an OLAP database, you can create automations that are quite difficult to create with a closed product.

Elasticsearch

Elasticsearch is a powerful, distributed, and open-source search and analytics engine designed to handle large volumes of data quickly and in near real-time. It is part of the Elastic Stack (also known as the ELK Stack, which includes Elasticsearch, Logstash, and Kibana) and is widely used for searching, analyzing, and visualizing structured and unstructured data.

The key features of Elasticsearch are:

- **Full-text search:** Elasticsearch is renowned for its full-text search capabilities. It supports complex search queries such as fuzzy search, phrase search, and wildcard search, allowing for precise data retrieval. It also provides features like relevance ranking, synonyms, and language-specific text analysis.

- **Distributed architecture:** Elasticsearch is designed to be distributed, meaning it can run on a cluster of servers, providing scalability and high availability. Data is automatically divided into multiple shards (smaller data partitions) and distributed across the nodes in the cluster, ensuring efficient load balancing and redundancy.

- **Near real-time search and analytics:** Elasticsearch provides near real-time indexing and searching capabilities, which makes it ideal for use cases where immediate visibility into the data is required, such as log analysis, monitoring, and real-time data analytics.

- **RESTful API JSON-based data format:** Elasticsearch uses a RESTful API with data stored in JSON format. This makes interacting with and integrating into various applications, platforms, and programming languages easy.

- **Schema-free data model:** Elasticsearch has a flexible schema design, meaning it can automatically recognize new fields in documents. This allows it to accommodate changing data structures easily, making it suitable for diverse and dynamic data types.

- **Advanced analytics:** Elasticsearch supports complex queries and aggregations to perform advanced analytics, such as statistical analysis, machine learning, trend analysis, and geospatial data queries. These capabilities are built-in and allow users to analyze large datasets efficiently.

- **Inverted index:** At its core, Elasticsearch uses an inverted index, which is a data structure that maps terms (keywords) to their locations in the documents. This structure is optimized for fast full-text searches, enabling Elasticsearch to locate and retrieve relevant documents based on search queries quickly.

- **Integration with the Elastic Stack:** Elasticsearch is part of the Elastic Stack, which also includes **Logstash** (a data collection and processing engine), **Kibana** (a visualization and dashboarding tool), and **Beats** (lightweight data shippers). This integration allows for a complete end-to-end solution for data ingestion, processing, storage, and visualization.

Elasticsearch is a versatile, fast, and scalable search and analytics engine that is widely used for full-text search, log analysis, real-time data analytics, and more. Its distributed architecture, real-time capabilities, and powerful query language make it an ideal choice for businesses seeking insights from large volumes of structured and unstructured data. As part of the Elastic Stack, Elasticsearch provides a comprehensive platform for ingesting, processing, storing, and visualizing data, making it a key tool in the modern data ecosystem.

Ingesting data into Elasticsearch

As in the previous example with Clickhouse, we can use the pumper script provided with the Fl0wer collector. As usual, the Python script can be run in background and is located in **/opt/fl0wer/flowpumper** named **pumper.py** that is already supporting multiple ingesting platforms like:

- Clickhouse
- MySQL
- Elasticsearch
- OpenSearch
- Syslog

So, if you check the script, you can provide the parameters for the database using command line options or prepare a **pumper.ini** file to be stored inside the same directory of the script, something like:

```
root@syslog:/opt/fl0wer/flowpumper# cat pumper.ini
[main]
ch_server = 10.1.20.17
ch_port = 8123
ch_user = fl0wer
ch_password = fl0werr0x
my_server =
my_port =
my_user =
my_password =
elk_server = 10.1.20.91
elk_port = 9200
```

```
elk_user = elastic
elk_password = 7GH6Tgtm1123rtbsdaasixco
elk_opensearch = False
k_server =
k_port =
k_user =
k_password =
i_server =
i_port =
i_user =
i_password =
s_server =
s_port =
datapath = /opt/fl0wer/data/bricks/
nodelete =
```

If **pumper.py** fails, check logs in **/opt/flower/logs** and verify database connectivity.

You can easily run it using the screen system tool to detach it from the running console and have it running in background. As we can see, it can ingest multiple different platforms at the same time; in our example both Clickhouse and Elasticsearch 8.15:

```
08/09/2024 17:35:22 Clickhouse - Processing flows file: /opt/fl0wer/data/
bricks/flowbrick-tid-3342849792-20240908-031326.csv
08/09/2024 17:35:22 Clickhouse - inserted flows data in Clickhouse, it took:
0.2310080691240728 seconds
08/09/2024 17:35:22 Clickhouse - flows processed from file: /opt/fl0wer/data/
bricks/flowbrick-tid-3342849792-20240908-031326.csv
08/09/2024 17:35:22 Elasticsearch - Processing flows file: /opt/fl0wer/data/
bricks/flowbrick-tid-3342849792-20240908-031326.csv
08/09/2024 17:35:22 Elasticsearch - loaded file: /opt/fl0wer/data/bricks/
flowbrick-tid-3342849792-20240908-031326.csv - Records: 2000
08/09/2024 17:35:22 Elasticsearch - Fixing up data in dataframe
08/09/2024 17:35:24 Elasticsearch - flow dataframe fixup took:
2.023171761073172 seconds
08/09/2024 17:35:24 Elasticsearch - Converted flow dataframe to dict for
ElasticSearch took: 0.12688345508649945 seconds
08/09/2024 17:35:24 Elasticsearch - Pumping flow data to ElasticSearch to
index: fl0wer-2024.09.08

08/09/2024 17:35:27 Elasticsearch - Pumping Flows into ElasticSearch
(127.0.0.1:9300) index: fl0wer-2024.09.08 took 2.804528950713575 seconds
08/09/2024 17:35:27 Elasticsearch - Result of Flows pumping was: 2000
loaded documents
```

To make practical use of the data, simply use Kibana to build your favorite dashboards and views.

Just point to your properly configure Kibana installation on web port 5601, as shown:

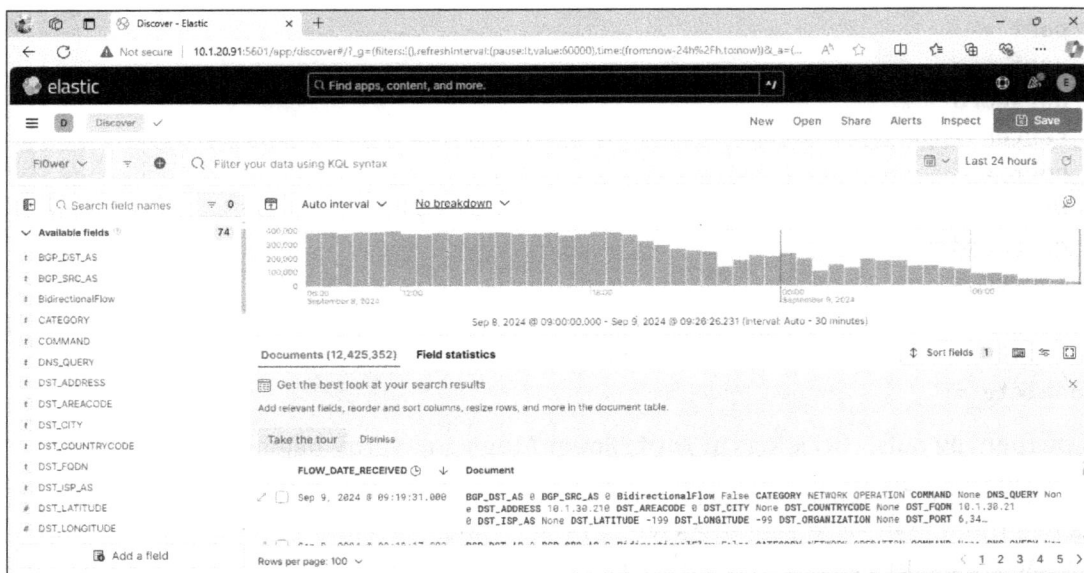

Figure 8.2: Browsing Fl0wer data in Kibana

Conclusion

In this chapter, we have seen how to receive all the traffic flows data from the network and ingest it into some tools to use it. Using an OLAP database, you can quickly analyze your data and build scripts and automation to react to specific flows. Instead, using an analytics tool like Elasticsearch, you can drill down quickly inside your traffic flows and understand how things work better in your network.

In the next chapter, we will dig into ways to analyze traffic.

Join our book's Discord space

Join the book's Discord Workspace for Latest updates, Offers, Tech happenings around the world, New Release and Sessions with the Authors:

https://discord.bpbonline.com

## CHAPTER 9

Flow Data Analysis: Exploring Data for Fun and Profit

Introduction

After so much work, from understanding what a flow is, to preparing an environment for flow data analysis, we can finally explore what is really happening inside our network.

In this chapter, we will examine two real-world case studies that can prove quite useful to improve our overall network security posture and have a better understanding of how we can put flow data at work for us. The first use case is regarding the DNS traffic, which mostly happens on UDP port 53 of the network and is the basis for proper working of our network infrastructure. We will see how simply knowing the source and destination addresses of queries can reveal both practical problems and security issues. The second use case will show us how to better hunt (in a large and structured enterprise network) for anomalies in systems management.

Structure

In this chapter, we will discuss the following topics:

- Understanding what we collected
- Interacting with Clickhouse
- Interacting with Elasticsearch
- Fl0wer data model

- Fl0wer RTE
- Traffic classification
- Data analysis examples
- Rogue VTEPs
- OUT OF POLICY SNMP

Objectives

The chapter will discuss how we can do interesting analysis of the flow data we are getting from the network. It will teach the reader to understand better what is happening inside his network infrastructure, by showing a lot of examples. It will also give the reader further in-depth knowledge about identifying patterns and anomalies, and how to detect security threats.

Understanding what we collected

In the previous chapter, we configured our flow collector to store its data both in an OLAP database (Clickhouse) and in a search and analytics engine like Elasticsearch. For now, we are creating a data redundancy that can be used in different ways, and it will be up to you to choose your preferred analysis method. Let us take these points of view:

- Using Elasticsearch or OpenSearch, you can easily create quick charts and drill down in data by means of the very useful Kibana web interface

- Using Clickhouse, you can work on a compressed database and you can create and automate a lot of analysis tasks by means of scripts.

One suggestion is to begin using Elasticsearch/OpenSearch to explore, and then once you have a good understanding of your network, move to using only the Clickhouse database, which is way faster and scalable.

Interacting with Clickhouse

As said in *Chapter 8, Ingesting Data into Clickhouse and Elasticsearch*, Clickhouse is an OLAP database following the classic client-server model. All data is stored on a server and we interact with it using clients, which can be clients like the CLI application Clickhouse-client in the Linux world, the free DBeaver application with the proper driver, or even using Python scripts (and other languages, but for us they are out of scope; you can refer to the product documentation) which, in combination with the Pandas framework are an excellent tool for our arsenal.

Interacting with Elasticsearch

Elasticsearch and its derivatives like OpenSearch, given their scalability capabilities and their features in managing big data, are search and analyze engines that are greatly used for first steps of data analysis, as we can see in the next paragraphs. They store their data in so-called indexes that can be grouped by index patterns and queried using the web interface named Kibana, through which you can easily create wonderful and useful views of your data.

Fl0wer data model

Fl0wer is simply a network flow collector and by itself it is not tied to any specific storage model. Its full focus is on performance, and it is by definition storage agnostic so that it writes its output to simple CSV text files, that can be easily used by tons of different applications. In its default configuration, it writes bricks of data in the folder **/opt/fl0wer/data/bricks**, and in the commercial edition, it can also write the same in **/opt/fl0wer/data/worm**, which can easily be an NFS-shared **Write Once Read Many** (**WORM**) folder from a dedicated storage or as example from a GlusterFS WORM folder.

This feature allows the user to store the raw flow data on a readable but immutable storage (once written, it can only be read). It is useful in environments where repudiation of data is not an option, typically for big enterprises. The data bricks, once written, are processed by the pumper process as we have seen in the previous chapter and loaded into your favorite platform.

In its current implementation, Fl0wer writes two types of data bricks, one about flows and one about events. Flows are the enriched data flows coming from the network and it is a very big record to deal with. Events, as the word says, are meaningful events happening on the network that Fl0wer is monitoring and that deserve attention from the network manager.

The pumper loads these two types of data in different ways depending on the target engine:

- **On Clickhouse, a database named Fl0wer is created with two tables**: FLOWS and EVENTS.

- **On Elasticsearch, two different indexes are created**: fl0wer-yyyy.mm.dd and netevent-yyyy.mm.dd.

Flows

The following table of the flows is quite simple, and it contains one row for each flow received by flower from the network:

Column name	#	Data type	Default description
FLOWID	1	UInt64	Unique flow ID generated by Fl0wer
IP_Version	2	UInt8	IP version of the fl0w
IP_SRC_FLOWEXPORTER	3	String	IP of the exporter that sent this flow
FLOW_DATE_RECEIVED	4	DateTime	Datetime of reception of this flow by Fl0wer
FLOWSEQUENCE	5	UInt64	Flow sequence number by NetFlow/IPFIX
IP_PROTOCOL	6	String	IP Protocol by NetFlow/IPFIX
FLOW_START_DATE	7	DateTime	Datetime of flow start by NetFlow/IPFIX
FLOW_END_DATE	8	DateTime	Datetime of flow end by NetFlow/IPFIX
FLOW_BYTE_DELTA_COUNT	9	UInt64	Number of bytes in the flow by NetFlow/IPFIX
FLOW_PACKET_DELTA_COUNT	10	UInt64	Number of packets in the flow by NetFlow/IPFIX
IP_CLASSOFSERVICE	11	UInt8	IP CoS by NetFlow/IPFIX
TCP_CONTROL_BITS	12	UInt8	For TCP Flows, TCP Flags by NetFlow/IPFIX
IP_FLOW_DIRECTION	13	String	Flow direction according to fl0wer networks
NPAR	14	String	Network probabilistic application recognition
CATEGORY	15	String	Macro category of the flow
SRC_PORT	16	UInt16	Source port by NetFlow/IPFIX
DST_PORT	17	UInt16	Destination port by NetFlow/IPFIX
SRC_ADDRESS	18	String	Source address by NetFlow/IPFIX
DST_ADDRESS	19	String	Destination address by NetFlow/IPFIX
XINFO	20	String	Extra info by Fl0wer traffic rules/checks
RULE	21	String	Fl0wer traffic rule matched by the flow
SRC_ORGANIZATION	22	String	Organization of the source address from geodata (if available)
SRC_ISP_AS	23	String	Autonomous system of the ISP of the source address from geodata (if available)
SRC_COUNTRYCODE	24	String	Country code of the source address from geodata (if available)
SRC_REGION	25	String	Geographical region of the source address from geodata (if available)
SRC_REGION_NAME	26	String	Geographical region name of the source address from geodata (if available)
SRC_CITY	27	String	City of the source address from geodata (if available)

Column name	#	Data type	Default description
SRC_POSTALCODE	28	String	Postal code of the source address from geodata (if available)
SRC_LONGITUDE	29	Float64	Longitude of the source address from geodata (if available)
SRC_LATITUDE	30	Float64	Latitude of the source address from geodata (if available)
SRC_AREACODE	31	String	Area code of the source address from geodata (if available)
SRC_TIMEZONE	32	String	Time zone of the source address from geodata (if available)
DST_ORGANIZATION	33	String	Organization of the destination address from geodata (if available)
DST_ISP_AS	34	String	Autonomous system of the ISP of the destination address from geodata (if available)
DST_COUNTRYCODE	35	String	Country code of the destination address from geodata (if available)
DST_REGION	36	String	Geographical region of the destination address from geodata (if available)
DST_REGION_NAME	37	String	Geographical region name of the destination address from geodata (if available)
DST_CITY	38	String	City of the destination address from geodata (if available)
DST_POSTALCODE	39	String	Postal code of the destination address from geodata (if available)
DST_LONGITUDE	40	Float64	Longitude of the destination address from geodata (if available)
DST_LATITUDE	41	Float64	Latitude of the destination address from geodata (if available)
DST_AREACODE	42	String	Area code of the destination address from geodata (if available)
DST_TIMEZONE	43	String	Time zone of the destination address from geodata (if available)
SRC_FQDN	44	String	Full FQDN of the source IP if available.
DST_FQDN	45	String	Full FQDN of the destination IP if available.
USERNAME	46	String	Username of the flow if available (mostly from Cisco ASA)
RISK_INDEX	47	UInt16	Risk Index computed by Fl0wer
NEXTHOP_ADDRESS	48	String	NextHop address if available by NetFlow/IPFIX
BGP_SRC_AS	49	String	Source BGP autonomous system if available by NetFlow/IPFIX
BGP_DST_AS	50	String	Destination BGP autonomous system if available by NetFlow/IPFIX
VLAN_SRC	51	UInt32	Source VLAN of the packet if available from Fl0wer
VLAN_DST	52	UInt32	Destination VLAN of the packet if available from Fl0wer

Column name	#	Data type	Default description
NBAR	53	String	Cisco NBAR for the flow if available
FWD_STATUS	54	UInt8	Reserved for future features
SNMP_IN	55	UInt16	Reserved for future features
SNMP_OUT	56	UInt16	Reserved for future features
PLATFORM	57	String	Reserved for future features
PROCESS	58	String	Reserved for future features
PID	59	UInt32	Reserved for future features
COMMAND	60	String	Reserved for future features
DNS_QUERY	61	String	Reserved for future features
HTTP_URL	62	String	Reserved for future features
HTTP_CODE	63	UInt16	Reserved for future features
USER_AGENT	64	String	Reserved for future features
srcPrefix	65	String	Source subnet with prefix if available from Fl0wer
dstPrefix	66	String	Destination subnet with prefix if available from Fl0wer
srcZone	67	String	Source zone if available from Fl0wer
dstZone	68	String	Destination zone if available from Fl0wer
outOfMatrix	69	String	True or false if packet is not in the flow matrix table
BidirectionalFlow	70	String	Bidirectional flow flag from IPFIX if available
IN_PKTS	71	UInt64	No. of incoming packets from IPFIX if available
OUT_PKTS	72	UInt64	No. of outgoing packets from IPFIX if available
IN_BYTES	73	UInt64	No. of incoming bytes from IPFIX if available
OUT_BYTES	74	UInt64	No. of outgoing bytes from IPFIX if available

Table 9.1: Clickhouse flows table

As seen, the names of the fields are quite self-explaining and allow us to investigate a huge number of aspects of our network. *Table 9.1* reports the Clickhouse data format but the data is stored in the same way on Elasticsearch/OpenSearch.

Datatypes used are quite self-explanatory:

- **String:** A bunch of characters, dynamic size.
- **UInt64:** A 64-bit unsigned integer.
- **UInt32:** A 32-bit unsigned integer.
- **UInt16:** A 16-bit unsigned integer.

- **UInt8:** An 8-bit unsigned integer.
- **Float64:** A 64-bit floating-point number.
- **Datetime:** Date time field that can be represented by a string in yyyy-mm-dd hh:mm:ss format.

Events

One special feature of Fl0wer is the creation of network events files, which can report immediately (in near-real-time) some network events that are worthy of attention and analysis. These events are also imported both in the Elasticsearch/OpenSearch tools, both in the Clickhouse database. So, it is worth taking a look at them.

Some examples of network events are explained in the following table:

Eventid	Timestamp	Level	Category	Source	Message
1,730, 221,500, 071,457	2024-10-29 18:05:00. 000	Alert	Unwanted	10.1.30.251	Flow Exporter 10.1.30.251 is silent from more than 600 seconds. Can you please check up?
1,730, 221,499, 525,251	2024-10-29 18:04:59. 000	Rule	Data storage	10.1.61.2	FlowID: 1730226107245721 Protocol: tcp Src: 10.1.61.2/21 Dst: 10.1.30.25/37262 Packets: 5 Bytes: 350 Matches rule FTP - Classification is [SUSPICIOUS]
1,730, 221,499, 525,059	2024-10-29 18:04:59. 000	Rule	Data storage	10.1.61.2	FlowID: 1730226039586415 Protocol: tcp Src: 10.1.30.25/37262 Dst: 10.1.61.2/21 Packets: 7 Bytes: 384 Matches rule FTP - Classification is [SUSPICIOUS]
1,730, 221,498, 321,240	2024-10-29 18:04:58. 000	Rule	Management	10.1.30.21	FlowID: 1730225187480482 Protocol: tcp Src: 10.1.30.25/44034 Dst: 10.1.61.2/23 Packets: 3 Bytes: 164 Matches rule TELNET - Classification is [SUSPICIOUS]
1,730, 221,498, 526,013	2024-10-29 18:04:58. 000	Rule	Management	10.1.30.101	FlowID: 1730225668977693 Protocol: tcp Src: 10.1.30.101/23 Dst: 10.1.30.25/40464 Packets: 3 Bytes: 176 Matches rule TELNET - Classification is [SUSPICIOUS]

Table 9.2: Example of events in the Clickhouse database

As you can see, these events are quite self-explaining and already coded inside Fl0wer, so you do not need to configure anything, except you can improve their accuracy.

Fl0wer RTE

Fl0wer is normally installed with a so-called **RTE**, which stands for **run-time environment**. Although Fl0wer itself is written in C language, many tools use a Python environment with a collection of modules that are normally not installed. To ease the user experience, the Fl0wer RTE contains the full Python interpreter and PIP that was used to build the tools installed with Fl0wer, and we can use it to write and run our custom scripts.

Traffic classification

Fl0wer provides many features and configurations to improve traffic classification, which is the real driver in flow-based traffic analysis tools. **Network probabilistic application recognition (NPAR)** is very advanced and precise. Traffic rules can also be used to trigger actions when a certain pattern of IP traffic is matched. Custom network list allows you to detect traffic to most sites and change the NPAR for a flow. All this works for both IPv4 and IPv6, taking traffic classification to an unpaired level.

Data analysis examples

Now that we have a better understanding of the data model, the tools of trade and the actual data, let us see some examples of how to make a good use of the data that we are collecting.

DNS queries

As we all know, DNS is a key component of the Internet. For whatever IP network you use, it is the service that translates human-readable names into network addresses. Furthermore, if you use IPv6, it is practically mandatory. Even the most trained network engineer will never remember 128-bit network addresses. However, what companies usually do is leave the DNS port (UDP/53 and TCP/53) on the firewall and then configure the clients with known DNS services, internal or external.

Keeping UDP port 53 open on a firewall poses several security risks, as this port is typically used for DNS queries, and malicious actors can exploit it in various ways. Here are the primary risks:

- **DNS amplification attacks:** UDP port 53 can be abused in DDoS amplification attacks, where attackers send small DNS queries with spoofed IP addresses (pretending to be the victim) to a DNS server. The server responds with large DNS replies to the victim's IP address, overwhelming the target network with traffic.

- **DNS cache poisoning:** DNS cache poisoning (or spoofing) occurs when an attacker manipulates the DNS response to return a fake IP address for a legitimate domain, redirecting users to malicious websites. Keeping port 53 open makes it easier for attackers to target your DNS resolver with this kind of attack.

- **Exposing internal network information:** If DNS services on UDP port 53 are not configured properly (for example, exposing a DNS server to the Internet that was intended for internal use), sensitive internal domain and host information can be leaked to attackers. This could provide insight into internal infrastructure and open pathways for further attacks.

- **Data exfiltration via DNS tunneling:** Attackers can use DNS tunneling to bypass traditional firewalls and network security mechanisms. By sending data encoded within DNS queries and responses, they can exfiltrate information from your network without detection, especially if DNS traffic is not monitored carefully.

- **Open resolver exploitation:** If your DNS server is configured as an open resolver (responding to queries from anyone on the Internet), attackers can exploit it for various purposes, such as being part of DDoS attacks or scanning your network for vulnerabilities.

Some mitigation strategies are as follows:

- **Limit access:** Configure your firewall to allow UDP port 53 only for trusted internal DNS servers and block external DNS requests.

- **Use DNSSEC:** Implement **DNS Security Extensions (DNSSEC)** to ensure the authenticity and integrity of DNS responses, helping prevent cache poisoning.

- **Rate limiting:** Use rate limiting on DNS requests to reduce the risk of amplification attacks.

- **Monitor DNS traffic:** Actively monitor DNS traffic for unusual activity or anomalies to detect DNS tunneling or other malicious behavior.

- **Use alternatives:** Consider using more secure options such as **DNS over HTTPS (DoH)** or **DNS over TLS (DoT)**, which encrypt DNS traffic to prevent eavesdropping or manipulation.

In summary, keeping UDP port 53 open without proper security measures can expose your network to significant risks, from amplification attacks to data exfiltration, making it critical to restrict and secure DNS traffic.

Flow protocols come to rescue in the monitoring DNS traffic. Let us assume that we set up correctly (as described in *Chapter 8, Ingesting Data into Clickhouse and Elasticsearch*) the ingestion process to both Elasticsearch and Clickhouse, and let us try to create a browsing filter in Elasticsearch. We just to have an idea about how UDP Port 53 traffic flows inside and outside our network. Refer to the following figure:

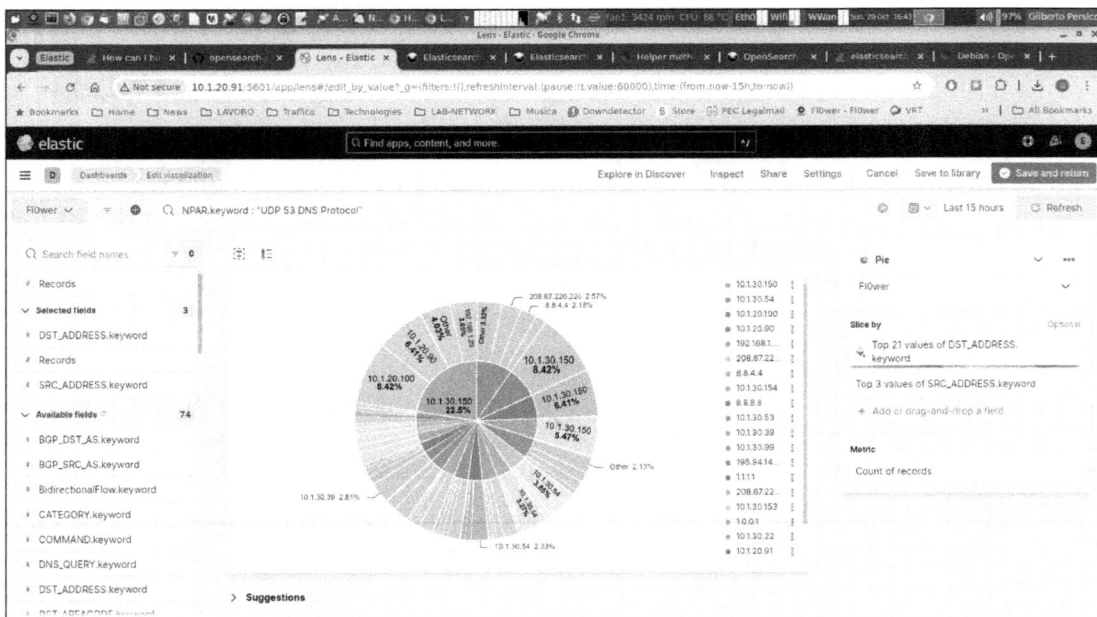

Figure 9.1: Kibana view of DNS usage distribution

As you see, it is quite easy to create a view with Kibana using the NPAR field set as a key. It is very useful to set up a view that identifies and summarizes by the amount of traffic (**FLOW_BYTE_DELTA_COUNT** field) towards the different DNS server (**DST_PORT 53**) used inside our organization.

In our example, a DNS tunnel and exfiltration tool (dnscat2 – **https://github.com/iagox86/dnscat2**) was installed on test systems to show how the DNS tunnels work and how we can identify it. The scenario assumes that the server tool was installed on host 192.168.179.111 system (let us pretend it is a public Internet server) and an internal system (10.1.30.222) was compromised and the client was installed on it. Refer to the following figure:

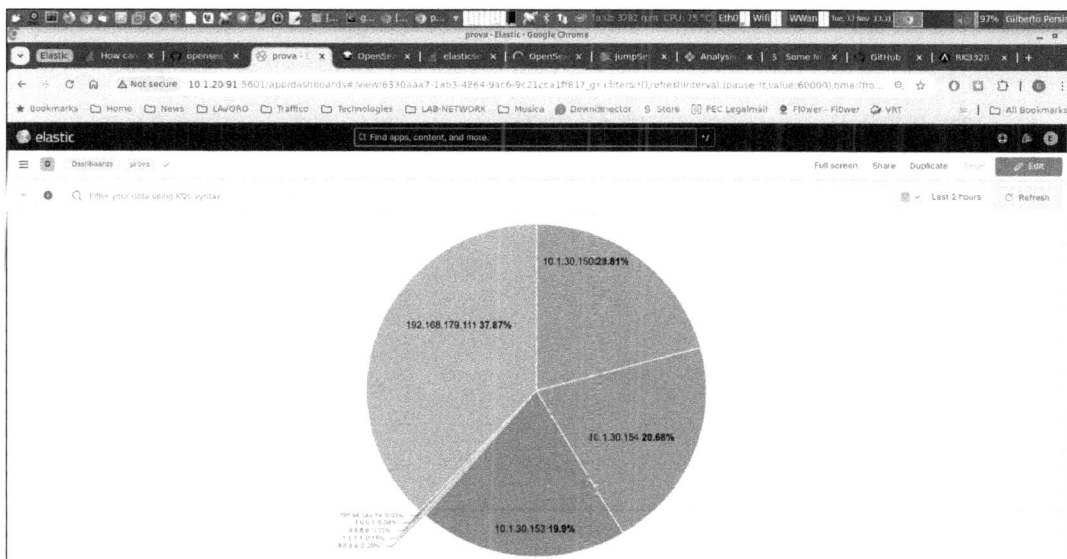

Figure 9.2: Deep filtering of DNS servers usage in Kibana

As we can see, an interesting percentage of the DNS traffic is going towards the 192.168.179.111 server. If we investigate and investigate the flows, we can see something like the following figure:

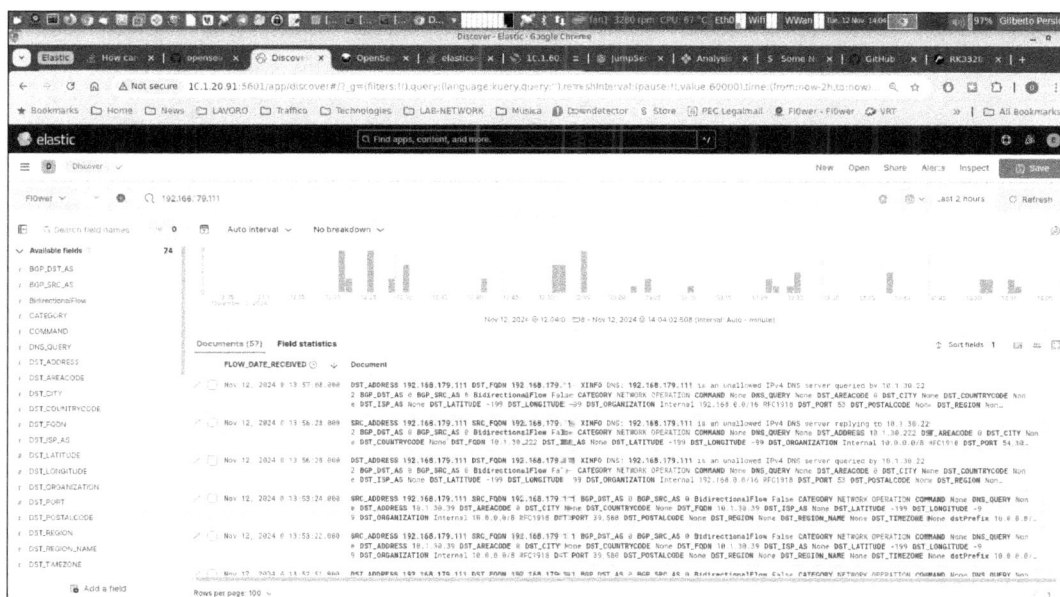

Figure 9.3: Elastisearch detail of DNS flows

If we drill down inside a single flow, we can see in the details as follows:

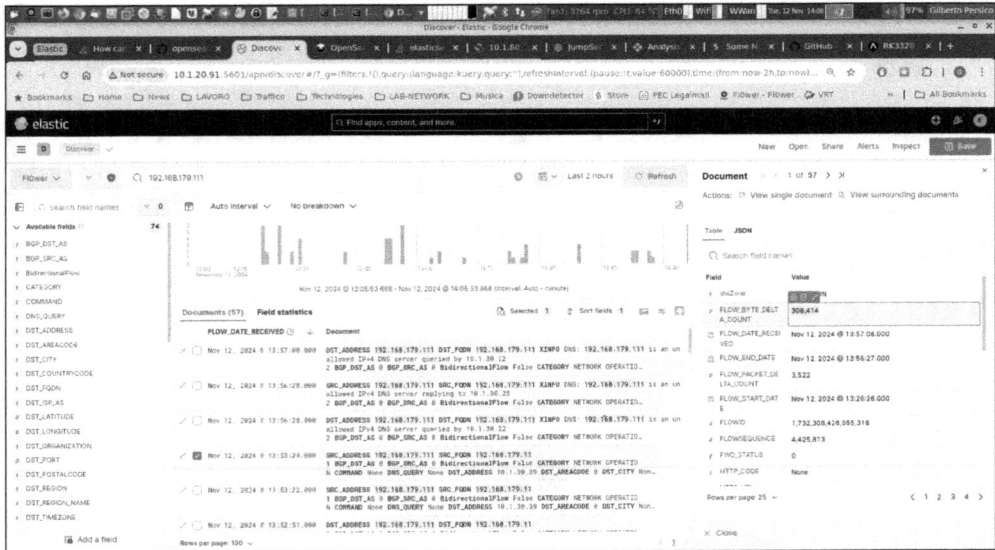

Figure 9.4: *DNS abnormal byte count in flow*

Actually, the **FLOW_BYTE_DELTA_COUNT** value of this flow (which should be a DNS query) reports 306.414 bytes and **FLOW_PACKET_DELTA_COUNT** reports 3522 packets, which is definitely not a DNS query.

Also, if we check in the **Events** (where unusual activities are reported as soon as they are detected) we can see the following:

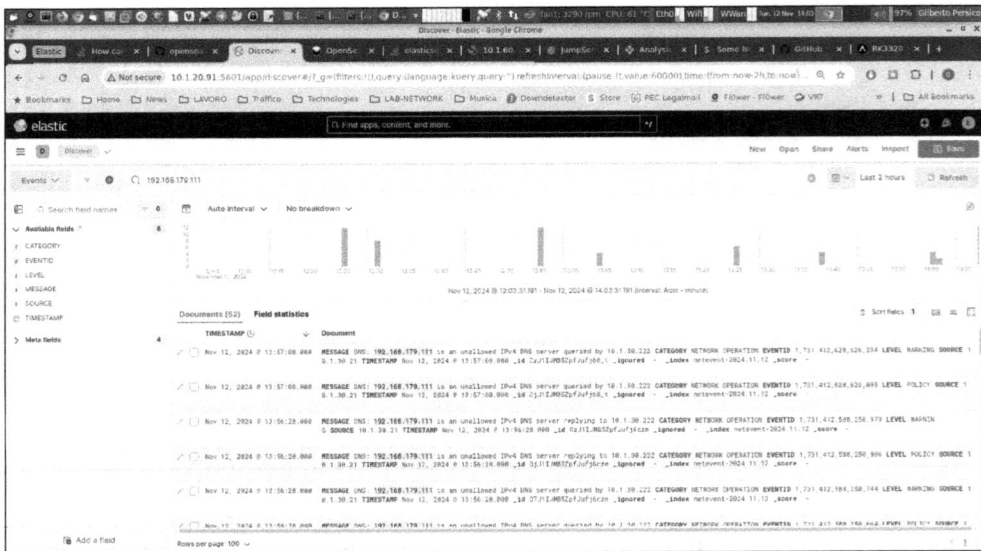

Figure 9.5: *View of the Events flows reporting unofficial DNS flows*

In Fl0wer, you can configure the company-established DNS and NTP servers, and the 192.168.179.111 address is not in the list (which are placed in **/opt/fl0wer/list** folder and are named **dns4list.txt** and **dns6list.txt** for IPv4 and IPv6 DNS servers and **ntp4list.txt** and **ntp6list.txt** for IPv4 and IPv6 NTP servers).

This simple feature can set you quite ahead of the 292 days (roughly 9 months) for business to identify and report a data breach (source: **https://www.ibm.com/security/data-breach** - *IBM Cost of a Data Breach Report 2024*). Flow data can help a lot in cybersecurity.

PAM access

Most modern and large organizations nowadays make use of **Privileged Access Management** (**PAM**) solutions to allow remote management of systems, making it easy to track management connections and be compliant with a lot of security laws.

PAM solutions are security tools designed to protect, monitor, and manage privileged accounts within an organization. These accounts have access to sensitive data, systems, or applications, often with elevated permissions, and are typically used by administrators, IT staff, or automated processes. PAM solutions aim to reduce risks associated with these accounts, such as insider threats, accidental misuse, or external attacks that exploit privileged credentials.

The key features of a PAM solution are as follows:

- **Credential management:** PAM solutions secure privileged credentials (for example, passwords, SSH keys) by storing them in a centralized, encrypted vault. This way, access is tightly controlled, and credentials are rotated frequently to reduce risks.

- **Session management and monitoring:** PAM enables organizations to track and record sessions involving privileged access. It allows real-time monitoring, logging, and even video recordings of sessions, which can help in identifying unusual behavior and ensuring compliance.

- **Access control and policy enforcement:** PAM enforces rules on who can access privileged accounts and what actions they can perform. It often uses **Multi-Factor Authentication** (**MFA**) and RBAC to ensure only authorized individuals access privileged assets.

- **Auditing and reporting:** PAM solutions log activities related to privileged accounts, providing detailed audit trails for compliance reporting and incident investigation. They often include predefined reports and dashboards for security audits.

- **Just-In-Time (JIT) access:** Some PAM solutions provide temporary access based on the principle of least privilege, granting users only the permissions they need for a specific task and for a limited time, which helps minimize exposure.

- **Automation and policy management:** PAM tools can automate tasks such as password rotation, policy enforcement, and access requests, helping streamline workflows and reduce human error.

The benefits of PAM solutions are as follows:

- **Reduced security risks:** PAM reduces the risk of unauthorized access and insider threats by limiting access to sensitive data and critical systems.

- **Compliance and governance:** Many regulatory standards, such as GDPR, HIPAA, and PCI DSS, require privileged access management controls, which PAM solutions help organizations meet.

- **Improved operational efficiency:** Automating access requests and credential management streamlines IT operations and reduces the administrative burden of managing privileged accounts.

Some common use cases for PAM are as follows:

- **Protecting access to critical systems:** PAM ensures that only authorized personnel can access systems with sensitive data, such as financial or critical infrastructure.

- **Securing DevOps and cloud environments:** By managing credentials used in dynamic environments like DevOps and cloud services, PAM can help prevent the exposure of secrets and privileged access.

- **Third-party access management:** PAM can restrict and monitor access given to external vendors or contractors, providing additional security for outsourced tasks.

Some of the leading PAM providers include CyberArk, BeyondTrust and One Identity. Each offers various features and integrations tailored to fit different enterprise needs.

PAM is increasingly essential as organizations face complex cybersecurity challenges and compliance requirements. It provides critical tools to secure privileged accounts and improve organizational security posture.

But how does network traffic control fit in all this scenario? Quite easy.

All management connections, when a PAM solution is deployed, should come from so-called Bastion Hosts (PSM in CyberArk terminology), which are part of the PAM solution itself. There can be some cases in which the connection (for emergency or technical reasons) could bypass the PAM solution. However, in a normal scenario, all other management connections should be worthy of investigation, especially during out-of-working areas. And that is where Fl0wer comes to work.

By using the Fl0wer traffic rules, we can tag the normal Bastion Host | System traffic (whatever, RDP, SSH, and so on) as normal traffic, thus removing it from due diligence, and investigate all other "unexpected" management traffic.

Let us, as an example, say that our Bastion Hosts are 10.1.30.120 and 10.1.30.121. SSH and RDP connections will originate from them, and all system administrators will connect to the 192.168.1.0/24 network via wired connections and 192.168.2.0/24 via wireless connections. All our servers are on the 10.1.10/24 network.

We can create an **ipgroup** containing the **Client Systems** like:

```
ipgroup clients
{
        description = "Client Systems"
        address = {
                "192.168.1.0/24",
                "192.168.2.0/24"
        }
}
```

Then one for the servers:

```
ipgroup servers
{
        description = "Server Systems"
        address = {
                "10.1.10.0/24"
        }
}
```

As well as a group for the **Bastion Hosts**:

```
ipgroup bastion
{
        description = "Bastion Hosts"
        address = {
                "10.1.30.120/32",
                "10.1.30.121/32"
        }
}
```

Then, we define the services that must be matched, such as:

```
servicegroup ManagementProtocols
{
        description = "System Management Protocols"
        services = {
                "22/tcp",
                "3389/tcp"
        }
}
```

Now we can create a simple rule to tag the traffic:

```
traffic_rule ManagementTraffic
{
        exporter = any
        ipversion = 4
```

```
        protocol = any
        tcp_flags = any
        tos = any
        add_to_nst = yes
        username = ""
        src_addr = @bastion
        src_mask = any
        src_port = any
        dst_addr = @servers
        dst_mask = any
        dst_port = @ManagementTraffic
        maxpacketsize = any
        classification = normal
        action = mark_npar
        description = "TRAFFIC FROM BASTIONHOST"
        negaterule = no
        store = yes
        continue = no
        enable_reverse = yes
        category = CATEGORY_MANAGEMENT
}
```

All these directives, the ipgroup, the servicegroup and the traffic_rule ones, are read at Fl0wer startup from the file **/opt/fl0wer/etc/fl0wer_rules.conf** and parsed accordingly. They are all documented in the user manual. In our example, the rule marks all the traffic from Bastion Hosts (**@bastion**) to servers (**@servers**) for the chosen services (**@ManagementTraffic**) replacing the NPAR field in the flow with the provided description. So, all the management traffic not marked as **TRAFFIC FROM BASTIONHOST** is worth investigating. Since we know it, we could also choose to completely ignore this kind of traffic by setting the **store = no** and **add_to_nst = no** fields in the traffic rule, so that we would only see the management traffic not originating from the Bastion Hosts.

Rogue VTEPs

A very useful feature of Fl0wer is its capability of identifying Rogue VTEPs and VXLAN tunnels inside the network. In Fl0wer, it is possible to configure well-known and established IPv4 and IPv6 VTEPs by simply adding their IP addresses in **/opt/fl0wer/iplist/vtep4list.txt** and **/opt/fl0wer/iplist/vtep6list.txt** for IPv4 and IPv6. This comes especially handy if you want to keep full control in structured OpenStack installations.

For example, if we have a broken cable in an area of our lab where we did not want to rewire, we resorted to configuring a couple of Mikrotik routerboards with Wi-Fi using VXLAN to transport our management network and avoid reconfiguring the printer too. In case we forget to update the previously mentioned files, we get the following notifications by Fl0wer:

```
clickhouse.ip6net.me :) SELECT TIMESTAMP,LEVEL,CATEGORY,SOURCE,MESSAGE
FROM FL0WER.EVENTS WHERE LEVEL LIKE '%POLICY%' AND MESSAGE LIKE '%VTEP%'
ORDER BY TIMESTAMP DESCENDING LIMIT 5;

SELECT
    TIMESTAMP,
    LEVEL,
    CATEGORY,
    SOURCE,
    MESSAGE
FROM FL0WER.EVENTS
WHERE (LEVEL LIKE '%POLICY%') AND (MESSAGE LIKE '%VTEP%')
ORDER BY TIMESTAMP DESC

Query id: b5daafe1-3b23-471c-bfdf-9128ba63d7a0
```

Timestamp	Level	Category	Source	Message
2024-11-10 11:52:43	Policy	Network Tunnel	10.1.30.21	TUNNEL: possibly TUNNEL Traffic (UDP 8472 possibly Linux 3.7 VTEP VXLAN Protocol) from 10.100.1.1/50610 to 10.100.1.20/8472 (7232 bytes in 32 packets)
2024-11-10 11:52:43	Policy	Network Tunnel	10.1.30.21	TUNNEL: possibly TUNNEL Traffic (UDP 8472 possibly Linux 3.7 VTEP VXLAN Protocol) from 10.100.1.1/50068 to 10.100.1.20/8472 (7360 bytes in 32 packets)
2024-11-10 11:52:43	Policy	Network Tunnel	10.1.30.21	TUNNEL: possibly TUNNEL Traffic (UDP 8472 possibly Linux 3.7 VTEP VXLAN Protocol) from 10.100.1.1/45058 to 10.100.1.20/8472 (8000 bytes in 32 packets)
2024-11-10 11:52:43	Policy	Network Tunnel	10.1.30.21	TUNNEL: possibly TUNNEL Traffic (UDP 8472 possibly Linux 3.7 VTEP VXLAN Protocol) from 10.100.1.1/60488 to 10.100.1.20/8472 (7456 bytes in 32 packets)

Table 9.3: Example of events regarding rogue VTEPs

As you see, a simple query on Clickhouse (that can be easily automated) can reveal misconfigurations and trickeries that maybe can be fixed with a more structured approach.

Out of policy SNMP

Most companies running services are normally using monitoring tools such as Centreon, Nagios, Icinga or BMC Patrol to check the availability of systems from specific management consoles, and these monitoring systems often make use of one of the more abused and misconfigured network management protocol: SNMP.

The **Simple Network Management Protocol** (**SNMP**) is primarily used for monitoring and managing devices on a network. However, when misconfigured or poorly secured, it can be exploited by attackers in the context of hacking. Here is an overview of how SNMP is used maliciously:

- **Information gathering (Reconnaissance)**
  - ○ **Exploiting public community strings:** SNMP uses community strings for access control. The default community string public is often left unchanged, allowing attackers to query devices.

- **Enumerating network details:** Attackers use SNMP to extract sensitive information such as:
  - ○ Device names and types
  - ○ IP addresses and subnet details
  - ○ Routing tables
  - ○ Installed software versions (useful for finding vulnerabilities)
  - ○ Exploiting Weak Configurations

- **SNMPv1 and SNMPv2 weaknesses:** These older versions lack encryption, making them vulnerable to:
  - ○ **Man-in-the-middle attacks:** Intercepting and modifying SNMP traffic.
  - ○ **Eavesdropping:** Capturing plaintext data, including community strings.
  - ○ **Default credentials:** Many devices ship with default SNMP configurations, which attackers can exploit.

- **Gaining unauthorized access**
  - ○ Using SNMP set commands (if improperly configured) to:
    - ▪ Change device configurations.
    - ▪ Redirect traffic (for example, altering routing tables).
    - ▪ Disable or disrupt services by modifying system settings.
    - ▪ Launching further attacks
  - ○ **Amplification attacks:** SNMP can be abused in DDoS attacks via amplification, where small queries generate large amounts of traffic to overwhelm targets.
  - ○ **Pivoting:** Information gathered via SNMP can help an attacker move laterally within the network.

- **Tools and techniques**
  - ○ Common tools used in SNMP-based attacks include:
    - ▪ **Snmpwalk:** For querying SNMP devices.
    - ▪ **Snmpcheck:** To audit and enumerate SNMP-enabled devices.
    - ▪ **Metasploit framework:** Includes modules for SNMP exploitation.

- **Mitigation strategies**
    - o   Disable SNMP if not needed.
    - o   Use SNMPv3, which supports encryption and authentication.
    - o   Change default community strings and enforce strong ones.
    - o   Limit SNMP access to trusted IP ranges via firewall rules.
    - o   Monitor SNMP traffic for unusual patterns.

SNMP exploitation highlights the risks of poor configuration management in network security.

That is why in Fl0wer you can set a list of allowed SNMP management systems that are authorized to issue queries to SNMP enabled devices without raising an Event. You just need to add the IP address in the file **/opt/fl0wer/iplist/snmp4list.txt** for IPv4 addresses and in **/opt/fl0wer/iplist/snmp6list.txt** for IPv6 SNMP managers. All the matching traffic will be considered normal system management and will not raise events like in the following example:

```
clickhouse.ip6net.me :) SELECT * FROM FL0WER.EVENTS WHERE (MESSAGE LIKE
'%10.1.61.221%' AND MESSAGE LIKE '%SNMP%')  ORDER BY TIMESTAMP ASCENDING LIMIT 1;

Query id: 9fd3bd00-5d10-42f3-96fd-cb4a673bfd14
Connecting to localhost:9000 as user default.
Connected to ClickHouse server version 24.7.3.
```

Output:

EventID	Timestamp	Level	Category	Source	Message
173189102 4139813	2024-11-18 01:50:24	Policy	Management	10.1.30.21	SNMP: Unallowed SNMP Traffic (UDP 16992 possible Intel AMT HTTP Protocol) from 10.1.20.202/161 to 10.1.61.221/16992 (3042 bytes in 33 packets)

Table 9.4: Example of out of policy SNMP traffic reported in events

We can easily automate this task by means of a simple Python script using the bundled RTE environment, as follows:

```
#!/opt/fl0wer/bin/fl0py
import os
import time
import csv
import pandas as pd
import datetime as datetime
import pathlib
import sys
import lz4
```

```
from os import system
from collections import Counter
from tabulate import tabulate

import clickhouse_driver as CH
from clickhouse_driver import Client

def dumpcsv(dataframe,filename):
        dataframe.to_csv(filename, encoding='utf-8', index=False)

# self-explaining values ☺
server = "10.1.20.17"
csvoutput = "/tmp/snmp_alerts.csv"

try:
        conn = CH.Client(    server,
                             secure=False,
                             verify=False,
                             compression=True)
except:
        print("Can't connect to Clickhouse server at: "+server)
        sys.exit(2)
print("Retrieving SNMP data into "+csvoutput)

try:
        df = conn.query_dataframe ("SELECT
TIMESTAMP,LEVEL,CATEGORY,SOURCE,MESSAGE FROM FL0WER.EVENTS WHERE LEVEL LIKE
\'%POLICY%\' AND MESSAGE LIKE \'%SNMP%\' ORDER BY TIMESTAMP DESCENDING;")
except:
        print("Can't retrieve data from Clickhouse server at: "+server)
        sys.exit(2)
print("Data fetched, formatting ...")
dumpcsv(df,csvoutput)
print(tabulate(df, headers='keys', tablefmt='psql'))
```

This script simply connects to the Clickhouse database, performs a query filtering the SNMP alerts and creates both a CSV file with the events while printing them on screen. Scheduling in crontab and sending it via mail is left as an exercise to the reader.

Conclusion

What we started in this chapter is to try to give the reader an understanding of the possibilities that are available by means of using two such powerful technologies, like OLAP and search and analysis tools like Elasticsearch. Obviously, a good knowledge of the behavior of network protocols is a requirement, but working with a good foundation is going to save your network a lot of trouble.

## CHAPTER 10

Understanding the Flow Matrix

Introduction

In the previous chapters, we have seen what network flows are, how to receive them from a variety of infrastructure devices, how to collect them and how to use them in ways to improve our security posture. This is certainly not as precise as a deep inspection of network packet contents, but it is surely effective and has some advantages considering that it is scalable. You can check a 100Mbit network as well as a 1 Terabit network without big issues since you work on flows and not on packets. Moreover, it is also reliable. Nowadays, more than 95% of Internet (and not only) network traffic is encrypted, as opposed to 2012, when it was only about 57%. So, even using deep packet inspection with packet decryption by means of certificates (possibly up to TLS 1.2 but not further) is a huge waste of CPU cycles. There must be other means to perform successful network traffic analysis, and Flow analysis is one of them.

Given that, one of the biggest advantages of having a flow traffic analysis infrastructure is the ability to create, update and monitor a flow matrix table, to have a clear view of what is happening inside our network.

Structure

In this chapter, we will discuss the following topics:

- Flow matrix
- Making good use of Fl0wer's flow matrix
- Capacity planning
- Network security with the flow matrix

Objectives

This chapter introduces an often underestimated concept: the flow matrix inside the company network. A deep dive into the concept will allow the reader to use it to improve the security of the whole network.

Flow matrix

In a network environment, a flow matrix is a tabular or graphical representation of traffic flows between different entities within the network. It is used to visualize and analyse how data is transferred between devices, applications, or network segments.

The key characteristics of a flow matrix are as follows:

- **Structure**:
  - o The matrix rows typically represent source entities (for example, IP addresses, VLANs, or devices).
  - o The columns represent destination entities.
  - o Each cell shows the volume, type, or characteristics of traffic flowing between the corresponding source and destination.
- **Traffic metrics**: The data in the matrix often includes:
  - o Traffic volume (bytes or packets)
  - o Protocols used (for example, TCP, UDP)
  - o Applications (for example, HTTP, DNS, FTP)
  - o Flow durations and timestamps.
- **Granularity**: The matric can represent traffic at various levels of granularity:
  - o Individual devices or IPs.
  - o Subnets or VLANs.
  - o Logical groupings like application clusters.

- **Dynamic nature**: Flow matrices can be static (captured at a specific moment) or dynamic, updated in real-time for monitoring.

The uses of a flow matrix are as follows:

- **Traffic analysis**:
    - o Identifying high-volume traffic sources or destinations.
    - o Pinpointing potential bottlenecks or overloaded links.

- **Security monitoring**:
    - o Detecting anomalous traffic patterns (for example, unusual flows to unknown destinations).
    - o Visualizing lateral movement during an attack.

- **Capacity planning**: Analysing which parts of the network are under or over-utilized to guide upgrades.

- **Policy enforcement**: Validating access control policies by reviewing traffic flows against allowed source-destination pairs.

- **Incident response**: Understanding the spread of an attack or malware by observing unauthorized flows.

Some tools for generating flow matrices are as follows:

- **NetFlow/IPFIX**: Protocols used to capture flow data from routers or switches.

- **sFlow**: Provides flow sampling for traffic analysis.

- **SIEM tools**: Security-focused tools like Splunk or Elastic stack can create flow matrices for analysis from network flow data.

A flow matrix provides invaluable insights into network behaviour, aiding in operational efficiency and security. The flow matrix in Fl0wer works very easily, and if enabled, it is automatically built while the software receives flows. The logic is quite simple: mostly used flows get higher positions in the flow matrix, less used ones are moved to lower positions, or they are removed if a flow limit is set in the Fl0wer parameters.

Making good use of Fl0wer's flow matrix

Fl0wer is a network flow analysis tool that automatically builds and updates a flow matrix based on collected flows, designed for security and capacity planning. The default installation of Fl0wer comes with reasoned defaults. The evaluation version has a limit of 50 entries for the flow matrix, but these often can be more than enough to have a good idea of what is happening in our network.

The basic reasoning about Fl0wer is that it considers everything that is not adequately described as external traffic. This is why in the file **/opt/fl0wer/etc/fl0wer_internal_ networks.conf** we have the following default values:

```
network Internal10
{
        subnet = 10.0.0.0
        netmask = 8
        description = "Internal 10.0.0.0/8 RFC1918"
}

network Internal172
{
        subnet = 172.16.0.0
        netmask = 12
        description = "Internal 172.16.0.0/12 RFC1918"
}

network Internal192
{
        subnet = 192.168.0.0
        netmask = 16
        description = "Internal 192.168.0.0/16 RFC1918"
}
```

Understandably, most companies adopted RFC1918 internal IP addressing, and as such this can be considered a safe assumption, although your case could be different. In this case, nobody prevents you from inserting the correct values for your internal networks and getting good results.

When Fl0wer is started, it reads its configuration values from **/opt/fl0wer/etc/fl0wer. conf** and if the flow matrix is enabled with the following lines:

```
###########################
# Flow Matrix
###########################
enable_flow_matrix = yes
enable_matrix_unknown = no
```

Then it will keep its internal flow matrix updated and create a dump of it in CSV every 10 minutes in **/opt/fl0wer/data/flowmatrix.csv** as well as an **/opt/fl0wer/data/ flowmatrix.dat** in binary format to reload it if the software is stopped for any reason.

Let us say we started Fl0wer with the default values, and wait for 10 minutes of traffic to be viewed and collected. We are going to get a first flow matrix of the entire network (depending on where we placed or configured our NetFlow/IPFIX exporters, as can be seen in the following table:

srcZone	dstZone	srcSubnet	srcNetmask	dstSubnet	dstNetmask	srcDescription	dstDescription	FlowDirection	Protocol	dstPort	NPAR	RULE	hits	bytes	packets	firstSeen	lastSeen	trafficCategory	riskLevel	riskType	classification
UNKNOWN	UNKNOWN	10.0.0.0	8	10.0.0.0	8	Internal 10.0.0.0/8 RFC1918	Internal 10.0.0.0/8 RFC1918	INTERNAL_TO_INTERNAL	udp	2056	UDP 2056 probably Cisco Netflow/IPFIX Protocol		287959	2.02E+10	25247779	2024-10-03 13:45:02	2024-10-20 13:47:21	NETWORK OPERATION	UNRATED	71	UNRATED
UNKNOWN	UNKNOWN	10.0.0.0	8	10.0.0.0	8	Internal 10.0.0.0/8 RFC1918	Internal 10.0.0.0/8 RFC1918	INTERNAL_TO_INTERNAL	icmp	0	ICMP Protocol Code: Not available		375908	1.55E+09	7729107	2024-10-03 13:45:05	2024-10-20 13:47:23	NETWORK OPERATION	UNRATED	64	UNRATED
UNKNOWN	UNKNOWN	10.0.0.0	8	10.0.0.0	8	Internal 10.0.0.0/8 RFC1918	Internal 10.0.0.0/8 RFC1918	INTERNAL_TO_INTERNAL	tcp	8291	TCP 8291 Mikrotik Winbox management protocol		93096	77621545	712443	2024-10-03 13:45:07	2024-10-20 13:47:28	NETWORK OPERATION	UNRATED	71	UNRATED
UNKNOWN	UNKNOWN	10.0.0.0	8	10.0.0.0	8	Internal 10.0.0.0/8 RFC1918	Internal 10.0.0.0/8 RFC1918	INTERNAL_TO_INTERNAL	udp	5353	UDP 5353 Multicast DNS Apple Bunjour		80340	2.96E+08	213807	2024-10-03 13:45:15	2024-10-20 13:47:31	NETWORK OPERATION	UNRATED	76	UNRATED
UNKNOWN	UNKNOWN	10.0.0.0	8	10.0.0.0	8	Internal 10.0.0.0/8 RFC1918	Internal 10.0.0.0/8 RFC1918	INTERNAL_TO_INTERNAL	tcp	80	TCP 80 HTTP Protocol		54061	24135326	249144	2024-10-03 13:45:20	2024-10-20 13:47:35	WEB	UNRATED	7	SUSPICIOUS
UNKNOWN	UNKNOWN	10.0.0.0	8	10.0.0.0	8	Internal 10.0.0.0/8 RFC1918	Internal 10.0.0.0/8 RFC1918	INTERNAL_TO_INTERNAL	tcp	21	TCP 21 FTP-Control Protocol	FTP	240027	65965916	1202991	2024-10-03 13:45:25	2024-10-20 13:47:37	UNWANTED	UNRATED	71	UNRATED
UNKNOWN	UNKNOWN	10.0.0.0	8	10.0.0.0	8	Internal 10.0.0.0/8 RFC1918	Internal 10.0.0.0/8 RFC1918	INTERNAL_TO_INTERNAL	tcp	22	TCP 22 SSH/SFTP Protocol		51289	2.45E+09	10968197	2024-10-03 13:45:30	2024-10-20 13:47:40	MANAGEMENT	UNRATED	78	UNRATED

Table 10.1: *A sample flow matrix*

As we can see, we just took the first seven flow types in the matrix to get an idea. The start is good; we know which flows go from where to where and how many hits, bytes, and packets there are, but we did not add any detail!

Let us start to improve our **/opt/fl0wer/etc/fl0wer_internal_networks.conf** by means of adding the subnets we know and see if things improve:

```
network FrontEnd
{
        subnet = 10.1.10.0
        netmask = 24
        description = "FrontEnd"
        zone = "PUBLIC"
}
network Backend
{
        subnet = 10.1.20.0
        netmask = 24
        description = "Backend"
        zone = "SECURE"
}
network Management
{
        subnet = 10.1.30.0
        netmask = 24
        description = "Management"
        zone = "INTERNAL"
}
network Wifiold
{
        subnet = 10.1.60.0
        netmask = 24
        description = "Wifi OLD"
        zone = "INTERNAL"
}
network Wifi
{
        subnet = 10.1.61.0
        netmask = 24
        description = "Wifi"
        zone = "INTERNAL"
}
```

```
network router-external
{
        subnet = 192.168.179.0
        netmask = 24
        description = "ROUTER-EXTERNAL"
        zone = "PUBLIC"
}

network DMZ
{
        subnet = 192.168.1.0
        netmask = 24
        description = "DMZ"
        zone = "PUBLIC"
}

network Internal10
{
        subnet = 10.0.0.0
        netmask = 8
        description = "Internal 10.0.0.0/8 RFC1918"
}

network Internal172
{
        subnet = 172.16.0.0
        netmask = 12
        description = "Internal 172.16.0.0/12 RFC1918"
}

network Internal192
{
        subnet = 192.168.0.0
        netmask = 16
        description = "Internal 192.168.0.0/16 RFC1918"
}
```

Now, besides adding the subnets, we also added a zone to our internal networks and left the defaults untouched. As such, every other network we have will be considered internal. Remove the **/opt/fl0wer/etc/flow** matrix files and restart collecting.

We get the following table now:

srcZone	dstZone	srcSubnet	srcNetmask	dstSubnet	dstNetmask	srcDescription	dstDescription	FlowDirection	Protocol	dstPort	NPAR	RULE	hits	bytes	packets	firstSeen	lastSeen	trafficCategory	risklevel	risktype	classification
INTERNAL	INTERNAL	10.1.30.0	24	10.1.30.0	24	Management	Management	INTERNAL_TO_INTERNAL	tcp	80	TCP 80 HTTP Protocol		252649	99637180	1298899	2024-10-03 13:45:02	2024-10-20 13:47:21	WEB	UNRATED	7	UNRATED
INTERNAL	INTERNAL	10.1.61.0	24	10.1.61.0	24	Wifi	Wifi	INTERNAL_TO_INTERNAL	udp	5353	UDP 5353 Multicast DNS Apple Bonjour		776777	2.86E+09	2064659	2024-10-03 13:45:05	2024-10-20 13:47:23	NETWORK OPERATION	UNRATED	76	UNRATED
INTERNAL	INTERNAL	10.1.30.0	24	10.1.30.0	24	Management	Management	INTERNAL_TO_INTERNAL	udp	161	UDP 161 SNMP Protocol		1834551	2.81E+09	36577934	2024-10-03 13:45:07	2024-10-20 13:47:28	NETWORK OPERATION	UNRATED	71	UNRATED
INTERNAL	INTERNAL	10.1.61.0	24	10.1.61.0	24	Wifi	Wifi	INTERNAL_TO_INTERNAL	tcp	23	TCP 23 Telnet Protocol	TELNET	192465	29375168	593419	2024-10-03 13:45:15	2024-10-20 13:47:31	UNWANTED	UNRATED	71	SUSPICIOUS
INTERNAL	INTERNAL	10.1.30.0	24	10.1.30.0	24	Management	Management	INTERNAL_TO_INTERNAL	tcp	23	TCP 23 Telnet Protocol	TELNET	127827	25632408	444889	2024-10-03 13:45:20	2024-10-20 13:47:35	UNWANTED	UNRATED	71	SUSPICIOUS
INTERNAL	INTERNAL	10.1.61.0	24	10.1.61.0	24	Wifi	Wifi	INTERNAL_TO_INTERNAL	tcp	8291	TCP 8291 Mikrotik Winbox management protocol		351561	1.82E+08	2158253	2024-10-03 13:45:25	2024-10-20 13:47:37	NETWORK OPERATION	UNRATED	71	UNRATED
INTERNAL	INTERNAL	10.1.30.0	24	10.1.30.0	24	Management	Management	INTERNAL_TO_INTERNAL	tcp	8291	TCP 8291 Mikrotik Winbox management protocol		222373	2.33E+08	1760849	2024-10-03 13:45:30	2024-10-20 13:47:40	NETWORK OPERATION	UNRATED	71	UNRATED
INTERNAL	INTERNAL	10.1.61.0	24	10.1.30.0	24	Wifi	Management	INTERNAL_TO_INTERNAL	udp	514	UDP 514 SYSLOG Protocol		17879	60530792	540318	2024-10-03 13:45:32	2024-10-20 13:47:45	MANAGEMENT	UNRATED	71	UNRATED
PUBLIC	SECURE	192.168.1.0	24	10.1.20.0	24	DMZ	Backend	INTERNAL_TO_INTERNAL	udp	2056	UDP 2056 probably Cisco Netflow/IPFIX Protocol		135395	4.71E+09	35194612	2024-10-03 13:45:35	2024-10-20 13:47:47	NETWORK OPERATION	UNRATED	71	UNRATED
SECURE	PUBLIC	10.1.20.0	24	192.168.1.0	24	Backend	DMZ	INTERNAL_TO_INTERNAL	icmp	0	ICMP Protocol Code: Not available		39355	9.11E+08	5352692	2024-10-03 13:45:40	2024-10-20 13:47:50	NETWORK OPERATION	UNRATED	64	UNRATED
INTERNAL	SECURE	10.1.30.0	24	10.1.20.0	24	Management	Backend	INTERNAL_TO_INTERNAL	icmp	0	ICMP Protocol Code: Not available		48138	2.19E+09	7063995	2024-10-03 13:45:45	2024-10-20 13:47:55	NETWORK OPERATION	UNRATED	64	UNRATED

Table 10.2: A sample of a real flow matrix

As you can see, we have the following values added:

- Source zone
- Destination zone
- Source subnet
- Destination subnet
- Source subnet description
- Source destination description

This can give us many more elements to classify our traffic relating to the complexity of our network. Maybe we have just a simple frontend/backend one, or we have an OpenStack infrastructure with several VPCs, and we can group traffic by source and destination VPC. We also have the capability to estimate traffic usage more precisely.

Being created as a CSV file, the flow matrix can be easily imported into your favorite spreadsheet, such as Excel or LibreOffice, and used for the previously described scopes.

You can easily retrieve the flow matrix by downloading the above-said file with a tool like FileZilla from the Fl0wer collector system, or you can install the Fl0wer Development Environment along with the Fl0wer RTE and write your own Python3.x scripts to retrieve it and properly use it. In the following example, we will use the provided Fl0wer Python module to interact with the running server using its authenticated and encrypted API over TCP port 7443.

```python
import argparse,socket,ssl
import hashlib
try:
    import simplejson as json
except ImportError:
    import json
import time
import tempfile
import shutil
import datetime
import zipfile
import pprint
import getpass
import platform

import os, sys, csv
import fl0wernet as flnet
from tabulate import tabulate
import pprint
```

```python
def comma_format(b):
    r =  str("{:,}".format(b))
    return r

def size_format(b):
    if b < 1024:
        h =  '%i' % b  + ' bytes'
    elif 1024 <= b < 1048576:
        h =  '%.1f' % float(b/1024) + ' KBytes'
    elif 1048576 <= b < 1073741824:
        h =  '%.1f' % float(b/1048576) + ' MBytes'
    elif 1073741824 <= b < 1099511627776:
        h =  '%.1f' % float(b/1073741824) + ' GBytes'
    elif 1099511627776 <= b < 1125899906842624:
        h =  '%.1f' % float(b/1099511627776) + ' TBytes'
    elif 1125899906842624 <= b:
        h = '%.1f' % float(b/1125899906842624) + ' PBytes'

    #r = comma_format(b) + " ("+h+")"
    r = h
    return r


user = "admin"
pw = "fl0werr0x"
server = "10.1.30.222"
server_port = 7443
port = server_port

lista = []

print("Retrieving Flowmatrix from Fl0wer server",server,"at port: ",port)
data_flowmatrix = flnet.GetFlowMatrix(user,pw,server,server_port)

datasource = data_flowmatrix

if (len(datasource) > 0):
    lista.append(
["srcZone","dstZone","srcSubnet","srcDescr","dstSubnet","dstDescr","flow_
direction","protocol","dst_port","hits","bytes","packets","NPAR","RULE",
"FlowDirection", "FirstSeen", "LastSeen", "Action","Category" ])
    for i in range(0,len(datasource)):
        srcZone = str(datasource[i]["FlowMatrixEntry"+str(i)]["srcZone"])
```

```
            dstZone = str(datasource[i]["FlowMatrixEntry"+str(i)]["dstZone"])
            srcNet = str(datasource[i]["FlowMatrixEntry"+str(i)]["srcSubnet"])
            srcDsc = str(datasource[i]["FlowMatrixEntry"+str(i)]["srcDescr"])
            srcMsk = int(datasource[i]["FlowMatrixEntry"+str(i)]["srcNetmask"])
            dstNet = str(datasource[i]["FlowMatrixEntry"+str(i)]["dstSubnet"])
            dstDsc = str(datasource[i]["FlowMatrixEntry"+str(i)]["dstDescr"])
            dstMsk = int(datasource[i]["FlowMatrixEntry"+str(i)]["dstNetmask"])
            protocol= str(datasource[i]["FlowMatrixEntry"+str(i)]["ipProtocol"])
            dstport= int(datasource[i]["FlowMatrixEntry"+str(i)]["dstPort"])
            NPAR    = str(datasource[i]["FlowMatrixEntry"+str(i)]["NPAR"])
            RULE    = str(datasource[i]["FlowMatrixEntry"+str(i)]["RULE"])
            hits    = int(datasource[i]["FlowMatrixEntry"+str(i)]["hits"])
            packets = int(datasource[i]["FlowMatrixEntry"+str(i)]["packets"])
            bytes   = int(datasource[i]['FlowMatrixEntry"+str(i)]["bytes"])
            flowdir = str(datasource[i]["FlowMatrixEntry"+str(i)]
["FlowDirection"])
            first   = str(datasource[i]["FlowMatrixEntry"+str(i)]["FirstSeen"])
            last    = str(datasource[i]["FlowMatrixEntry"+str(i)]["LastSeen"])
            action  = str(datasource[i]["FlowMatrixEntry"+str(i)]["action"])
            category= str(datasource[i]["FlowMatrixEntry"+str(i)]
["trafficCategory"])

            lista.append([srcZone,dstZone,str(srcNet)+"/"+str(srcMsk), srcDsc,
str(dstNet)+"/"+str(dstMsk),dstDsc,flowdir,protocol,dstport,hits,bytes,
packets,NPAR,RULE,flowdir,first,last,action,category])

    try:
            if (platform.system() == 'Windows'):
                    myfile = open('flowmatrix.csv', 'bw',encoding='utf-8')
            else:
                    myfile = open('flowmatrix.csv', 'w',encoding='utf-8')

            writer = csv.writer(myfile,quoting=csv.QUOTE_
ALL,lineterminator='\n')
            writer.writerows(lista)
            myfile.close()
    except:
            print("Can't write flowmatrix.csv")

pprint.pprint(datasource)
```

In the preceding code example, we connect to the running Fl0wer server, get the instant snapshot of the flow matrix, download it, save it as a **Comma Separated Value (CSV)** file, and make a pretty print of it in a way that can be easily used by a tool like grep and so on.

Capacity planning

The flow matrix is not only a tool for security and traffic visibility but also highly valuable for capacity planning. Capacity planning ensures that a network can handle current and future traffic demands without performance degradation. By mapping and analyzing the flows in a network, the matrix provides insights into bandwidth usage, traffic patterns, and potential bottlenecks.

It is often tough to estimate how much bandwidth will be used in a particular context, be it a new application or a well-established one. Nowadays, we consider it a bare minimum to have one or two (for high availability) 1Gbit connections inside our network, but depending on the application, it can be too many or too few. For example, think of a file-sharing system serving files to internal customers using NFS. We have over 500 clients who are continuously writing metering data for our NFS. We have 15k rpm drives backed by fast SSD for initial writing using ZFS, but our server has just a couple of gigabits. The result is that the network pipe is always full, and the server is perceived as slow, despite the bottleneck IS in the network part. Probably, providing a full 25 Gbit network path can turn the situation around.

Maybe instead of storing metered data, our file-sharing server is used by a bunch of **Virtual Desktop Infrastructure** (**VDI**) servers and the VDIs, once started, just run as normal Office desktops, with minimal I/O on the file-share. Still, the desktop protocol (VMware BLAST, RDP or X11) is killing the gigabit connection, and a 10Gbit network path can save the situation. But we need 10Gbit not on the file-sharing server, but on the VDI servers where the thin clients connect!

Another example of the opposite case could be a company that has some 2Mbit Wireless connections to a few nearby shops that use them only for end-of-day data synchronization of cash flows with the main office. In that case, probably a 100Mbit infrastructure for that network part would be more than enough.

The key aspects of capacity planning with a flow matrix are:

- **Traffic visibility**: The matrix gives a clear view of the traffic flows between different network entities, including source, destination, protocol, and volume.

- **Baseline establishment**: It helps establish a baseline for normal traffic patterns, including average and peak usage for each flow, which is crucial for predicting future capacity needs.

- **Bottleneck identification**: By analysing flow volumes, the matrix identifies over-utilized links or under-provisioned network devices.

- **Forecasting future demand**: Historical data from the matrix helps predict traffic growth trends and guides infrastructure scaling decisions.

To successfully use the flow matrix built by Fl0wer, you will simply need:

- **Analyse traffic patterns**:
  - **Volume analysis**: Identify high bandwidth flows that may require optimization or scaling.
  - **Peak usage**: Note peak traffic periods and associated entities or applications.
  - **Protocol trends**: Determine which protocols consume the most bandwidth (for example, HTTP/HTTPS, FTP, VoIP).

- **Identify bottlenecks**:
  - Highlight network links or devices operating near or at capacity.
  - Example: A link between the web and application tiers frequently exceeds 80% utilization, indicating potential congestion.

- **Forecast future needs**:
  - Use historical data to project future traffic growth:
    - Seasonal patterns (for example, e-commerce traffic spikes during holidays).
    - Organizational changes (for example, adding new services or users).
  - Calculate the required bandwidth increase or device upgrades for each flow.

- **Plan and implement upgrades**:
  - Upgrade network infrastructure based on the matrix's findings:
    - Increase link capacity for over-utilized connections.
    - Optimize traffic routing or load balancing.
    - Add more devices or instances (for example, additional servers or network switches).

Someone could argue that simple SNMP monitoring can reveal saturated links, and this is true, but capacity planning has several other applications like:

- **Data center scaling**: Monitor traffic between application servers, database servers, and storage systems to ensure sufficient bandwidth as user demand grows.
  - **Example**: Adding a 10 Gbps link between web and database tiers based on matrix analysis.

- **WAN optimization**: Use the matrix to analyse traffic between branch offices and the central data center. If the matrix shows high usage, consider upgrading MPLS links (if you use them) or upgrading the links of the saturated branches.

- **Cloud migration**: For hybrid cloud environments, the matrix helps predict bandwidth requirements between on-premises systems and cloud services.

  o **Example**: Allocating sufficient bandwidth for data replication flows to a cloud provider.

- **VoIP and video traffic planning**: Use the matrix to evaluate the impact of latency-sensitive traffic (like VoIP or video conferencing) on existing infrastructure.

  o **Example**: Reserving or prioritizing bandwidth for VoIP flows during office hours.

- **IoT network growth**: In IoT-heavy networks, the matrix tracks device-to-device and device-to-server traffic to ensure the network can handle increasing device numbers.

The flow matrix cannot help you decide how to design a brand-new infrastructure; only experience and budget can do that. However, it can give you tremendous insight into what is happening in the running production infrastructures, easing the task of deciding whether network infrastructure upgrades are needed and which ones.

Network security with the flow matrix

Flow matrix is a powerful conceptual and visualization tool used to understand, monitor, and secure network traffic. It provides a structured way to analyze communication patterns between entities (for example, devices, servers, users) in a network.

The matrix helps identify allowed, suspicious, or malicious traffic by mapping connections and ensures security policies are enforced.

Network flow matrix is instrumental in enhancing network security through the following means:

- **Traffic visibility**:

  o A flow matrix provides visibility into who communicates with whom on the network. It identifies legitimate and potentially unauthorized connections.

  o **Example**: Ensuring a web server can connect to a database but not directly to an internal development environment.

- **Policy definition and enforcement**:

  o The matrix helps define and enforce network security policies by specifying permissible traffic flows.

  o **Example**: Only HTTP(S) traffic is allowed from external clients to web servers, while SSH access is restricted to administrators.

- **Threat detection**:
  - Abnormal flows (for example, unexpected communication between unrelated systems) indicate potential threats like lateral movement during an attack.
  - **Example**: Detecting an internal workstation communicating directly with a database server, which might signal a compromised device.

- **Microsegmentation**:
  - Microsegmentation divides the network into smaller, isolated zones with strict control over inter-zone communication.
  - **Example**: Using the matrix to enforce isolation between production, development, and testing environments.

- **Incident response**:
  - During incidents, a flow matrix can help pinpoint anomalous traffic patterns and the scope of compromise.
  - **Example**: Tracking down unauthorized external connections initiated by malware.

- **Compliance and auditing**:
  - Regulatory requirements like PCI DSS, GDPR, or HIPAA often demand detailed records of data flows. The matrix simplifies auditing by documenting traffic flows and policies.

The steps to use a network flow matrix for security are as follows:

1. **Define entities**: Identify all entities (for example, servers, user groups, IoT devices, VPC) and group them based on roles or network zones. You can easily do it in Flower by adding the Zone attribute in the internal network's definition.

2. **Map traffic flows**: Document existing traffic flows capturing data with Flower and let it build the flow matrix for you.

3. **Establish a baseline**: Determine normal traffic patterns and flag unusual or unexpected flows.

4. **Apply security policies**: Update firewalls, ACLs, or SDN rules to enforce desired flows.

5. **Monitor continuously**: Continuously monitor the network for deviations from the expected flow matrix.

6. **Automate responses**: Use automated tools for real-time threat detection and mitigation based on the matrix.

The benefits of using a network flow matrix are:

- **Improved security**: Minimizes attack surface by restricting unnecessary communication.
- **Enhanced visibility**: Clear understanding of data flows aids in decision-making.
- **Efficient incident response**: Identifies and isolates malicious activity faster.
- **Compliance**: Simplifies auditing and ensures adherence to regulations.
- **Proactive defense**: Detects and prevents potential threats like lateral movement.

This can be even more efficient than inspecting single encrypted traffic packets (if you can) one by one looking for always changing dynamic malware patterns.

Conclusion

As we have seen, by leveraging the flow matrix, organizations can achieve a robust, scalable, and efficient approach to securing their networks while enabling better monitoring and control over data flows. However, besides network security and capacity planning, the flow matrix has other useful applications that we will describe in *Chapter 11, Firewall Rules Optimization Use Case.*

Join our book's Discord space

Join the book's Discord Workspace for Latest updates, Offers, Tech happenings around the world, New Release and Sessions with the Authors:

https://discord.bpbonline.com

CHAPTER 11
Firewall Rules Optimization Use Case

Introduction

In *Chapter 10, Understanding the Flow Matrix,* we delved into the main use cases for the flow matrix, discussing capacity planning and security. In this chapter, another use case will be discussed, based on the real experiences gained in the field to achieve a firewall rules optimization goal. Ironically, this is the practical reason for which the flow matrix has been implemented in Fl0wer, but as we have seen, in time it evolved quite substantially from the initial target.

Structure

In this chapter, we will discuss the following topics:

- Scenario
- Understanding firewall rules optimization criteria
- An interesting discovery
- Using simple shell scripting to split flow data
- Real-world case study

Objectives

This chapter describes a real use case of NetFlow data to approach a pretty complex problem of firewall optimization rules in a complex (but now becoming quite common) environment.

By the end of this chapter, the reader will better understand the capabilities of the tools he has available.

Scenario

In 2017, the author was hired as a freelance to overview Unix & network security as part of a project regarding deploying two highly integrated data center solutions in two different geographical sites by a huge Asian company for an Italian Telco.

The project was really intriguing. It involved a customized OpenStack solution with network devices managed using an integrated SDN solution from the Asian company. The solution was also integrated with VMWare virtualization infrastructure and provided VPCs protected by very powerful terabit speed firewalls. We have already met VPCs in *Chapter 3, Network Topologies,* and we have seen that they are the foundation for the so called cloud solutions, which was the main topic of the project.

The project was very ambitious and the author was also in charge of providing an integrated identity solution, which he successfully deployed using 14 geographically distributed replicas of FreeIPA (the Red Hat solution for identity management) integrated with FreeRadius, obviously running as virtual machines on the platform itself. The deployment went smoothly because he knew exactly the flows required for synchronization between the replicas and the ones required to make the service available to the entire platform.

The telco company decided to move their applications to the new infrastructure, compacting them in isolated VPCs. Each application had its own VPC, so the required separation criteria was effectively met and the different application teams started working in parallel to move the applications in the VPC. But a problem arose.

The OpenStack framework which was going to be deployed (which was stable although quite old) was heavily customized by the Asian vendor and unfortunately, the integrated SDN software part for the management of the Terabit firewalls was still relatively young. Therefore, its web interface only allowed for the punctual entry of rules with individual hosts and individual ports, leading to a proliferation of rules for all the VPCs. This by itself would not have been a big issue. Still, for their design, unfortunately, the Terabit firewalls had a global limit of 10000 rules, that was almost reached before the end of application migration.

The different applications teams, following the VPC logic, had separated access to each of their own VPCs for the applications, but there were some different kinds of problems, such as:

- Communication between teams because of pressure on delivery dates.

- Communication between teams because of different languages (Italian, English, Asian language).

- Traffic flows required by the application were not available or were incomplete, except in some cases.

- Limited web interface and strict rules requirements from the customer lead to an incredible proliferation of rules.

In this scenario, we needed to find a solution before the rules limit was exhausted, and so we started thinking about possible solutions. One hypothesis was to analyze the firewall logs, but the firewall was configured to log only the dropped traffic, and it was considered impractical because of the lack of information and logs size. Logging everything would be even worse because the size of the logs would be impractical, and a performance penalty was just waiting to happen. An additional problem was that successfully migrated applications could not be rolled back without causing data disruption; at least, it was very complicated, so no cleanup was possible. A firmware release to overcome the limit would have taken months, so this path could not be considered. After some reasoning, in the end, only the classical tuple [Src addr, Src port, Dst addr, Dst port, protocol, service, hits, bytes] was really needed to perform analysis, and data aggregation would be the mandatory step to make it successful.

The only possible solution was to receive flow data from the firewall, classify it, and create different sets of rules. Moreover, as the integrated SDN management code for the firewall was still immature, the decision was taken to disable the firewall rules management by SDN.

So, an analysis was done about the feasibility of the plan and it was agreed to use Fl0wer to receive the traffic flows, and it was enhanced to create the flow matrix and keep it updated.

In the meanwhile, we analyzed the firewall rules and decided to split them into different groups:

- Generic infrastructure related rules.

- Generic common rules that were shared between all the VPCs.

- VPC specific rules.

For the first two groups, having designed most of the infrastructure network, it was not so difficult to come up with a clear ruleset, but for the last one (the VPC specific rules), the Flow Matrix was really needed.

The first two groups contained basic rules such as public DNS usage, internal DNS usage, SYSLOG to internal collectors, LDAP/RADIUS/Kerberos authentication flows, **Privileged Access Management (PAM)** to VPCs and infrastructure, VMWare-related traffic, SDN-related traffic, and so on.

The VPC rules were then created using Fl0wer generated flow matrix.

Understanding firewall rules optimization criteria

Therefore, after a lot of coding, the flow matrix feature was implemented and we immediately deployed a couple of Fl0wer instances in the infrastructure, letting it collect about two weeks of data while producing the matrix in real time for both datacenters.

Luckily, the flow idiom spoken by the terabit firewalls was NetStream, which is basically NetFlow version 9 with some extra data, and it worked without problems. So, no code adaptations on Fl0wer side was needed. It should also be noticed that on each of these firewalls we had only one instance of flow exporter option, and this makes sense since having an instance for each VPC would be very complex for the vendor. Moreover, it would not allow us to receive the extra-VPC traffic.

A good job of describing the internal networks to Fl0wer was done, using the zone field as the VPC, so that we could have both generic traffic (which unsurprisingly matched what we crafted manually for the first two above points) and intra-VPC traffic, if any.

A great suggestion is for organizations (in large ones, it is quite mandatory) to use a network source of truth tool like **IP Address Management (IPAM)**. Be it a free one like Netbox or a completer and more integrated with DNS and DHCP like Infoblox, this kind of tool can really help when facing network problems.

Normally, the network is managed by a bunch of people, who are the company's historical memory. However, when there is outsourcing or people's retirement, minor networks or minor devices can be forgotten. When you do traffic analysis, you find them and do not know their scope, so you never know the impact of a change on them.

Nonetheless, we were working on a new infrastructure, so networks were well known. Once the flow data collection process was complete, it gave us a clear idea of the traffic that was happening.

At this point, grouping the traffic by VPC allowed us to finely tune the ruleset with real and effective traffic.

An interesting discovery

Incidentally, while analyzing the flow traffic, we discovered a combo of a lot of strange http and several (CIFS) connections to several servers around the world, from one of the jump hosts (a Windows system) that were used to connect to the new infrastructure.

Further investigations revealed that the contacted IP addresses via http protocol were becoming quite famous in those days, and there was always a search for an unregistered domain. We started analyzing the jump host and it was quickly revealed that the machine was infected with the infamous WannaCry ransomware (**https://en.wikipedia.org/wiki/WannaCry_ransomware_attack**). Luckily, our security team was able to remove it before the encryption process started, and so no further damage was done.

As you can see, we can learn some lessons from this discovery:

- Even the most structured and security-aware companies can fall due to human error.

- All active security controls (firewalls, PAM, Antivirus, and so on) can fall after some new threat.

- Flow data analysis goes beyond statistics, and it is a proactive way to improve your security posture.

- Network security nowadays is a must that cannot be procrastinated.

Using simple shell scripting to split flow data

If you had the opportunity to play a bit with Fl0wer, you should have seen that it comes with a rich and powerful Python API and an open-source CLI that we can use to retrieve the information that we need.

The workflow that was decided was to extract flow data grouped by VPC to develop different sections of rules for the terabit firewall. Therefore, we needed to split the flow matrix into groups, one per VPC. A simple Unix shell script with a couple of tools could do the job very easily.

In our case, we need two key pieces of information from Fl0wer:

- The flow matrix (**flowmatrix.csv**)

- The internal network definition to reconcile the matrix with the VPCs (**internal_ networks.neo4j**)

A single command, as we can see in the script, can retrieve this information for us, providing it in a handy CSV format that we can use.

A very handy tool that we can use and integrate in scripting is the wonderful SQLite, which is a simple local database (no network, no configuration, just a single binary) running on Linux machines that provides a standard SQL syntax to manipulate the needed data. Obviously, it can import standard CSV files and create reports from the command line, so it is a quite natural integration into a bash shell script.

We then load the provided CSV flow matrix information into SQLite3, iterate on the VPCs with a simple cycle, and extract the flow matrix specific to that VPC.

```bash
#!/bin/bash

rm -f flowmatrix.csv internal_networks.neo4j flowmatrix.db *.csv summary.txt

# Retrieve the flow matrix and the internal networks
```

```
/opt/fl0wer/bin/flcli admin fl0werr0x 10.1.30.210 7443 /flowmatrix 2>&1 > /dev/
null

# for ease of use, load everything on a small database to perform some
queries
sqlite3 -csv flowmatrix.db ".import flowmatrix.csv flowmatrix"
sqlite3 flowmatrix.db "CREATE INDEX srczone on flowmatrix(SRC_ZONE)"
sqlite3 flowmatrix.db "CREATE INDEX dstzone on flowmatrix(DST_ZONE)"

for i in `cat internal_networks.neo4j | grep -v ":ZONE" | awk -F, '{print
$1}' | sort | uniq | sed 's/\"//g'`
do
        echo "Processing "$i
        # Create per-VPC flow-matrix table in CSV for further analysis
        sqlite3 -header -csv flowmatrix.db "SELECT * FROM flowmatrix where\
SRC_ZONE=\""$i"\" OR DST_ZONE=\""$i"\" ORDER BY\ SRC_ZONE,SRC_SUBNET,DST_
SUBNET,CAST(HITS AS INTEGER) DESC" > TRAFFIC-$i.csv
        echo "Zone: "$i" Flows: "`wc -l TRAFFIC-$i.csv` >> summary.txt
done
```

Once the flow matrix is imported into the small database, a simple loop for the current **SRC_ZONE** (our VPC) will group and extract all flow data for that VPC, exporting it again in a handy CSV file that can be loaded in a spreadsheet for analysis and discussion.

This is exactly the script that was used to perform the firewall cleanup, so once we had the live flows documented in the Flow matrix, we used them to tune up the firewall ruleset specific for the chosen VPC.

The so-obtained flow matrix was then confronted with the application team to have the proper feedback, and in the end, translated in Firewall rules for the Terabit firewall. Once the new ruleset for the VPC was ready, we identified wrong rules for the VPC and put the new ruleset in front of the old rules (cleaning up the wrong rules counters). Then, after some days, we checked on the firewall the number of hits of the old ruleset, which was zero in all cases since the new rule encompassed the old rules. In the end, we proceeded with cleaning up the old and useless ruleset, freeing up rules for the other VPCs.

Conclusion

As we have seen, the flow matrix can be used in several use cases. Investigation of real network traffic can reveal many things, from unknown threats to misused or misconfigured devices. Of course, it can be time-consuming, like it was when it came to firewall logs analysis some years ago. However, it is a very proactive way of improving global network security posture for companies. Flower does a lot of the job for us and can be further automated, as we can see in the next chapter.

## CHAPTER 12

Simple Network Anomaly Detection System Based on Flow Data Analysis

Introduction

This is the last chapter of our journey in the flow data analysis, and we will see how we can detect most network anomalies by means of our Fl0wer flow-data collector. By performing near-real time analysis on incoming flows and blocks of flow, we can identify threats and network anomalies in a much faster way than using old-school tools like Wireshark or DPI (which are always helpful, but more limited). Let us get a glance at major network threats and how to deal with them.

Structure

In this chapter, we will discuss the following topics:

- Scenario
- Common cybersecurity threats
- Handling DNS threats
- Handling NTP threats
- Handling BGP threats
- Handling P2P threats
- Dealing with TOR threats

238 ■ Mastering Network Flow Traffic Analysis

- Dealing with covert channels
- Dealing with horizontal and vertical scans
- Dealing with VTEP and SDN controller attacks
- Automating checkups

Objectives

This chapter focuses on how to identify network anomalies and data breaches by means of using the flow matrix and some Python scripting using Pandas. It will show the reader how to automate continuous checking, trying to address the very long breach discovery-date of the breach event.

Scenario

Let us say that we want to improve our network posture. We have already deployed firewalls, IDS, and a **Network Source of Truth** (**NSOT**) and properly configured our Fl0wer network monitoring infrastructure.

Fl0wer is collecting data both in Elasticsearch and Clickhouse. It is constantly updating the flow matrix and traffic data is charted on our Elasticsearch. But we want to have a daily report about the situation of threats inside our infrastructure.

This can be accomplished with a structured approach:

- Proper configuration of the Fl0wer monitoring features
- A script that can be scheduled in a crontab to be run regularly

But let us try to understand first which are common threats that we should monitor for.

Common cybersecurity threats

There are several aspects of a network infrastructure that are worth monitoring and for several reasons.

Let us see the most common ones:

- **Domain Name Servers** (**DNS**) usage connections
- **Network Time Protocol** (**NTP**) connections
- **Border Gateway Protocol** (**BGP**) connections
- **Peer to Peer file transfers** (**P2P**) connections
- **The Onion Router** (**TOR**) connections
- Covert channels

- Network scans
- VTEPs and SDN connections

Monitoring the above protocols and connections can identify several threats, and a firewall will probably never identify most of them.

Let us see them one by one.

Handling DNS threats

The DNS is a fundamental component of the Internet, translating human-readable domain names (like example.com) into IP addresses that computers use to locate each other. However, DNS's openness and critical role make it a common target for various network attacks. DNS-based attacks exploit vulnerabilities or misuse DNS functionality to disrupt services, redirect traffic, or steal data.

Let us see some common type of DNS attacks:

- **DNS spoofing (cache poisoning)**: An attacker inserts malicious data into the DNS cache of a resolver, causing users to be redirected to malicious sites when they try to access legitimate domains. Impact can be that users may be tricked into entering sensitive information on fake websites or that users could be redirected to sites hosting malware.

- **DNS tunneling**: Encapsulates other types of traffic (for example, HTTP, SSH) within DNS queries and responses. This can be used to bypass firewalls and exfiltrate data covertly. We already saw this in *Chapter 9, Flow Data Analysis: Exploring Data for Fun and Profit*.

- **DNS reflection attack**: Attackers use a DNS server to reflect traffic toward a target by sending queries with a spoofed source IP (the target's IP). The impact is that it overwhelms the target with a large volume of DNS responses. That is why it is a good practice to keep secret the internal IP addressing of a company.

Flower can be configured to monitor DNS traffic (port 53 TCP/UDP) and alert on connections to servers not listed as legitimate. It is just a matter of adding the proper IPv4 addresses to **/opt/fl0wer/iplist/dns4list.txt** and **/opt/fl0wer/iplist/dns6list.txt** for IPv6 DNS servers.

Once done, Fl0wer will report the unqualified DNS servers in its events so you can fix the clients for the (hopefully) existing network security policy, pointing them to the safe internal DNS servers.

This script connects to Clickhouse, retrieves events from the past day, and exports them to a CSV file for analysis:

```
#!/opt/fl0wer/bin/fl0py

import os
import time
import csv
import pandas as pd
import datetime as datetime
import pathlib
import time
import lz4
from os import system
from collections import Counter
from tabulate import tabulate
from datetime import timedelta
from datetime import datetime

import clickhouse_driver as CH
from clickhouse_driver import Client

def dumpcsv(dataframe,filename):
      dataframe.to_csv(filename, encoding='utf-8', index=False)

server = "10.1.20.17"
csvoutput = "/tmp/alerts.csv"
days = 1

try:
      conn = CH.Client(   server,
                          secure=False,
                          verify=False,
                          compression=True)
except:
      print("Can't connect to Clickhouse server at: "+server)
      sys.exit(2)

# Let's retrieve data since yesterday
datefrom  = datetime.now() - timedelta(days)
dateto   = datetime.now()

strFrom  = datefrom.strftime("%Y/%m/%d %H:%M:%S")
strTo    = dateto.strftime("%Y/%m/%d %H:%M:%S")

print("Retrieving data into "+csvoutput)

try:
```

```
    # Load the data into a Pandas dataframe
    df = conn.query_dataframe ("SELECT
TIMESTAMP,LEVEL,CATEGORY,SOURCE,MESSAGE FROM FL0WER.EVENTS WHERE
LEVEL LIKE \'%POLICY%\' AND MESSAGE LIKE \'%DNS%\' AND ( TIMESTAMP >=
toDateTime(\'"+strFrom+"\') AND TIMESTAMP <= toDateTime(\'"+strTo+"\'))
ORDER BY TIMESTAMP DESCENDING;")
except:
    print("Can't retrieve data from Clickhouse server at: "+server)
    sys.exit(2)

print("Data fetched, formatting ...")
dumpcsv(df,csvoutput)
print(tabulate(df, headers='keys', tablefmt='psql'))
```

We will use this script as the basis for all the other examples.

Handling NTP threats

The NTP is used to synchronize clocks across computer systems over IP networks. While NTP plays a critical role in maintaining accurate time in distributed systems, it is vulnerable to several types of attacks. Exploiting NTP vulnerabilities can disrupt services, degrade network performance, or assist in further attacks. It is also a common source of problems for Active Directory authentication problems with Kerberos tickets.

A common type of NTP attack in the inside network is the time synchronization attacks. In this type of threat, attackers manipulate NTP responses to provide incorrect time information to clients, leading to disruptions in time-sensitive applications. The impact will be Authentication failures (for example, expired certificates), Log discrepancies (hindering forensic analysis), and out-of-sync processes, causing errors in distributed systems. Also, NTP can also be used in covert channels to exfiltrate data (the extension field and MAC fields can be used for this purpose) and a Python script to create a client/server covert-channel solution can be built easily by code-generating Ais like ChatGPT or DeepSeek.

Of course there are several other types of attacks, like joining an NTP based DDoS, but this can also be a source of malfunctions, so for now let us focus on how to be sure that all the infrastructure is aligned with the proper servers.

Again, Fl0wer allows us to configure a list of legitimate NTP servers and notice NTP traffic (port 123 TCP/UDP) to unknown servers.

It is just a matter of adding the proper IPv4 addresses to **/opt/fl0wer/iplist/ntp4list. txt** and **/opt/fl0wer/iplist/ntp6list.txt** for IPv6 NTP servers.

Once done, Fl0wer will report in its events the unqualified NTP servers so you can fix the clients for the (hopefully) existing network security policy pointing them to the safe internal NTP servers.

Like before, we can reuse the same script by simply changing the query to be like:

```
df = conn.query_dataframe ("SELECT TIMESTAMP,LEVEL,CATEGORY,SOURCE,MESSAGE
FROM FL0WER.EVENTS WHERE LEVEL LIKE \'%POLICY%\' AND MESSAGE LIKE
\'%NTP%\' AND ( TIMESTAMP >= toDateTime(\'"+strFrom+"\') AND TIMESTAMP <=
toDateTime(\'"+strTo+"\'))  ORDER BY TIMESTAMP DESCENDING;")
```

Handling BGP threats

BGP is a core component of the Internet's routing infrastructure, responsible for exchanging routing information between **Autonomous Systems** (**AS**). Despite its importance, BGP lacks inherent security mechanisms, making it susceptible to various attacks. It is mainly used in large organizations but also in SDN architectures. A good practice is to keep track of the running BGP infrastructure by monitoring with tools like ExaBGP (**https://github.com/Exa-Networks/exabgp**).

Here is a list of some possible BGP network attacks:

- **BGP route hijacking**: An attacker announces incorrect BGP routes to redirect or intercept traffic. Possible impacts are that the attacker can monitor traffic before forwarding it to the legitimate destination or may drop traffic, causing DoS.

- **BGP session hijacking**: An attacker intercepts and takes control of an established BGP session between two routers. Possible impacts are traffic redirection or interception and manipulation of routing tables for malicious purposes

- **BGP session reset attack**: An attacker disrupts an active BGP session by sending forged TCP RST (reset) or FIN (finish) packets. Since BGP sessions rely on long-lived TCP connections, an attacker sends spoofed RST or FIN packets with matching sequence numbers to terminate the session. If successful, the attack results in disruption of routing updates and temporary loss of connectivity.

- **BGP prefix deaggregation (routing table flooding)**: An attacker floods the network with excessively granular route announcements, overwhelming routers. Instead of announcing an aggregate route (for example, 192.0.0.0/16), the attacker announces numerous sub prefixes (such as, 192.0.1.0/24, 192.0.2.0/24). The results are increased memory and CPU load on routers, resulting in network instability or crashes

Yet again, Fl0wer allows us to configure a list of legitimate BGP peers and notice BGP traffic (port 179 TCP) to unknown addresses.

It is just a matter of adding the proper IPv4 addresses to **/opt/fl0wer/iplist/bgp4list.txt** and **/opt/fl0wer/iplist/bgp6list.txt** for IPv6 NTP servers.

Once done, Fl0wer will report in its events the unqualified BGP peers so you can take proper counter measures to secure your BGP infrastructure.

Like previously, we can reuse the same script by simply changing the query to be like:

```
df = conn.query_dataframe ("SELECT TIMESTAMP,LEVEL,CATEGORY,SOURCE,MESSAGE
FROM FL0WER.EVENTS WHERE LEVEL LIKE \'%POLICY%\' AND MESSAGE LIKE
\'%BGP%\' AND ( TIMESTAMP >= toDateTime(\'"+strFrom+"\') AND TIMESTAMP <=
toDateTime(\'"+strTo+"\'))  ORDER BY TIMESTAMP DESCENDING;")
```

Handling P2P threats

Using P2P tools within a corporate network can introduce a variety of risks that compromise security, compliance, productivity, and network stability. While P2P applications are useful for file sharing, collaborative projects, and decentralized communication, their use in corporate environments is often discouraged due to the following risks:

- **Malware and viruses**: P2P networks are notorious for hosting malicious files disguised as legitimate ones. Users inadvertently download malware, spyware, or ransomware from unverified sources, or some P2P applications themselves may contain bundled adware or harmful components. The impact can be as bad as malware propagation within the corporate network or even data breaches and system compromises.

- **Data exposure**: P2P tools may unintentionally share sensitive files stored on a user's device. Misconfigured P2P software settings allow sharing of entire folders, exposing sensitive corporate data. Shared files can be indexed by P2P search engines, making them accessible to unauthorized users, resulting in leakage of proprietary or confidential information, violation of data protection regulations, and loss of trust.

- **Intellectual property infringement**: P2P tools are often used to share copyrighted materials, such as software, music, and videos. Employees download or distribute copyrighted content without proper licenses. The impact is legal action against the company for copyright violations leading to fines, penalties, and reputational damage

- **Bandwidth consumption**: P2P tools often consume large amounts of network bandwidth. With continuous downloading and uploading of files by multiple users simultaneously participating in P2P activities. This can lead to network congestion and reduced performance for critical business applications and increased operational costs due to higher bandwidth usage.

- **Loss of productivity**: Employees using P2P tools for non-work-related purposes (for example, downloading media) can distract from business objectives. Work time is spent on P2P activities unrelated to job functions, reducing employee productivity and misusing company resources.

Fl0wer has very good capabilities to classify P2P traffic, so our query is still quite simple if we reuse the previous script.

```
df = conn.query_dataframe ("SELECT FLOW_DATE_RECEIVED,IP_Version,
IP_SRC_FLOWEXPORTER, IP_PROTOCOL, FLOW_BYTE_DELTA_COUNT, FLOW_PACKET_
DELTA_COUNT,IP_FLOW_DIRECTION, NPAR, CATEGORY, SRC_ADDRESS,SRC_PORT,DST_
ADDRESS,DST_PORT  FROM FL0WER.FLOWS WHERE CATEGORY LIKE \'%P2P%\' AND
FLOW_PACKET_DELTA_COUNT > 10 AND IP_FLOW_DIRECTION LIKE \'%Internet\'
AND ( TIMESTAMP >= toDateTime(\'"+strFrom+"\') AND TIMESTAMP <=
toDateTime(\'"+strTo+"\'))  ORDER BY FLOW_DATE_RECEIVED DESCENDING;")
```

Dealing with TOR threats

Using TOR within a corporate network introduces several risks, both technical and operational. While TOR provides anonymity and privacy for users, its use in a corporate environment can conflict with organizational policies, regulatory compliance, and security measures. Let us understand some of them:

- **Malware and exploits**: TOR traffic can connect to unregulated websites on the dark web, where malware, exploits, and phishing schemes are common. If employees access malicious websites, they could inadvertently download malware that compromises the corporate network.

- **Regulatory violations**: Many industries are subject to strict data protection regulations (for example, GDPR, HIPAA, PCI DSS). TOR traffic complicates tracking and auditing requirements for these regulations. The impact is that failure to comply with regulatory standards can result in fines and reputational damage.

- **Illegal activities**: TOR is often used to access dark web marketplaces, conduct illegal transactions, or engage in cybercriminal activities. If TOR is used for illegal purposes within the corporate network, the company could be held liable, even if management is unaware.

- **Attribution challenges**: Anonymity provided by TOR makes it difficult to identify the source of malicious or unauthorized activity, complicating incident investigations. TOR traffic obscures the origin and intent of connections, making it difficult for IT and security teams to detect and respond to potential threats effectively.

- **Suspicious activity**: TOR traffic can trigger scrutiny from **Internet Service Providers (ISP)**, government agencies, or other external entities monitoring for criminal activities. A corporate IP address flagged for TOR usage may attract unwanted attention or legal investigations.

Fl0wer can easily spot the TOR traffic to a very good degree, so our query is still quite simple if we are going to reuse the previous script.

```
df = conn.query_dataframe ("SELECT FLOW_DATE_RECEIVED,IP_Version,
IP_SRC_FLOWEXPORTER, IP_PROTOCOL, FLOW_BYTE_DELTA_COUNT, FLOW_PACKET_
DELTA_COUNT,IP_FLOW_DIRECTION, NPAR, CATEGORY, SRC_ADDRESS,SRC_PORT,DST_
```

```
ADDRESS,DST_PORT  FROM FL0WER.FLOWS WHERE XINFO LIKE \'%TOR%\' AND IP_FLOW_
DIRECTION LIKE \'%Internet\' AND ( TIMESTAMP >= toDateTime(\'"+strFrom+"\')
AND TIMESTAMP <= toDateTime(\'"+strTo+"\')) ORDER BY FLOW_DATE_RECEIVED
DESCENDING;")
```

Dealing with covert channels

A network covert channel is a method of transmitting data that hides the communication, making it difficult to detect by traditional security mechanisms. These channels exploit legitimate network protocols (like DNS, NTP, HTTP, HTTPS, and so on) or behaviors to encode and transfer information covertly. They are often used for data exfiltration, command-and-control communication, or bypassing security policies. An interesting repository where you can find and try a bunch of tools is on **https://github.com/cdpxe/ NetworkCovertChannels**.

Detecting covert channels bypassing a company firewall is challenging, as these channels are specifically designed to evade standard detection mechanisms. Covert channels can hide unauthorized communication in legitimate network traffic, often exploiting protocols, metadata, or other means of encoding information. It is also difficult to identify them by using firewall packet inspection since they mostly use encryption technology.

The most common protocols used are:

- **DNS**: Encoding data in DNS queries and responses. We already have seen an example in *Chapter 9, Flow Data Analysis: Exploring Data for Fun and Profit*.

- **HTTP/HTTPS**: Embedding data in headers or body content. An example tool can be found at **https://github.com/zaheercena/Covert-TCP-IP-Protocol**.

- **ICMP**: Using ping packets to exfiltrate data. An interesting implementation can be found at **https://cryptsus.com/blog/icmp-reverse-shell.html**.

- **TCP/UDP**: Encoding data in sequence numbers, flags, or payloads.

To successfully identify if there are any covert channels inside your network, you should follow the next steps:

1. **Create a baseline normal network behavior**: Use network monitoring tools to establish what normal traffic looks like for your environment. The flow matrix is an excellent tool to start with. Analyze patterns such as:

    a. Protocol usage (for example, volume of DNS queries).

    b. Typical packet sizes and frequencies.

    c. Destination addresses and domains.

2. **Anomaly detection**: You should look for unusual traffic patterns that deviate from the baseline:

a. **High volume DNS queries**: Frequent requests to unrecognized or dynamically changing domains.

b. **Unusual ICMP usage**: Large payloads or high-frequency pings.

c. **HTTP/HTTPS anomalies**: Repeated requests to obscure endpoints, unusual headers, or non-standard URL patterns.

d. **Timing irregularities**: Traffic with deliberate delays or consistent intervals between packets.

3. **Behavioral analysis**: You should monitor for endpoints consistently communicating with:

a. Unusual domains or IP addresses.

b. Locations outside the typical geographic scope of business operations.

Consider that in time new threats will appear and new ways of hiding channels will be discovered and used, so rely on a good traffic baseline with the flow matrix and always perform behavioral analysis.

In this case, we do not have a pre-built script, but we need to work on several steps, such as the following:

1. Improve the classification of your traffic in the best possible way. Bring it to the level that the flow matrix is self-speaking, and you can immediately identify every single flow to create the baseline of your traffic. Fl0wer does a tremendous job in doing this, but if you do not give it information about your network, hosts, zones, or VPC, it cannot make miracles. In this, the NSOT provides invaluable help.

2. Fl0wer dumps its flow matrix table in **/opt/fl0wer/data/flowmatrix.csv** every 10 minutes, so you can retrieve it via **scp/ssh** and simply make a difference between the previous and current one. Carefully check for the differences between the two versions. In Unix/Linux, since we are dealing with CSV files, which are basically text files, a simple **diff** command will reveal the differences, or if you are running a graphics environment with X11, **xxdiff** will be even more visually clear.

3. Investigate these differences carefully, even physically going to the source hosts (if needed) and performing manual analysis.

4. Make use of flower traffic rules to detect flows with **maxpacketsize** oversized for that kind of flow. The **maxpacketsize** parameter is computed dividing the bytes by the number of packets in the flow, and if it exceeds the **maxpacketsize**, the rule matches. So, if your ICMP flows towards the Internet and have an average of over 64 bytes (default for ping on most platforms), something strange could be in place. Moreover, DNS requests and replies are normally small in size, so exceeding 512 bytes is an alarm bell.

5. If you make use of geolocation of IP Addresses in Fl0wer, you can take advantage of checking for it in a number of ways (LUA scripts, address ranges, SQL queries, and so on)

As you can see, there are several ways to discover covert channels, but it is impossible to describe all possible ways, since threats are always evolving. Structurally, the usage of an HTTP Proxy (like Squid) in your network infrastructure is a good way to prevent unsolicited Internet access, but there are cases where this is overkill or simply cannot be applied. Reframe your reasoning by applying it to real-life situations.

Dealing with horizontal and vertical scans

Network scanning is a reconnaissance technique used to identify active devices, open ports, and services within a network. It often precedes cyberattacks, providing attackers with valuable information about network vulnerabilities. It can also be used by internal company auditing to verify the security posture of the infrastructure. But if this is not the case, it is the prelude of a network breach.

Horizontal scanning involves targeting the same port or service across multiple IP addresses in a network. An attacker scans a wide range of IP addresses to identify systems with a specific vulnerability or service. For example, Scanning all devices in a subnet (for example, 192.168.1.0/24) to find which ones have an open telnet port (TCP 23)

Vertical scanning involves targeting a single IP address to identify all open ports and services on that device. An attacker focuses on one device, probing multiple ports to identify its running services and their versions. For example, Scanning 192.168.1.10 for open ports (for example, 22, 80, 443, 3389) to enumerate running services.

The risks of having unauthorized scans inside the company network should be quite obvious and can be summarized in:

- Increased exposure to attacks
- Data exfiltration
- Disruption of services
- Evasion attempts
- Host-specific exploitation
- Privilege escalation
- Endpoint compromise
- Exposure of network topology

Normally, port scans from the Internet should be blocked at the firewall level if they arrive from the Internet. The problem is when they happen inside your company network. In that case, only flow-data monitoring can help. Fl0wer, by doing both single flow and group of flows (the so-called **bricks**), is quite successful in their detection, reporting them as alarms in the events database.

Still, we reuse the initial script and change the query to obtain our data.

For horizontal scans:

```
df = conn.query_dataframe ("SELECT
TIMESTAMP,LEVEL,CATEGORY,SOURCE,MESSAGE FROM FL0WER.EVENTS
WHERE MESSAGE LIKE \'%HORIZONTAL%\' AND ( TIMESTAMP >=
toDateTime(\'"+strFrom+"\') AND TIMESTAMP <= toDateTime(\'"+strTo+"\'))
ORDER BY TIMESTAMP DESCENDING;")
```

For vertical scans, the flows database in Clickhouse is updated with the proper NPAR, so the query will be changed into something like:

```
df = conn.query_dataframe ("SELECT FLOW_DATE_RECEIVED,IP_Version, IP_SRC_
FLOWEXPORTER, IP_PROTOCOL, FLOW_BYTE_DELTA_COUNT, FLOW_PACKET_DELTA_COUNT,
IP_FLOW_DIRECTION, NPAR, CATEGORY, SRC_ADDRESS, SRC_PORT,DST_ADDRESS,
DST_PORT FROM FL0WER.FLOWS WHERE NPAR LIKE \'%VERTICAL%\' AND ( TIMESTAMP
>= toDateTime(\'"+strFrom+"\') AND TIMESTAMP <= toDateTime(\'"+strTo+"\'))
ORDER BY FLOW_DATE_RECEIVED DESCENDING;")
```

Dealing with VTEP and SDN controller attacks

Virtual Tunnel Endpoints (**VTEP**) are critical components of network virtualization, especially in environments using **Virtual Extensible LAN** (**VXLAN**). VTEPs encapsulate Layer 2 Ethernet frames into Layer 3 IP/UDP packets for transport across an IP network, enabling scalable and flexible network overlays.

While VTEPs enhance network scalability and isolation, they also introduce potential vulnerabilities. Attackers targeting VTEPs can exploit misconfigurations or inherent protocol weaknesses to disrupt services, intercept data, or gain unauthorized access.

Some of the common attacks on the VTEP side can be:

- **VXLAN traffic interception**: An attacker captures or intercepts encapsulated VXLAN traffic between VTEPs to gain access to sensitive data. If VXLAN traffic is not encrypted, attackers on the same IP network can sniff encapsulated packets; analyzing VXLAN headers allows attackers to reconstruct original Layer 2 payloads. This can lead to data theft or exposure of sensitive information and compromised privacy and confidentiality.

- **Spoofed VTEP attack**: Attackers create a rogue VTEP to inject malicious traffic into the VXLAN network. A rogue VTEP is configured to mimic a legitimate VTEP by using the same **VXLAN Network Identifier** (**VNI**). The rogue VTEP participates in VXLAN communication, injecting unauthorized or malicious frames into the network. Results can be disruption of legitimate traffic and unauthorized access to VXLAN segments or even spread of malware or other malicious payloads. Once spot, a rogue VTEP should be immediately removed from the production infrastructure to avoid worst scenarios.

- **Flooding and broadcast amplification**: Attackers exploit the VXLAN replication mechanism to flood the network with unnecessary broadcast or multicast traffic. VXLAN replicates **broadcast, unknown unicast, and multicast (BUM)** traffic to all VTEPs in the same VNI. Attackers generate excessive BUM traffic, consuming bandwidth and resources across the network. This can lead to network congestion.

- **IP spoofing within VXLAN**: An attacker inside the VXLAN fabric spoofs an IP address within a VXLAN segment to impersonate another system. The attacker sends packets with a forged source IP address, which can confuse other devices, misdirect traffic, or enable MITM attacks. The impact could be traffic redirection and potential data theft or disruption.

A lot of work on Fl0wer has been done while working on the on-premises cloud solution described in *Chapter 11, Firewall Rules Optimization Use Case*, so adding support for VTEP and SDN was quite natural.

Fl0wer can track SDN VTEP connections and match them in a couple of files that are read at the daemon start up from the file **/opt/fl0wer/iplist/vtep4list.txt** and **/opt/fl0wer/iplist/vtep6list.txt**.

These files contain an IPv4 (for the **vtep4list.txt**) or IPv6 (for the **vtep6list.txt**) address per row and represent the allowed VTEP peers allowed to make traffic in an SDN context.

A VTEP is detected when VXLAN traffic (4789/udp or 8472/udp) is detected.

Again, to look for unallowed VTEP traffic, we can change our query to something like:

```
df = conn.query_dataframe ("SELECT TIMESTAMP,LEVEL,CATEGORY,SOURCE,MESSAGE
FROM FL0WER.EVENTS WHERE MESSAGE LIKE \'%VTEP%\' AND ( TIMESTAMP >=
toDateTime(\'"+strFrom+"\') AND TIMESTAMP <= toDateTime(\'"+strTo+"\'))
ORDER BY TIMESTAMP DESCENDING;")
```

SDN) centralizes network control through an SDN controller, which manages network devices and handles routing, forwarding, and policy enforcement. The controller operates as the brain of the SDN architecture, communicating with the network's data plane via southbound APIs (for example, OpenFlow) and interacting with management applications via northbound APIs.

This centralization improves network flexibility and programmability but introduces a single point of failure. Compromising the SDN controller can lead to severe disruptions, data breaches, or loss of network control.

Some types of threats can be:

- **DDoS attack on the controller**: Overloading the SDN controller with excessive requests to render it unresponsive or unavailable. Attackers flood the controller with large numbers of malicious or malformed packets, overwhelming its processing capacity. Legitimate control plane operations are delayed or fail entirely. The result can lead to network downtime and inability to reconfigure or manage network flows.

- **MitM attack on southbound APIs**: Intercepting or tampering with communication between the SDN controller and network devices. Attackers position themselves between the controller and data plane devices like switches or routers. Southbound protocols like OpenFlow may lack sufficient encryption or authentication, making them susceptible to interception or modification. Impact can be eavesdropping on sensitive network information and injection of malicious flow rules or communication disruption.

- **Flow rule exhaustion**: Overloading the flow table of switches by flooding the controller with new flow requests. Attackers generate a high volume of packets with unique headers, forcing switches to request new flow entries from the controller. The switch flow table fills up, leading to dropped packets or degraded performance. Results are reduced switch performance, network congestion and packet loss.

Fl0wer can also track SDN controller connections and match them in a couple of files that are read at the daemon start up from the file **/opt/fl0wer/iplist/sdncontrollers4list.txt** and

/opt/fl0wer/iplist/sdncontrollers6list.txt.

These files contain an IPv4 (for the **sdncontrollers4list.txt**) or IPv6 (for the **sdncontrollers6list.txt**) address per row and represent the allowed SDN controllers in an SDN context.

An SDN controller is considered such when making traffic on:

- OpenFlow (port range 6633-6653/tcp-udp)
- NETCONF (port range 830-833/tcp-udp)

If we want to take care of SDN controllers' traffic, we simply change our query in the script to:

```
df = conn.query_dataframe ("SELECT TIMESTAMP,LEVEL,CATEGORY,SOURCE,MESSAGE
FROM FL0WER.EVENTS WHERE MESSAGE LIKE \'%SDN%\' AND ( TIMESTAMP >=
toDateTime(\'"+strFrom+"\') AND TIMESTAMP <= toDateTime(\'"+strTo+"\'))
ORDER BY TIMESTAMP DESCENDING;")
```

Automating checkups

As we said in the scenario, we can automate the checkups that should be done regularly with a script run in crontab. This will create a scheduled report of network traffic that can give us the status of our network posture, acting like a Penetration testing report.

To ease your work, Fl0wer provides in its Fl0wer development environment (the fl0wer-devel packages) a quite complete script performing most of the things described previously and even more, in source form.

It will create:

- An HTML document with all CSV that you can share by using an internal web server.
- PDF version of the report for a handier reading.

It is not included here for size and reading reasons, but it is provided in full source code that you can customize at ease. It is written in Python 3 and uses the Fl0wer RTE, so you should have all dependencies. For immediate reaction to threats, you can also make use of the embedded LUA interpreter in Fl0wer, which can run user-customized LUA scripts that you can program to perform whatever action you prefer, including executing system commands or shell scripts. Just schedule it to run according to your requirements, and you will have the network situation at your fingertips whenever you need it. The sky is your limit.

Conclusion

Throughout this book, we've explored how flow data analysis provides unique insights into network traffic that traditional monitoring tools like packet capture and DPI cannot match. This final chapter has demonstrated how to transform theoretical knowledge into practical security controls by detecting and responding to a comprehensive range of threats—from DNS poisoning to covert channels and SDN controller attacks.

The power of flow-based anomaly detection lies in its ability to spot patterns across vast volumes of network traffic without the processing overhead of deep packet inspection. By implementing the techniques described in this chapter, organizations typically reduce their threat detection time from days or weeks to minutes or hours.

As you implement these controls in your environment, consider following a phased approach:

1. Begin with critical infrastructure protocols (DNS, NTP, BGP).
2. Progress to user-driven threats (P2P, TOR).
3. Finally, implement the more complex detection mechanisms for covert channels and scanning.

Remember that flow analysis is not a static implementation but an evolving practice. As attackers develop new evasion techniques, your detection methods must likewise evolve. Regular reviews of your flow matrix will help identify emerging patterns that might indicate novel threats.

The scripts and methods provided in this book serve as a foundation that you can customize and extend to meet your organization's specific security requirements. The combination of automated checks with human analysis creates a powerful security posture that makes your network significantly more resilient to both current and emerging threats.

Thank you for joining this journey through the world of flow data analysis. Hopefully, the knowledge and techniques shared in this book will help you build more secure, reliable, and observable networks.

Join our book's Discord space

Join the book's Discord Workspace for Latest updates, Offers, Tech happenings around the world, New Release and Sessions with the Authors:

https://discord.bpbonline.com

Index

www.ingramcontent.com/pod-product-compliance
Lightning Source LLC
Chambersburg PA
CBHW061807210326
41599CB00034B/6906